Attacking Inequality in the Health Sector

A Synthesis of Evidence and Tools

Abdo S. Yazbeck

THE WORLD BANK

ATTACKING INEQUALITY IN THE HEALTH SECTOR

ATTACKING INEQUALITY IN THE HEALTH SECTOR

A Synthesis of Evidence and Tools

Abdo S. Yazbeck

THE WORLD BANK
Washington, DC

ISBN: 978-0-8213-7444-3   eISBN: 978-0-8213-7740-6
DOI: 10.1596/978-0-8213-7444-3

Library of Congress Cataloging-in-Publication Data
Yazbeck, Abdo.
  Attacking inequality in the health sector : a synthesis of evidence and tools/
  Abdo S. Yazbeck.
    p. cm.
  Includes bibliographical references and index.
  ISBN 978-0-8213-7444-3
  1. Equality—Health aspects.   2. Health services accessibility.   3. Poor—Medical care—Cross-cultural studies.   4. World health.   I. World Bank.   II. Title.
  [DNLM: 1. Healthcare Disparities.   2. Cross-Cultural Comparison.   3. Developing Countries.   4. Health Policy.   5. Health Status Disparities.   6. Socioeconomic Factors. WA 395 Y35a 2009]
  RA418.Y39 2009
  362.1'042—dc22

                                                              2008036215

Contents

FIGURES

TABLES

BOXES

Foreword

The overwhelming evidence of inequalities in health outcomes and in the use of health services calculated and disseminated by the World Bank and other development agencies in the last 10 years has energized global efforts to address the needs of the poor and socially vulnerable. These efforts have led to a renewed interest at the global and national levels in both understanding the causes of health sector inequalities and developing policies to tackle them. It is time to synthesize the new knowledge being generated from research and experimentation on addressing inequality.

The main purpose of this book is to make available the accumulated knowledge of successful policy and analytical tools in this fight to reverse the vicious circle of income-poverty and ill health. The book presents both a practical set of analytical tools for understanding the causes of inequality in the use of health services and a menu of proven pro-poor policy actions. It is based on the evaluation of 14 successful policy changes in low- and middle-income countries in Africa, Asia, and Latin America, and a review of the published literature on inequality in the health sector. As this book shows, however, policy answers are neither easy nor uniform.

We now have ample evidence about the levels of inequality in more than 50 low- and middle-income countries. We know which outcomes and which services show the highest levels of inequality. We have proven analytical tools for understanding the causes of service use inequality. Most important, we have evaluations of experiences from countries designing and implementing pro-poor polices that are having measurable success. This book puts all this knowledge in one place. The next challenge is turning this knowledge into further action in the global effort to reduce poverty.

Joy Phumaphi
Vice President
Human Development Network
The World Bank

Rakesh Nangia
Acting Vice President
World Bank Institute

Preface

We know some important facts about the health of the poor throughout the world. For example, they are generally more in need of health care than the better-off. And their use of quality health services has a direct and immediate influence on their current and future health. Unfortunately, within low- and middle-income countries, where most of the world's poor live, the poorest use the health sector less than do the better-off.

We know these facts on inequalities because of breakthroughs in the late 1990s in the use of vast amounts of previously collected data on health and wealth in low- and middle-income countries. Indeed, the data contain information that is even more detailed; they can tell us, for example, how the use of health care in those countries varies by the location, gender, and wealth of the clientele and the high degree to which such use may impact the health of the population. The data and other sources of information also tell us that spending by the government on health in those countries often is more likely to reach the better-off households rather than the poorest—which are generally the neediest.

Until these hard (and hard-to-take) facts linking wealth to health status and health care began to emerge, health-sector advocates for the poor had little to go on *factually* in most countries. They could not demonstrate *objectively* that the poor in a specific country were not only sicker than the better-off, and more vulnerable to illness, but that the health system itself was slighting them in favor of wealthier households.

Now, the tide is turning. The data have been available for several years, and policy and practice are beginning to shift because of the stunning picture of inequality the data can reveal when expertly deployed.

This book was written to show that the new window on inequality has energized the spirit of empiricism among those seeking to improve the health status of the poor.[1] Empiricism paves the way for implementing four basic tasks necessary to creating effective policy and programs. With the data available now, we can (i) measure the extent of inequality of health service use and (ii) identify its causes. By extending the empirical approach, we can (iii) learn from policies tried elsewhere; and by empirically gauging the effectiveness of new, locally tuned policies, we can (iv) make informed and productive course corrections to bring us closer to our goal.

The Path of Empiricism

The first step for empiricism in the attack against inequality in health outcomes and service use is measuring the extent of the problem. Doing so frames the objectives of the health sector, helps better allocate resources, contributes to target setting, and informs internal and external advocacy. Chapter 1 portrays some of what is known of the inequality both in health outcomes and in the use of the health care systems in low- and middle-income countries.

After defining the problem, one must discover its causes. Causes are the link between the problem and evidence-based policy design. The contextual nature of poverty and inequality, described in chapter 2, is likely to doom the application of universal answers to health care inequality unless they are adapted to local constraints and institutions. The need for sensitivity to local conditions puts a premium on a diagnosis of the system that is both quantitative and qualitative in nature. Qualitative diagnoses come from asking participants in the system—practitioners and clients alike—open-ended questions that can elicit information and reveal issues that may not have been previously considered. Chapter 3 provides a menu and examples of such diagnoses that support policy design, implementation, and monitoring.

The evaluation of global experience must also play a role in the selection of policy directions. There has been no shortage of prescriptions for attacking inequality, but until recently there has been a shortage of empirical evidence on what worked. The emergence of projects like the Reaching the Poor Program and Equitap has injected new life into the work of evaluation and building a solid base of evidence for policy dialogue and design. Chapters 4 through 18 distill the relevant operational knowledge in this area.

The work of empiricism in attacking health inequality is completed by establishing a monitoring capability simultaneously with the design of policies. Monitoring tools capture changes in service use by the poor and the extent to which constraints are being eliminated as policies are implemented. The persistent nature of inequality in the health sector, highlighted in chapter 1, and the complex and contextual nature of inequality, described in chapters 2 and 3, speak to the importance of building in monitoring mechanisms. Chapter 19 surveys available monitoring tools and gives examples of applications.

Scope of the Book

The main aim of this book is to synthesize, for operational applications, the growing volume of empirical research in the area of inequalities in health care (O'Donnell and others 2007; Gwatkin, Wagstaff, and Yazbeck 2005). The book is thus directed at policy makers, advocates in civil society, and development agencies. The short list below highlights the information included and excluded.

Inequality versus Inequity

- The simpler, more readily measured incidence of *inequality* is the main focus of the book instead of the more complex question of *inequity*, which is related to medical need.[2] Because it is the more straightforward of the two problems, inequality has been the subject of considerably more research than has inequity. However, as chapter 1 highlights, the poor demonstrably suffer considerably more than the better-off in mortality, morbidity, malnutrition, and undesirably high rates of fertility. Given those facts, a focus on inequality can directly address inequity.
- Inequality in the use of health *services* across wealth groups dominates the volume instead of the larger problem of inequality of health *outcomes*. Chapters 1 and 2 touch on outcome inequalities, but the overall focus is on service use.

The Measurement of Poverty

- The book addresses relative poverty (for examples, quintiles and quartiles of wealth) rather than absolute poverty. While both approaches have their advantages, the choice was determined mainly by the availability of relative poverty data and the ease of measurement.
- Poverty is measured by assets rather than consumption. Once again, the choice was driven by the availability of data and research output. Consumption-based approaches are known as the gold standard for measuring distribution (O'Donnell and others 2007). Near the other

end of the robustness scale are socioeconomic measures of economic status, like education or location. The asset-based approach used here is somewhere in the middle in robustness and practicality and has the added advantage of being the most used approach in published research during the past five years.

Sources and Data

Composing the book involved an extensive literature review.[3] In addition, large segments of the book were derived from a selection of books and resources developed by the World Bank and other agencies and networks over the past 10 years. That selection includes the following resources:

Reaching the Poor Program (RPP). RPP was funded by the World Bank, the Bill and Melinda Gates Foundation, and the governments of the Netherlands and Sweden. Chapters 5–18 of this book are based on the following products of the project:

- A book that summarizes the main findings of the research financed by RPP (Gwatkin, Wagstaff, and Yazbeck 2005)
- An issue of *Development Outreach* that included findings from the RPP conference held in February 2004 and additional evaluation work
- The RPP Policy Briefs, which are available in English, French, Russian, and Spanish (http://go.worldbank.org/PUJ2E7T1Z0)
- A book on methodologies used in researching inequalities in health (O'Donnell and others 2007)
- A Population Reference Bureau book that expands on the RPP findings (Ashford, Gwatkin, and Yazbeck 2006)

Poverty Reduction Strategy Papers (PRSPs) for the health sector. The PRSP process was launched by the International Monitory Fund and the World Bank in September 1999. At that time, a resource book, the PRSP Sourcebook, was put together to support the process, and it covered most sectors of the economy, including health. The health, nutrition, and population chapter of the PRSP Sourcebook and an accompanying series of technical annexes provide some of the framework for chapter 2 and the backbone for chapter 3.

World Bank's data on inequality in 56 low- and middle-income countries. Starting in 1999, the World Bank began re-analyzing Demographic and Health Surveys (DHS) using a new asset-based approach developed by the World Bank's Research Group (Gwatkin and others 2007;

http://go.worldbank.org/6LO8OUOUR0). Most of the analysis in chapter 1 uses this database.

Publications on the Millennium Development Goals (MDGs). The launch of the MDG development agenda produced a number of books and resource guidelines that touched on inequality in the health sector. Two synthesis publications were used in chapter 2; they covered multisectoral determinants of health outcomes, especially for the poor; and the importance of household actions and resources and community influences on both outcomes for, and health services usage by, the poor (Wagstaff and Claeson 2004; Campbell White, Merrick, and Yazbeck 2006).

World Bank Institute (WBI) courses on equity in health. WBI, along with the World Health Organization (WHO) and Semmelweis University, has developed two courses focused on inequality. The first, a Web-based course, "Health Outcomes and the Poor," was launched in 2002 and has been delivered in a partnership between WBI and WHO in English, French, Chinese, and Spanish. The second, a face-to-face course held in Budapest, Hungary, has been led by Semmelweis University and WHO/Euro since 2003. Content developed for both courses has been used throughout the book.

World Development Report 2004: Making Services Work for the Poor (WDR04). In 2004, the World Bank's flagship annual publication, *World Development Report*, focused on the need to increase the benefits received by the poor in several sectors, including health. Chapter 8 of WDR04 focused on health and is used in chapters 2, 3, and 4. Moreover, one of the background papers for WDR04, which collected all available evidence on the distributional orientation of public spending, is used in chapters 1 and 3 (Filmer 2004).

Equitap research products. Funded since 2000 by a grant from the European Commission, the Equitap research project is implemented by a network of Asian researchers with a focus on comparing equity in regional health systems in countries that range geographically from Bangladesh to Japan (http://www.equitap.org).

India health sector research. Detailed data from India are used throughout the book to provide examples of country-specific analysis. The data and findings are from two books and several research papers (Peters and others 2002; Yazbeck and Peters 2003; Mahal and others 2002; Pande and Yazbeck 2003; Gaudin and Yazbeck 2006).

Notes

1. From the Wikipedia article on "Empiricism": "In philosophy, *empiricism* means, roughly, 'try it and see.' It is a theory of knowledge that is practical rather than abstract, and asserts that knowledge arises from experience rather than revelation. . . . It is a fundamental part of the scientific method that all hypotheses and theories must be tested against observations of the natural world, rather than resting solely on *a priori* reasoning, intuition, or revelation. Hence, science is considered to be *methodologically* empirical in nature." Of interest for our purposes here, the article notes that one of the origins of *empiricism* is the Greek and Roman term *empiric*, "referring to a physician whose skill derives from practical experience as opposed to instruction in theory" (http://en.wikipedia.org/wiki/Empiricism, accessed June 15, 2008).

2. Inequity and inequality are not the same thing but are unfortunately used interchangeably in the literature. Inequality is a simpler concept; in health service use, inequality refers to simple proportional measures of use relative to population scaled by some measure of socioeconomic status (for example, the poorest half of the population used less than half of the available resources for health care provided by the government). Inequity refers to use of health services relative to medical need, and medical need is a fairly difficult concept to quantify.

3. An annotated bibliography of the relevant papers from the literature review was developed as a companion product to this book, Goldman and others (Forthcoming). Selected references from the annotated bibliography, and shortened descriptions of each selected reference, are located in annexes for chapters 1, 2, 3, 4, and 19 linking the most relevant papers from the published literature to the topics of each chapter.

Acknowledgments

Putting together this book was a labor of love, in large part because of the opportunity to work with a wonderful group of people who are passionate about improving the health of the poor. Special thanks go to Davidson Gwatkin and Adam Wagstaff, who co-led the first phase of the Reaching the Poor Program (RPP), which laid the foundation for this work and was financially supported by the Bill and Melinda Gates Foundation, the governments of the Netherlands and Sweden, and the World Bank's Research Support Budget. Most of the work on this book took place during the second phase of RPP, which was financially supported by the government of the Netherlands and the World Bank Institute. I am deeply indebted to the RPP II team for all their hard work and support: Christina (Tina) Chang, Ann Goldman, Jo Hindriks, Michelle Morris, Mary Mugala, Tanya Ringland, and Chailing Yang. In addition to the RPP II team at WBI, thanks go to Bruno A. Laporte, the WBI manager under whose leadership and support RPP II thrived.

Early drafts of the book were reviewed by a wonderful group of experts from within and outside the World Bank, including Agnès Couffinhal, Maria-Luisa Escobar, Davidson Gwatkin, April Harding, Melitta Jakab, Dan Kress, Aparnaa Somanathan, and Marko Vucici. Effective editorial assistance was provided by Gregg Forte and Melody Molinoff as well as the editors working for the World Bank's Office of the Publisher. Thanks also go to the production team at the Bank's Office of the Publisher, especially the acquiring editor Stephen McGroarty, production editor Cindy Fisher, print coordinator Stuart Tucker, and their teams. Finally, a special thanks to the great team at Steam Cafe.

Abbreviations

ANM	auxiliary nurse midwife
ARI	acute respiratory infection
BA	beneficiary assessment
BEMFAM	Brazilian Family Well-Being Society
BIA	benefit incidence analysis; also, beneficiary incidence analysis
BKKBN	National Family Planning Coordinating Board
CASEN	Chile's biannual national socioeconomic household survey
CBHI	community-based health insurance
CHI	community health insurance
CI	concentration index
DALY	disability-adjusted life year
DHMT	district health management team
DHS	Demographic and Health Survey
DOTS	directly observed treatment
DPT	diphtheria, pertussis, and tetanus
DRG	Diagnosis-Related Group
FLS	Family Life Survey
FONASA	Fondo Nacional de Salud (Chile's national health insurance program)
FOSIS	Fondo Solidario de Inversion Social (Solidarity and Social Investment Fund)
FOSYGA	Fondo de Solidaridad y Garantía
HEF	health equity fund
HIS	health information systems
IAP	indoor air pollution
IHRDC	Ifakara Health Research and Development Centre
IMCI	Integrated Management of Childhood Illness
IMF	International Monetary Fund
IMR	infant mortality rate

JPS	Jarang Pengaman Sosial
KINET	Kilombero Treated Net Project
LSMS	Living Standards Measurement Study
M&E	monitoring and evaluation
MAP	macroeconomic adjustment program
MBB	Marginal Budgeting for Bottlenecks
MCE	multi-country evaluation
MCH	maternal and child health
MDG	Millennium Development Goal
MHIF	Mandatory Health Insurance Fund
MICS	Multiple Indicator Cluster Surveys
MOH	Ministry of Health
NAP	Nepal Adolescent Project
NGO	nongovernmental organization
NHA	national health accounts
NSSO	National Sample Survey Organization
PER	Public Expenditure Review
PETS	public expenditure tracking survey
POS	Plan Obligatorio de Salud
POSS	Plan Obligatorio de Salud Subsidiado
PROGRESA	Health, Nutrition and Education Program
PRSP	Poverty Reduction Strategy Paper
PSF	Programa de Saúde da Família (Family Health Program)
RC	contributory regime
RH	reproductive health
RPP	Reaching the Poor Program
RS	subsidized regime
SES	socioeconomic status
SEWA	Self-Employed Women's Association
SIAs	supplementary immunization activities
SISBEN	Selection System of Beneficiaries for Social Programs
SP	Seguro Popular
UNFPA	United Nations Population Fund
UNICEF	United Nations Children's Fund
USAID	U.S. Agency for International Development
WBI	World Bank Institute
WHO	World Health Organization
WHS	World Health Survey

1

An Unacceptable Reality

Recently published data show that health inequality is rampant among 56 low- and middle-income countries representing 2.8 billion people. In relation to the most well-off 20 percent of the population in these countries, the data show that, *in the poorest 20 percent, on average,*

- an infant is more than twice as likely to die before reaching the age of 1,
- a child is more than three times as likely to suffer from severe stunting, and
- the adolescent fertility rate is three times higher (Gwatkin and others 2007).[1]

These data suggest that the health sector should allocate more resources to the poor. Yet, the data documenting these disparities also show that the health sector is a contributor to the inequality. Again in relation to the wealthiest quintile of the population, the data show that, in the poorest quintile, on average,

- a pregnant woman is more than three times as likely to deliver at home, instead of at a health facility;
- births are more than two-thirds less likely to be attended by a trained professional;
- children are half as likely to have received full basic childhood immunization; and
- women of childbearing age are 40 percent less likely to practice contraception.[2]

Numbers and statistics like those cited above are dramatically changing the research agenda and policy dialogue in the health sector, particularly as it relates to inequality (Yazbeck 2007). A number of factors are contributing to this renewed attention to equity and equality, but a critical driving force is a new emphasis on empiricism, the results of which are focusing the attention of researchers, policy makers, and a growing civil society.

A Light at the End of the Tunnel: A New Way to Measure Inequalities

Nothing mobilizes policy action and political attention like evidence, especially evidence that paints a terrible picture of neglect or inequality. Until recently, advocates for health sector equity were limited in their ability to effectively tackle inequity and inequality in low- and middle-income countries. The dearth of data, analysis, and systematic evaluation regarding the effects of policy reforms and prescriptions posed a critical constraint. In the absence of country-specific data, most published work on inequality focused on cross-country inequality in health outcomes (like infant mortality and life expectancy) and health services utilization. The published data often neglected or underemphasized intracountry inequalities.

At the heart of the problem were fragmented approaches to the collection of data by international development agencies. The disparity was most prominent in two of the largest programs of the past 20 years for the collection of household data: the Demographic and Health Surveys (DHS), conducted by the U.S. Agency for International Development (USAID), and the Living Standards Measurement Study (LSMS) surveys, conducted by the World Bank. The DHS data are focused on population, health, choice of providers within the public and private sectors, health knowledge, and some household characteristics. The DHS data, however, lack direct information about household wealth or health-sector-related expenditures.

The LSMS, on the other hand, measures the distribution of economic status, and uses the gold standard of methods for doing so—household production, consumption, and expenditures. That approach allows researchers to rank each household in the income continuum and makes it feasible to examine distributional dimensions. What the LSMS lacks, however, are the detailed modules on health, health consumption, and choices. In other words, LSMS data sets are able to capture overall inequality but are limited in the ability to look at the distribution of health sector indicators.

The absence of household-level measures of economic status in the health sector data led to the use of proxy measures or to the use of geographic residence and nationality as the basis of equity analysis in the health sector. None of those approaches could convincingly portray the data needed to drive innovations in policy.

A breakthrough came in the late 1990s when researchers at the World Bank and those working on USAID programs developed the ability to measure wealth distribution using asset and access variables that existed in DHS data sets but had not been previously exploited.[3] Historically, the DHS and other health surveys have not covered expenditures and consumption in detail but did include questions about ownership of radios, TVs, cars, bicycles, and other assets. They also contained data on access to water and heating, and household characteristics like types of toilets and roof materials. Information from such household asset and access questions can now be used to identify the economic status of a household relative to other households in a region or a country. This innovation is now known as the asset-score approach. (Annex 1.1 has information on calculating asset scores as well as references for technical notes, computer programs, and examples.)

This breakthrough, together with the publication of data for 44 low- and middle-income countries by the World Bank in 1999 and 2000 using this technique, brought country-specific inequality back into the debates over health sector policy, and changed the research landscape in the following ways.[4]

First, researchers found themselves with a large number of nationally representative household surveys (the DHS) that permitted them to capture the inequality of health outcomes and health system outputs over large parts of the world. For large countries, the data were also used to look at inequalities at the subnational level.[5]

Second, the asset-score approach changed the way new household surveys were collected by other agencies. Capturing economic status through a household, facility, or patient survey was much easier with an asset-score approach than with the more complex consumption and expenditure approach. The United Nations Children's Fund (UNICEF), which funds the Multiple Indicator Cluster Surveys (MICS), and the World Health Organization (WHO), which funds World Health Surveys, now include asset questions in their surveys and by doing so facilitate the analysis of inequality.

The breakthrough in empirical analysis has enhanced the abilities of researchers in the following areas:

- *Problem identification.* By analyzing (i) health, nutrition, and population outcomes and health system outputs, such as the use of critical services or outputs; and (ii) variations across socioeconomic groups, researchers can identify the nature of the inequality problem.

- *Identification of causes.* As will be summarized in chapter 2, many determinants of both health outcomes and inequality are outside the health sector. Those factors are thus outside the scope of this book, but knowledge of how the health sector interacts with them deepens understanding and response at the policy level. Chapter 3 focuses on the quantitative and qualitative tools available for identifying the causes of inequality in health service use and provides examples of applications.
- *Designing policies and setting targets.* Problem identification and analysis of causes should form the technical foundation for policy development and operational planning. Chapter 4 outlines policies for addressing inequality in health service use. Chapters 5 through 18 give examples of policies and programs that decreased inequality in health service use and increased the availability of services in low- and middle-income countries in Africa, Asia, and Latin America.

Not a Pretty Picture

The reanalysis of the DHS data by the World Bank for 56 low- and middle-income countries has enabled researchers to look at inequality within countries and across countries and regions. To illustrate the starkness of the results, and the large variations in them, we consider three measures of health sector outcomes: infant mortality, adolescent fertility, and severe stunting. Figure 1.1 summarizes the regional inequalities for each of these outcomes, and in annex 1.2, tables A1.3 through A1.5 show similar data by country and wealth quintile.

First, as figure 1.1 shows for each of those outcomes, the poorest 20 percent of the population in every region suffer more than the wealthiest 20 percent.

But, second, the *level of inequality* between the wealthiest and poorest groups does not necessarily track the outcomes for the poor. (The level of inequality is measured by the concentration index, a measure shown in parentheses for each region in the figures and defined later in the chapter.) For example, although the poorest families in East Asia and Pacific and in Latin America had the lowest levels of infant mortality (deaths before the age of one, per 1,000 live births), the level of inequality in each of those regions was higher than in all the other regions. That fact seems to indicate that as countries become better at addressing infant mortality, wealthier families are much more able than others to take advantage of such advances (Victora and others 2000).

Third, the averages for each region obscure the large heterogeneity across the countries of each region and across the 56 countries. Infant mortality in the poorest quintile of a country ranges from a low of 32 in

Figure 1.1 *Regional Inequalities in Health Sector Outcomes*

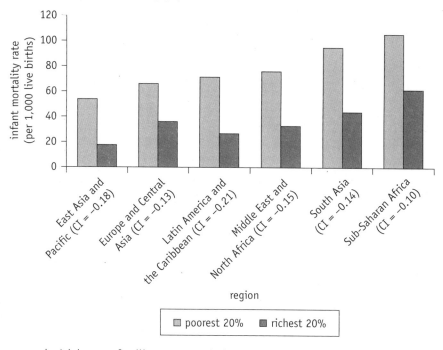

a. Infant mortality gaps in low- and middle-income countries

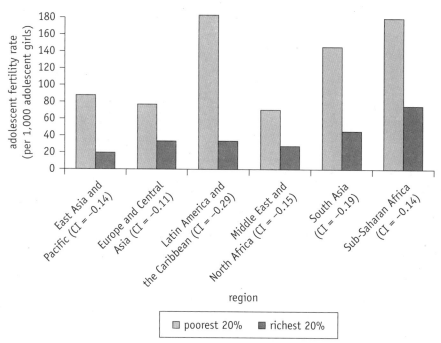

b. Adolescent fertility rate gaps in low- and middle-income countries

Figure 1.1 *(continued)*

c. Severe stunting in children in low- and middle-income countries

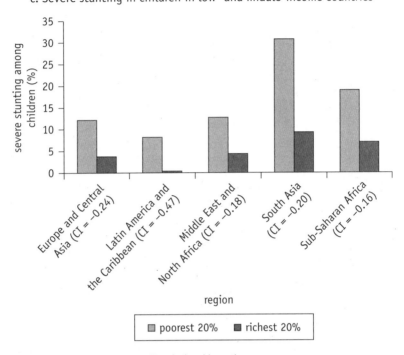

Source: Gwatkin and others 2007. CIs calculated by author.
Note: The East Asia and Pacific region does not appear in figure c because there were not enough data on stunting to allow aggregation to regional average by quintile.

Colombia (surveyed in 2000 and 2005) to a high of more than 140 in Mozambique (1997 and 2003). In Brazil (survey dated 1996), the concentration index for infant mortality was −0.25 (a high level of inequality), whereas in Kazakhstan (1995) there was no statistically significant level of inequality.

The points just made with regard to infant mortality hold for the other two outcomes treated here. Some clear variations exist, however, in results among the three outcomes. Looking at the data for the Latin American region, across the three outcome variables we find that while inequality is consistently the highest of the regions, the average measures for the poorest quintile rank differently. The poorest of Latin America do much better on average than the poorest in all other regions in severe stunting, in the middle range with respect to infant mortality, but rank last for adolescent fertility. Tremendous variations exist across variables, regions, countries, and even by subnational groupings (box 1.1).

Box 1.1 *Variations in Health and Fertility Outcomes in India*

The variations in health and fertility outcomes across regions and countries, shown in the main text of this chapter and in annex 1.2, can be examined within large countries such as India. As shown in the table below, the average infant mortality rate (IMR) in all India is 73, but the rate for infants in the poorest 20 percent of the population is more than 2.6 times that for infants in the wealthiest 20 percent (95.6 versus 36.1). The variation between urban and rural areas is very large, both on average and across wealth quintiles. The variations by selected states are also large on average, and much more so across wealth groups. An infant born to a family in the wealthiest quintile in Tamil Nadu is almost five times more likely to survive until age one than an infant born to a family in the poorest quintile in Uttar Pradesh.

Total fertility shows a similar pattern of variation across India. At the national level, the poor have much higher fertility rates. The gap between fertility among the urban and rural populations is not as large as the IMR gap, but the variations are considerable across the selected states.

Inequality in Health and Fertility Outcomes in Rural and Urban India and by Selected States, 1998–99

Quintiles of wealth	All India	Rural India	Urban India	Tamil Nadu	Maharashtra	Uttar Pradesh	Rajasthan	Punjab
Infant mortality								
1st (poorest)	95.61	94.15	74.17	62.16	68.86	125.57	110.52	83.02
2nd	82.72	92.18	50.85	59.86	65.27	100.26	85.99	62.37
3rd	75.28	77.89	41.32	52.79	60.15	94.90	100.96	54.45
4th	55.90	73.08	41.56	46.26	31.33	87.11	71.00	31.70
5th	36.09	49.46	23.64	27.68	26.06	52.15	59.34	33.80
Average	73.02	79.67	49.22	50.97	53.22	95.36	88.09	56.80
Total fertility								
1st (poorest)	3.73	3.75	3.04	2.51	3.18	5.07	4.62	3.45
2nd	3.33	3.46	2.60	2.26	2.72	4.57	4.67	2.80
3rd	2.80	3.11	2.26	2.14	2.75	4.18	3.80	2.12
4th	2.56	2.73	1.84	2.02	2.32	3.77	3.53	1.84
5th	1.96	2.39	1.73	2.03	1.73	2.64	2.49	1.56
Average	2.85	3.07	2.27	2.19	2.52	3.99	3.78	2.28

Source: Recalculated from IIPS (2000).

Some obvious and strong findings can be summarized from the outcomes data detailed here and in annex 1.2:

1. *Large gaps between the poor and wealthy.* The overwhelming majority of low- and middle-income countries (representing more than 2.8 billion people in 2001) show a large gap in outcomes between the poor and the wealthiest. The health sector should play a role in addressing this gap in outcomes because the poor need health care services much more than the rich.

2. *Persistence of inequality.* In the countries for which data exist for multiple time periods, the large gap appears to be persistent over time. Additionally, more countries experience growth in inequality of outcomes than experience contractions of the gap. The persistence of inequality points to systematic constraints and long-term failures in the health sector and argues for the need to truly understand these constraints and failures, particularly as policies are devised to address them. In other words, simplistic policy answers are likely to fail.

3. *Variation in sources of inequality.* The inequality gaps appear to be consistent across regions for some outcomes, like infant mortality, but not for others. This finding reinforces the need to understand the determinants of the outcomes and recognize that factors outside the health sector may play a stronger role for some outcomes than for others.

4. *A need for local solutions.* The considerable variability in outcome inequality at the country and subnational levels (box 1.1) suggests that global or regional answers will not work for all countries. Therefore, national and subnational analysis should be integral to developing effective policies.

The wealth of data can and should be exploited considerably more than has been done to date. Such analysis can produce a range of policy-relevant findings. Because the main focus of this book is health services use, the inequality data regarding outcomes are used mainly to provide motivation for addressing inequality in the use of critical health, nutrition, and fertility services.

Health Sector May Exacerbate Inequality

The pervasive inequality in health outcomes is not surprising considering the many ways in which the poor face critical handicaps, including in education, transportation (in both access to hospitals and to safety), water and sanitation access, and security in their sources of heating and cooking fuel.

In all countries, many of those constraints are outside the direct control of the ministry of health and the overall health sector. However, the use of important and life-saving *health services* is within the sphere of influence of health policy makers and is critical to health outcomes for the poor.

Unfortunately, as we saw at the beginning of this chapter, global estimates show that health services in low- and middle-income countries tend to serve the wealthier more than the poor. We examine that point in more detail here, for if the health sector is already serving the wealthy more than the poor, one could well expect that simply providing more resources to the health sector would *worsen* the inequality of outcomes. With the tools discussed in chapters 3 and 4, however, direct and focused efforts to correct the pro-wealthy bias of the health sector can benefit the poor and reduce inequality, as the examples summarized in chapters 5–18 illustrate.

As with pro-wealth bias of health outcomes, the reanalyzed data from the DHS provide ample evidence of a pro-wealth bias in the use of health services in low- and middle-income countries. First, we provide some global perspective on the use of health services in those countries: When the services are ranked by the global concentration index, which presents a single point measure of inequality, the seven with the largest measure of inequality are all related to reproductive health (table 1.1). In the world of inequality of health services, reproductive health services stand out as the worst of the worst (Campbell White, Merrick, and Yazbeck 2006; Yazbeck 2004).

Expanding the global analysis of these countries to encompass basic maternal and child health services, we find again that the wealthy use the services more than the poor (figure 1.2). Indeed, for all basic health services for which data are available, and regardless of the source of financing or

Table 1.1 *Health Services with the Largest Measure of Inequality*

DELIVERY IN A PRIVATE FACILITY
CONTRACEPTIVE PREVALENCE AMONG MEN
DELIVERY AT HOME
DELIVERY IN A PUBLIC FACILITY
DELIVERY ATTENDED BY A MEDICALLY TRAINED PERSON
CONTRACEPTIVE PREVALENCE AMONG WOMEN
ANTENATAL CARE VISITS TO A MEDICALLY TRAINED PERSON MULTIPLE TIMES

Source: Gwatkin and others 2007.

Figure 1.2 *Use of Basic Maternal and Child Health Services, Coverage Rates among the Poorest and Wealthiest 20 Percent of the Population in 56 Low- and Middle-Income Countries*

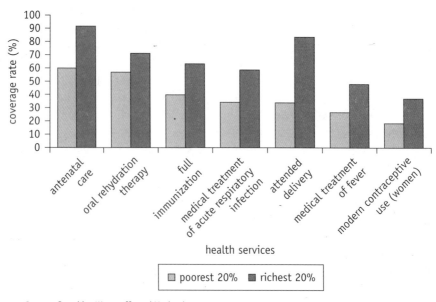

Source: Gwatkin, Wagstaff, and Yazbeck 2005.

delivery (public or private), the better-off are much more likely to obtain access even though the poor need them more.

The *size* of the gap between the lowest and highest wealth groups varies by service, by region, by country, and within countries. To see that variation by service, we recalculate the service data in figure 1.2 as odds ratios, that is, as the probability that a person from a household in the wealthiest 20 percent of the population, on average, receives a specific service relative to a person from a household in the poorest 20 percent (figure 1.3). All the health services in figure 1.3 have an odds ratio higher than 1, which means that the wealthiest households are more likely than the poorest to use them. However, the odds ratio is much higher than 1 for deliveries attended by a trained provider (the wealthiest are three times more likely to obtain that service than the poorest) and much higher than 1 for the use of modern contraceptives by women (two times more likely). Again, the health sector not only fails the poor, but poor women in particular.

Figure 1.3 *Inequalities in the Use of Basic Maternal and Child Health Services: Coverage Rate Ratios for the Wealthiest and Poorest 20 Percent, 56 Low- and Middle-Income Countries*

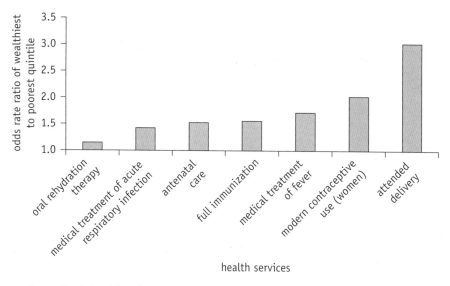

Source: Recalculated from figure 1.2.

We also find considerable variability in the inequality of service use by region and country. To illustrate, we have selected four services: (i) full immunization for children, (ii) three or more antenatal checkups for pregnant women, (iii) contraceptive prevalence rates for women, and (iv) deliveries attended by trained providers. All four exhibit strong pro-wealthy inequality across regions and countries (annex 1.2, tables A1.6, A1.7, A1.8, and A1.9). Population-weighted regional averages for antenatal care visits reveal large gaps between the rich and poor in every region (figure 1.4). The poorest women in the Middle East and North Africa region and in the South Asia region had the lowest rates of access to care. Unlike the findings in outcome inequalities, however, the same two regions also had the highest levels of inequality as measured by the concentration index.

Differences across countries in inequality of service use are large. Therefore, examining inequalities at the national level—or, in the case of large countries, the subnational level (box 1.2)—is a much more practical and effective use of the data, given that the goal is to apply new policies in specific countries. For example, the country-level data show tremendous

Figure 1.4 *Population-Weighted Regional Averages of Percentage of Pregnant Women in the Poorest and Wealthiest Quintiles Who Receive Three or More Antenatal Visits*

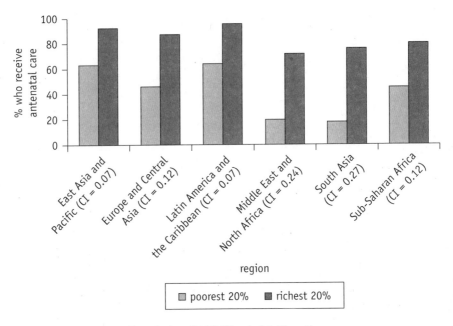

Source: Data from Gwatkin and others (2007). CIs calculated by author.

Box 1.2 *Variations in Health Service Use in India*

In a large country such as India, a subnational analysis is essential to reveal details hidden by national, not to mention regional, analyses. The use of three reproductive and child health services illustrates the point (table). Starting at the national level, all three variables reveal significant inequalities.

The most interesting findings, however, are the tremendous variation by state, both in averages and across wealth groups. Those findings raise many questions. Why would two states in the same country have such large differences in the use of the same service (for example, full immunization for all children—almost 89 percent in Tamil Nadu and only 16.5 percent in Rajasthan)? Why do only 5 percent of the poorest women in Uttar Pradesh get antenatal care while over 80 percent of the poorest in Tamil Nadu get this service?

Box 1.2 *(continued)*

Service Use Inequality in India and Selected States, 1998–99
(percentage of relevant population who receive service)

Quintiles of wealth	All India	Rural India	Urban India	Tamil Nadu	Maharashtra	Uttar Pradesh	Rajasthan	Punjab
Full immunization								
1st (poorest)	22.19	22.44	39.85	79.91	64.35	10.19	4.53	42.25
2nd	29.27	24.27	53.34	88.42	70.61	16.27	11.87	74.33[a]
3rd	42.92	36.56	58.45	87.37	74.85	18.70	8.66	71.05
4th	54.54	45.10	65.92	90.32	79.66	32.13	23.44	84.89[a]
5th	66.19	59.56	72.81	97.92	79.40	38.06	45.35	100.0[a]
Average	41.13	36.51	56.62	88.65	73.17	22.07	16.51	71.28
Antenatal care, three or more visits								
1st (poorest)	20.30	20.92	48.64	82.22	38.35	5.29	10.36	30.49
2nd	30.02	25.31	64.72	83.81	56.27	7.20	15.16	50.71
3rd	45.01	35.70	73.84	95.88	69.11	9.67	16.05	57.63
4th	61.55	46.89	82.70	97.14	85.43	15.26	26.79	78.28
5th	81.31	64.34	92.47	97.42	93.99	47.48	62.90	97.44
Average	44.24	36.90	70.13	90.94	66.20	14.86	23.59	58.42
Use of modern contraceptives among women								
1st (poorest)	28.90	29.48	42.48	48.44	54.66	12.66	25.41	52.45
2nd	34.42	31.12	49.54	45.27	60.95	14.37	29.43	55.70
3rd	45.42	39.42	51.73	51.73	60.31	17.87	39.01	55.09
4th	49.89	46.80	55.18	50.26	61.26	24.22	40.47	53.03
5th	54.91	51.89	56.28	55.33	62.08	40.18	55.08	52.92
Average	42.85	39.89	51.22	50.27	59.88	21.97	38.06	53.83

Source: Recalculated from IIPS (2000).
a. Average based on small sample size and may not be representative.

Figure 1.5 *Population-Weighted Regional Averages of Percentage of Deliveries for the Poorest and Wealthiest Quintiles That Were Attended by a Medically Trained Person*

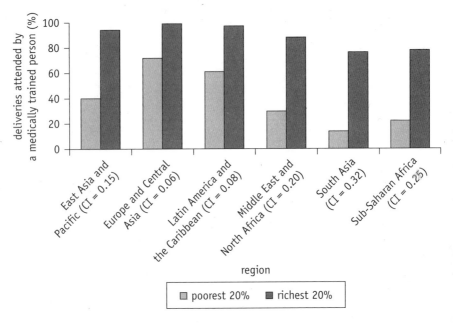

Source: Data from Gwatkin and others (2007). CIs calculated by author.

variations for the proportion of women in the poorest quintile who have three or more antenatal care visits (table A1.7), with a low of only 3.4 percent in the Republic of Yemen (1997) and a high of 92.4 percent in the Dominican Republic (2002). A large variation also exists in the level of inequality as measured by the concentration index. The highest level of inequality for the use of this health service was found in Pakistan and the lowest in Zimbabwe.

By region, the wealth-group gaps are much larger for deliveries attended by a professional (figure 1.5) than for full immunization for children (figure 1.6). Once again, the country-specific variations for these two service-use variables are about as extreme as they can be (tables A1.9 and A1.6). The percentage of deliveries for poor women that are attended by medically trained personnel ranges from a low of less than 1 percent in Ethiopia (2000) to over 99 percent in Kazakhstan (1999). Considerable country-level variation also exists for immunization.

Figure 1.6 *Population-Weighted Regional Averages of Percentage of Fully Immunized Children from the Poorest and Wealthiest Quintiles*

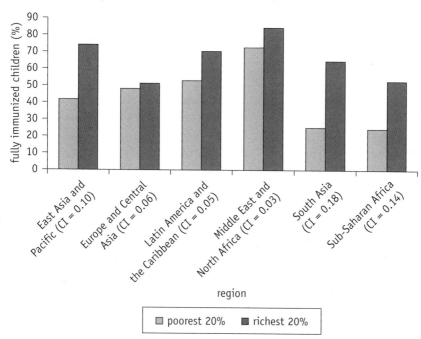

Source: Data from Gwatkin and others (2007). CIs calculated by author.

The Misallocation of Public Spending on Health

The overwhelming evidence of inequality in health service use addressed so far is based on surveys like the DHS, which focus mostly on primary health care or family planning services. In most countries, primary care services constitute only a small percentage of what the public sector typically spends in the health sector. Missing from the DHS data and our analysis so far are the large and expensive secondary and tertiary hospital-based health care services. Because the evidence suggests that public spending on primary health care goes mainly to the wealthy, it should not come as a surprise that public spending on hospital-based services is even more biased toward the wealthy. The next chapter examines the many barriers that the poor face in seeking health care. These barriers are even more binding when it comes to expensive hospital services.

An analytical technique that allows us to capture the distributional nature of public health spending is benefit incidence analysis (BIA).[6] BIA is an indirect method of estimating the allocation of the benefits of public spending across wealth groups. The method starts with the public cost of providing various services—for example, the cost of providing an inpatient hospital stay is considerably higher than an outpatient visit; similarly, an overnight stay in a small rural clinic is considerably less expensive than an overnight stay in an oncology hospital. By tracking use of various services by socioeconomic group, BIA helps to answer the politically important question of who is benefiting from public spending on various services.[7] More to the point, are governments allocating their resources to address the needs of the poor and disadvantaged?

Additionally, BIA can be used to aggregate health service use inequality by capturing the magnitude of inequality in a government's total health sector spending. A literature review of BIA analyses, conducted for the World Bank's 2004 *World Development Report*, found BIA data on the health sector for 22 countries (Filmer 2004; World Bank 2004). The data confirmed that the overwhelming majority of public health budgets were pro-wealthy.

A number of issues are immediately noticeable if we examine the findings from eight of those countries (figure 1.7). The most obvious finding is

Figure 1.7 *Selected Benefit Incidence Findings for Public Spending on Health*

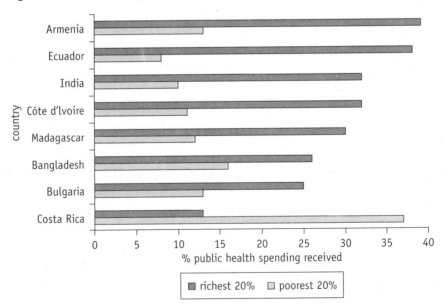

Source: Filmer 2004.

the disparity between the poor and the wealthy—in all eight countries except Costa Rica, the poorest 20 percent of the population capture considerably less than 20 percent of the benefits (especially in Ecuador); and in all eight except Costa Rica, the wealthiest 20 percent capture much more than 20 percent (in Armenia, almost double). As implied by the exceptional position of Costa Rica in figure 1.7, another obvious finding is that the gap between the incidence of public subsidies across wealth groups varies considerably by country.

A BIA can also be conducted at the subnational level for large countries. India was the site of one of the most detailed BIA studies ever conducted (box 1.3). The data show that while public spending in the overwhelming majority of states and at the national level is pro-wealthy, it is pro-poor in at least one state (Kerala). A motivating force behind the present book is that the world can learn from the examples of success in attacking inequality even amid the overwhelming evidence that health sectors fail the poor.

Presenting Inequality Data

Throughout this book and in the wider literature, the data on inequality are presented in a number of ways, each chosen in accord with several practical, technical, and strategic factors. To take just the strategic perspective, it is important to match the presentation to the targeted audience. Policy makers need simple, easy to explain to a wide audience, politically powerful tools, while researchers prefer more complex, comprehensive analyses. The remainder of this chapter summarizes the choices made here for presenting inequality data.

The Wealth Gap

The most direct way of presenting inequality data is to compare averages for the poorest and wealthiest in society. This method was used for the health outcomes in figure 1.1; for service use in figures 1.2, 1.4, 1.5, and 1.6; and for capturing the public subsidy for health spending in figure 1.7. Wealth gaps are attractive because they are simple to understand and politically powerful, well suited to capturing the attention of senior politicians, parliaments, civil society, and the media.

For example, the wealth gap in immunizations in India (box 1.2) is captured in figure 1.8. The result highlights the simple and powerful message that poor children are exposed to vaccine-preventable illnesses considerably

Box 1.3 *Benefit Incidence Analysis at the Subnational Level*

The BIA conducted in India in 1995 shows that, for the whole country, the share of the government subsidy of the health sector for curative care that goes to the wealthiest 20 percent is more than three times the size of the subsidy going to the poorest quintile (table). The subnational BIA shows that the poor fare much better in some states (Kerala, Gujarat, Tamil Nadu, and Maharashtra) than in others. The finding for the state of Bihar is especially dire—there, the share of the public health subsidy received by the rich for curative care is more than 10 times greater than that received by the poor.

Benefit Incidence Analysis, India, 1995

Rank	State	Ratio of curative care subsidy to richest versus poorest quintile	Concentration index
1	Kerala	1.10	−0.041
2	Gujarat	1.14	0.001
3	Tamil Nadu	1.46	0.059
4	Maharashtra	1.21	0.060
5	Punjab	2.93	0.102
6	Andhra Pradesh	1.85	0.116
7	West Bengal	2.73	0.157
8	Haryana	2.98	0.201
9	Karnataka	3.58	0.208
	All India	**3.28**	**0.214**
10	North East	3.16	0.220
11	Orissa	4.87	0.282
12	Madhya Pradesh	4.16	0.292
13	Uttar Pradesh	4.09	0.304
14	Rajasthan	4.95	0.334
15	Himachal Pradesh	5.88	0.340
16	Bihar	10.3	0.419

Source: Based on findings from Mahal and others (2002) and Peters and others (2002).

Figure 1.8 *Wealth Gap for Full Immunization, India, 1998–99*

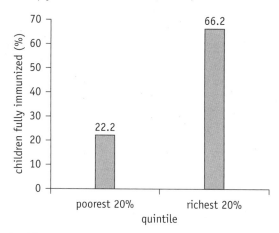

Source: Recalculated from IIPS (2000).

more than the children of better-off families. A disadvantage of wealth-gap analyses is that they capture the statistics of only the extreme groups, missing the rest of the population. Another limitation is the difficulty in comparing gaps across a number of variables or countries.

Odds Ratio

The data in the wealth gap can be presented as an odds ratio. This method was used for transforming figure 1.2 into figure 1.3. Odds ratios are visually less striking than wealth gaps, but they are easier to explain and allow comparisons across different variables (as in figure 1.3) or across different countries or regions.

Although odds ratios easily produce comparisons, the magnitude of the variable is lost. For example, the data on infant mortality in India for the poorest and wealthiest quintiles and for urban and rural populations (box 1.1) can be presented as odds ratios (figure 1.9). We know from other measures that rural infants have a much lower survival rate than urban infants, but that fact—the magnitude of the urban-rural difference—is hidden in the odds-ratio presentation. Instead, the latter presentation reveals that the wealth gap for infant mortality *within* the urban population is about 50 percent greater than in the rural population (that is, compared with infants in the wealthiest quintile of families, infants in the poorest quintile

Figure 1.9 *Odds Ratios for Infant Morality: The Likelihood of Infant Death in the Poorest Quintile of Families Relative to That in the Wealthiest Quintile, Rural and Urban India, 1998–99*

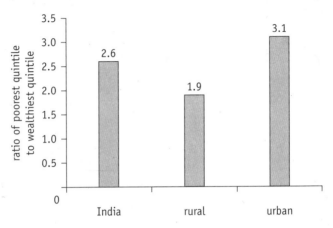

Source: Recalculated from IIPS (2000).

are 3.1 times as likely to die before age one in urban areas but only 1.9 times as likely in rural areas). Another limitation of the odds ratio is that, like the wealth-gap approach, it captures only the data from the poorest and richest groups, excluding information on the remaining middle of the population.

Full Gradient

Another approach to presenting inequality data is to simply show the full gradient, that is, the result for every grouping in the analysis. This method was used in most of the tables in this chapter, especially in annex 1.2. The obvious advantage of this approach is that it shows the complete distribution. However, more information is both good and bad. While it adds the important dimension of understanding inequality across the whole population, it hinders communication with nontechnical or policy audiences. Figure 1.10 captures the full inequality picture, by wealth quintile, for all of India as well as for its rural and urban populations.

Concentration Curves

The same full distribution of inequality in outcomes or outputs of the health sector is depicted in the cumulative form called a concentration curve.

Figure 1.10 *Inequality in Full Immunization, India, 1998–99*

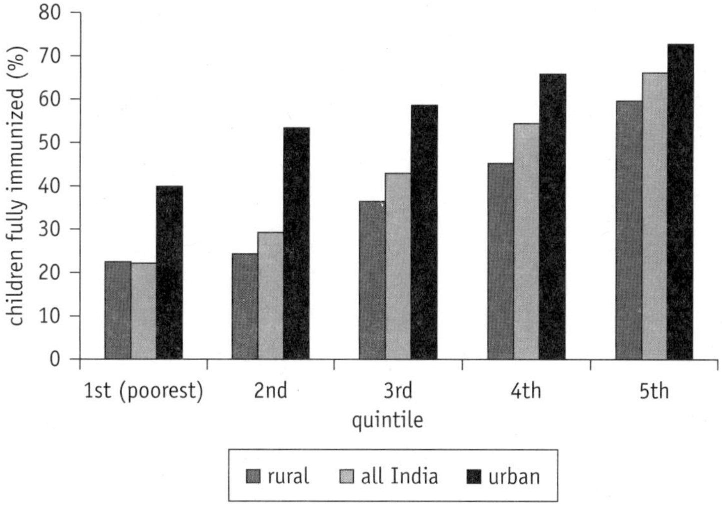

Source: Gaudin and Yazbeck 2006.

Concentration curves capture the burden of health outcomes, or the benefit of using a health service, cumulatively for the poorest 20 percent, the poorest 40 percent, the poorest 60 percent, and so on until the full population is represented.[8] Using the India data (presented in boxes 1.1 and 1.2), figures 1.11 and 1.12 represent the concentration curves of infant mortality (IMR) and full immunization, respectively. The concentration curves for IMR are above the 45 degree line, which means that the poorest quintiles of the population shoulder a higher burden of mortality than the wealthiest. Also, the concentration curve for IMR in urban India is above the concentration curve for IMR in rural India, which reflects the fact that while IMR, on average, is lower among the urban population, inequality (as shown in figure 1.9) is lower among the rural population.

A concentration curve of a negative health outcome like infant mortality reflects inequality when above the 45 degree, or equality, line, but the opposite is true for concentration curves for health service usage. Figure 1.12 depicts concentration curves for full immunization of children in four states in India (based on the data in box 1.2). Two of the curves, those for Rajasthan and Uttar Pradesh, are considerably below the equality line (the diagonal in the figure) and those for the other two, Tamil Nadu and Maharashtra, are almost the same as the equality line. A concentration curve for

Figure 1.11 *Concentration Curves of Infant Mortality Rates in India, 1998–99*

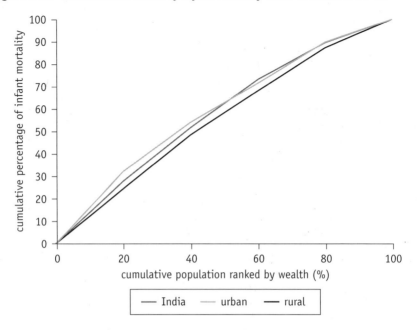

Source: Based on data from Gaudin and Yazbeck (2006).

Figure 1.12 *Immunization Concentration Curves, Selected Indian States, 1998–99*

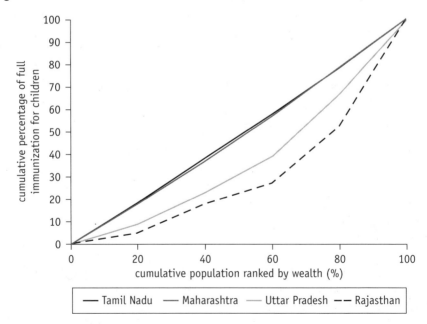

Source: Based on data from Gaudin and Yazbeck (2006).

health service use that is below the equality line means that the poorest populations are consuming less than the wealthiest.

Concentration Index

The above methods are not easily used to compare services, or countries and regions, with each other. Odds ratios and wealth gaps can be used to compare services or regions with each other but do so at the expense of eliminating considerable information about large segments of society. In contrast, the concentration index (CI) is a numeric measure that uses all the available data and readily permits comparisons across groupings. A CI is calculated as twice the area between the concentration curve and the equality line (the diagonal). A CI ranges between −1 and 1 in value; it ranges from −1 to 0 if the concentration curve is above the equality line and from 0 to 1 if the curve is below the equality line.

The ability of the CI to capture all available inequality data makes it extremely useful for researchers, and it thus represents the most used statistic in studies of health sector inequality. Correspondingly, the significant drawback to the use of CIs is precisely that they are not intuitive to nonresearch audiences. A CI of 0.4 means very little to a policy maker or nontechnical advocate, whereas they are much more likely to understand an odds ratio of 2 or a wealth gap of 30 percent. As with every approach to presenting inequality, CIs have clear advantages and disadvantages.

Annex 1.1   Asset Index as a Measure of Relative Wealth

Why Use Asset Index as a Proxy for Socioeconomic Status?

There are two approaches to measuring living standards, direct and indirect (O'Donnell and others 2007). The direct method involves gathering income, expenditure, or consumption data; however, such data are expensive and difficult to collect. The indirect method uses a proxy measure such as an asset index. An asset index measures living standards by using data on household assets such as bicycles, automobiles, and radio receivers; household materials such as wood or concrete flooring; and access to superior sources of household necessities, such as water. Such information can be easily and quickly collected in household and facility surveys. Although this method has been criticized for lacking a theoretical foundation, it is by far the most convenient method for measuring standards of living. Furthermore, recent studies suggest a close relationship between assets and consumption, indicating that an asset index is indeed a reasonable proxy for standard of living.

Data Needs

To construct an asset index, household asset data are required. Household asset data can be obtained from a multipurpose household survey, such as the DHS.

Where to Find Resources for Constructing an Asset Index

The research group at the World Bank has developed a technical note on how to construct and use an asset index from household survey data. This documentation includes computer software code and case examples to help researchers. The technical note can be found in *Analyzing Health Equity Using Household Survey Data: A Guide to Techniques and Their Implementation* (O'Donnell and others 2007). The same information can also be accessed through the Web at http://go.worldbank.org/LVSSZJX9O0. See chapter 6 of that volume.

An Example

Asset information from India's National Family Health Survey 1998–99 (IIPS 2000) was used by Gaudin and Yazbeck (2006) to examine inequality in access to immunization services at the national level, in urban versus rural populations, and in 16 of the largest states in the country. Table A1.1 summarizes the

Table A1.1 *Assets and Factor Scores, Urban India, 1998–99*

Asset	Asset ownership		Principal components results		
		Unweighted		Household score	
	Unweighted mean	standard deviation	Asset factor scores	Owns asset	Does not own asset
Telephone	0.20078	0.40059	0.3772	0.7526	−0.1891
Electricity	0.91341	0.28123	0.3686	0.1135	−1.1972
Drinking water piped into residence	0.51646	0.49974	0.3413	0.3303	−0.3527
Gas as cooking fuel source	0.46922	0.49906	0.2384	0.2535	−0.2241
Pressure cooker	0.65112	0.47662	0.2269	0.1661	−0.3100
TV	0.69189	0.46172	0.2165	0.1445	−0.3245
Table	0.65003	0.47697	0.2113	0.1551	−0.2880
Mattress	0.71707	0.45043	0.2104	0.1321	−0.3349
Fan	0.82162	0.38284	0.2083	0.0971	−0.4471
Chair	0.71298	0.45238	0.2072	0.1314	−0.3265
Refrigerator	0.28817	0.45292	0.2057	0.3233	−0.1309
Own flush toilet	0.47621	0.49944	0.1983	0.2080	−0.1891
Pucca house	0.65904	0.47404	0.1974	0.1420	−0.2745
Motorcycle	0.24961	0.43280	0.1794	0.3111	−0.1035
Separate room used as kitchen	0.64010	0.47998	0.1786	0.1339	−0.2382
Clock	0.90105	0.29860	0.1733	0.0574	−0.5228
Sewing machine	0.35412	0.47825	0.1561	0.2108	−0.1156
Radio	0.53163	0.49901	0.1428	0.1340	−0.1521
Cot	0.86096	0.34599	0.1314	0.0528	−0.3271
Drinking water hand pump in residence	0.09888	0.29851	0.0957	0.2889	−0.0317
Water pump	0.09306	0.29052	0.0952	0.2971	−0.0305
Car	0.04369	0.20440	0.0928	0.4344	−0.0198
Bicycle	0.53444	0.49882	0.0818	0.0764	−0.0877
Owns house	0.78185	0.41300	0.0329	0.0174	−0.0624
Drinking water from own well	0.00685	0.08249	0.0310	0.3730	−0.0026
Acres of irrigated land under cultivation	6.10423	40.47415	0.0275	n.a.	n.a.

(continued)

Table A1.1 *(continued)*

Asset	Asset ownership		Principal components results		
				Household score	
	Unweighted mean	Unweighted standard deviation	Asset factor scores	Owns asset	Does not own asset
Tractor	0.00761	0.08688	0.0272	0.3113	−0.0024
Drinking water from public well	0.05357	0.22516	0.0267	0.1122	−0.0064
Acres of cultivated land	10.72356	55.83063	0.0257	n.a.	n.a.
Drinking water from public pump	0.08252	0.27517	0.0182	0.0606	−0.0054
Drinking water from a tanker truck	0.00325	0.05691	0.0150	0.2625	−0.0009
Biogas as cooking fuel source	0.00566	0.07499	0.0145	0.1925	−0.0011
Thresher	0.00684	0.08241	0.0129	0.1552	−0.0011
Other source of drinking water	0.00664	0.08124	0.0125	0.1525	−0.0010
Owns agricultural land	0.19916	0.39938	0.0107	0.0214	−0.0053
Bullock cart	0.01423	0.11845	0.0039	0.0325	−0.0005
Drinking water from a spring	0.00086	0.02922	0.0038	0.1282	−0.0001
Drinking water from a pond or lake	0.00278	0.05261	0.0031	0.0584	−0.0002
Electricity as cooking fuel source	0.00826	0.09052	0.0023	0.0255	−0.0002
Drinking water from a river or stream	0.00077	0.02769	0.0022	0.0776	−0.0001
Drinking water from rainwater	0.00005	0.00681	0.0019	0.2823	0.0000
Own pit latrine	0.13384	0.34049	0.0016	0.0041	−0.0006
Drinking water from a dam	0.00001	0.00294	0.0006	0.2178	0.0000
Drinking water from a public tap	0.22736	0.41913	0	0	0
Gas as main source of lighting	0.00003	0.00570	−0.0006	−0.1000	0

| Asset | Asset ownership | | | Principal components results | | |
| | Unweighted mean | Unweighted standard deviation | Asset factor scores | | Household score | |
				Owns asset	Does not own asset
Other source of lighting	0.00039	0.01982	−0.0060	−0.3031	0.0001
Other toilet facility	0.00028	0.01664	−0.0075	−0.4488	0.0001
Other source of cooking fuel	0.00218	0.04669	−0.0112	−0.2394	0.0005
Oil as main source of lighting	0.00041	0.02030	−0.0128	−0.6277	0.0003
Coal as cooking fuel source	0.00553	0.07419	−0.0151	−0.2027	0.0011
Shared flush toilet	0.07728	0.26704	−0.0175	−0.0605	0.0051
Shared pit latrine	0.02186	0.14624	−0.0202	−0.1354	0.0030
Public pit latrine	0.01294	0.11300	−0.0246	−0.2153	0.0028
Crop residue as main fuel source	0.00516	0.07163	−0.0302	−0.4189	0.0022
Dung as cooking fuel source	0.01376	0.11649	−0.0326	−0.2760	0.0039
Coke as cooking fuel source	0.04349	0.20395	−0.0353	−0.1654	0.0075
Owns livestock	0.13712	0.34398	−0.0362	−0.0908	0.0144
Public flush toilet	0.08558	0.27975	−0.0536	−0.1751	0.0164
Kerosene as cooking fuel source	0.21441	0.41042	−0.0757	−0.1449	0.0396
Semi-Pucca house	0.24381	0.42939	−0.1227	−0.2161	0.0697
Number of members per sleeping room	2.54588	1.87060	−0.1325	n.a.	n.a.
Kachha house	0.09562	0.29408	−0.1391	−0.4278	0.0452
Wood as main fuel source	0.23198	0.42210	−0.1762	−0.3206	0.0968
Kerosene as main source of lighting	0.08537	0.27944	−0.1841	−0.6025	0.0562
Bush or no toilet facility	0.19196	0.39385	−0.1880	−0.3858	0.0917

Source: Gaudin and Yazbeck 2006.
Note: n.a. = not applicable (these variables are not ownership questions).

Table A1.2 *Household Wealth Quintiles, Urban India, 1998–99*

Wealth quintile	Unweighted sample size	Asset index score			
		Mean	Standard deviation	Lowest	Highest
1st (poorest)	5,683	−4.350	1.743	−12.971	−0.363
2nd	5,987	−1.466	1.166	−7.750	2.057
3rd	6,009	0.434	1.097	−5.114	4.342
4th	6,272	2.097	0.950	−2.192	5.554
5th (wealthiest)	6,735	3.735	1.025	0.377	9.240

Source: Gaudin and Yazbeck 2006.

Figure A1.1 *Concentration Curves for Full Immunization, Rural and Urban India*

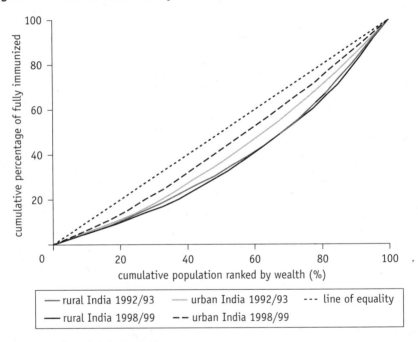

Source: Gaudin and Yazbeck 2006.

asset scores produced for the urban population and table A1.2 shows how the resulting quintiles were derived from the asset index. Figure A1.1 shows how the asset-based quintiles allowed the analysis of inequality in immunization in urban and rural India and over time. Immunization inequality improved over time in urban India but remains very deep in rural India.

Annex 1.2 Health, Nutrition, and Population Inequality Data

Table A1.3 *Infant Mortality Inequalities in Low- and Middle-Income Countries*

Region, country, and year of survey	Infant mortality rate (per 1,000 live births)						Ratio of poorest to wealthiest quintiles	Difference between poorest and wealthiest quintiles (absolute value)	Concentration index	
	Poorest quintile	2nd	3rd	4th	Wealthiest quintile	Population average			Value	Standard error
East Asia and Pacific	**54.1**	**43.9**	**36.7**	**30.9**	**18.0**	**38.2**	**3.0**	**36.1**	**−0.18536**	**0.05559**
Cambodia 2000	109.7		88.2	88.7	50.3	92.7	2.2	59.4	−0.10515	0.00090
Indonesia 1997	78.1	57.3	51.4	39.4	23.3	52.2	3.4	54.8	−0.19544	0.00077
Indonesia 2002/03	60.6	50.3	44.0	36.4	17.1	43.0	3.6	43.6	−0.18722	0.07300
Philippines 1998	48.8	39.2	33.7	24.9	20.9	36.0	2.3	27.9	−0.15659	0.00085
Philippines 2003	42.0	32.2	25.8	22.2	19.5	30.0	2.2	22.5	−0.15380	0.02569
Vietnam 1997	42.8	43.2	35.2	27.2	16.9	34.8	2.5	25.9	−0.14272	0.00188
Vietnam 2002	39.3	27.7	19.7	15.2	13.8	24.8	2.8	25.5	−0.21740	0.00259
Europe and Central Asia	**66.3**	**54.4**	**45.6**	**38.3**	**36.3**	**49.7**	**1.8**	**30.0**	**−0.12637**	**0.02107**
Armenia 2000	52.3	50.0	36.8	49.6	27.3	44.1	1.9	25.0	−0.09061	0.00253
Kazakhstan 1995	39.2	43.1	36.6	48.9	35.1	40.7	1.1	4.1	0.00351	0.00280
Kazakhstan 1999	67.6	65.3	65.8	27.3	42.3	54.9	1.6	25.3	−0.08479	0.00200
Kyrgyz Republic 1997	83.3	73.3	67.5	49.6	45.8	66.2	1.8	37.5	−0.11881	0.00172
Turkey 1993	99.9	72.7	72.1	54.4	25.4	68.3	3.9	74.5	−0.18849	0.00199
Turkey 1998	68.3	54.6	42.1	37.5	29.8	48.4	2.3	38.5	−0.15829	0.00132
Turkmenistan 2000	89.3	78.6	68.2	62.4	58.4	71.6	1.5	30.9	—	—
Uzbekistan 1996	54.4	39.8	36.0	39.0	45.9	43.5	1.2	8.5	−0.05153	0.00226

	71.3	45.3	34.7	26.6	26.9	44.8	2.6	44.4	−0.20970	0.04025
Latin America and the Caribbean										
Bolivia 1998	106.5	85.0	75.5	38.6	25.5	73.5	4.2	81.0	−0.21073	0.00156
Bolivia 2003	87.3	82.0	63.3	50.9	32.3	67.8	2.7	55.0	−0.15046	0.05333
Brazil 1996	83.2	46.7	32.9	24.7	28.6	48.1	2.9	54.6	−0.25125	0.00091
Colombia 1995	40.8	31.4	27.0	31.5	16.2	30.8	2.5	24.6	−0.12046	0.00153
Colombia 2000	32.0	31.6	22.0	11.9	17.6	24.4	1.8	14.4	−0.16024	0.00135
Colombia 2005	32.0	23.8	20.9	14.2	14.4	22.1	2.2	17.6	−0.16460	0.03389
Dominican Republic 1996	66.7	54.5	52.3	33.5	23.4	48.6	2.9	43.3	−0.16907	0.00162
Dominican Republic 2002	50.2	37.1	35.6	24.3	20.0	34.6	2.5	30.2	−0.16337	0.04503
Guatemala 1995	56.9	79.7	55.7	46.7	35.0	57.2	1.6	21.9	−0.08179	0.00108
Guatemala 1998/99	58.0	50.8	52.1	39.6	39.2	49.1	1.5	18.8	−0.07858	0.00173
Haiti 1994/95	93.7	93.6	85.6	81.7	74.3	87.1	1.3	19.4	−0.04306	0.00083
Haiti 2000	99.5	70.0	93.4	88.4	97.2	89.4	1.0	2.3	0.00684	0.00088
Nicaragua 1997/98	50.7	53.7	45.7	40.2	25.8	45.2	2.0	24.9	−0.09431	0.00100
Nicaragua 2001	49.6	40.6	32.2	25.7	16.3	35.3	3.0	33.3	−0.18253	0.00116
Paraguay 1990	42.9	36.5	46.1	33.5	15.7	35.9	2.7	27.2	−0.11423	0.00219
Peru 1996	78.3	53.6	34.4	36.0	19.5	49.9	4.0	58.8	−0.22243	0.00069
Peru 2000	63.5	53.9	32.6	26.5	13.9	43.2	4.6	49.6	−0.22660	0.00102
Middle East and North Africa	**75.8**	**65.7**	**54.2**	**46.3**	**32.7**	**56.4**	**2.3**	**43.1**	**−0.15381**	**0.03862**
Egypt, Arab Rep. of 1995	109.7	88.7	64.6	50.6	31.8	72.9	3.4	77.9	−0.21609	0.00084

(continued)

Table A1.3 *(continued)*

Region, country, and year of survey	Infant mortality rate (per 1,000 live births)						Ratio of poorest to wealthiest quintiles	Difference between poorest and wealthiest quintiles (absolute value)	Concentration index	
	Poorest quintile	2nd	3rd	4th	Wealthiest quintile	Population average			Value	Standard error
Egypt, Arab Rep. of 2000	75.6	63.9	53.9	43.9	29.6	54.7	2.6	46.0	−0.16266	0.00073
Jordan 1997	35.4	28.8	30.1	25.9	23.4	29.0	1.5	12.0	−0.07201	0.00089
Morocco 1992	79.7	67.7	62.4	58.5	35.1	63.1	2.3	44.6	−0.11659	0.00122
Morocco 2003/04	62.2	53.1	36.8	33.4	24.0	44.0	2.6	38.1	−0.17514	0.03796
Yemen, Rep. of 1997	108.5	102.0	88.9	80.9	60.0	89.5	1.8	48.5	−0.10202	0.00053
South Asia	**94.8**	**82.3**	**79.7**	**60.3**	**43.6**	**75.3**	**2.2**	**51.2**	**−0.13795**	**0.04254**
Bangladesh 1996/97	96.5	98.8	96.7	88.8	56.6	89.6	1.7	39.9	−0.06703	0.00101
Bangladesh 1999/2000	92.9	93.6	78.1	62.8	57.9	79.7	1.6	35.0	−0.09663	0.00059
Bangladesh 2004	89.7	65.9	75.1	59.1	64.8	72.4	1.4	25.0	−0.06962	0.02592
India 1992/93	109.2	106.3	89.7	65.6	44.0	86.3	2.5	65.2	0.10960	0.00248
India 1998/99	96.5	80.7	76.3	55.3	38.1	73.0	2.5	58.4	−0.11780	0.00028
Nepal 1996	96.3	107.2	103.6	84.7	63.9	93.0	1.5	32.4	−0.06020	0.00087
Nepal 2001	85.5	87.7	76.6	72.8	53.2	77.2	1.6	32.3	−0.07241	0.00076
Pakistan 1990/91	88.7	108.7	109.3	95.7	62.5	94.0	1.4	26.2	−0.05100	0.00112

Sub-Saharan Africa	105.8	107.1	100.6	83.9	61.8	94.2	1.7	44.0	−0.09693	0.03805
Benin 1996	119.4	111.1	105.8	103.8	63.3	103.5	1.9	56.1	−0.07999	0.00118
Benin 2001	111.5	108.2	106.3	78.1	50.0	94.8	2.2	61.5	−0.11209	0.00136
Burkina Faso 1992/93	112.5	119.5	120.8	99.7	80.9	107.6	1.4	31.6	−0.05841	0.03273
Burkina Faso 1998/99	106.2	118.5	118.0	116.5	76.7	108.6	1.4	29.5	−0.03108	0.00101
Burkina Faso 2003	97.1	108.4	81.9	94.1	77.9	92.1	1.2	19.2	−0.04306	0.01952
Cameroon 1991	103.9	101.0	78.8	65.1	51.2	80.3	2.0	52.7	−0.14046	0.00109
Cameroon 1998	108.4	86.3	72.6	58.7	55.8	79.8	1.9	52.6	−0.14262	0.00081
Cameroon 2004	100.5	90.3	82.9	64.2	52.0	81.3	1.9	48.6	−0.11688	0.03581
Central African Republic 1994/95	132.3	116.8	99.2	97.6	53.7	101.8	2.5	78.6	−0.13742	0.00138
Chad 1996/97	79.8	136.7	120.2	115.0	89.3	109.8	0.9	9.5	−0.00122	0.00127
Chad 2004	109.2	122.5	117.4	122.4	100.9	115.2	1.1	8.3	−0.01038	0.02443
Comoros 1996	87.2	108.5	83.7	62.6	64.6	83.7	1.3	22.6	−0.07847	0.00176
Côte d'Ivoire 1994	117.2	97.3	88.9	78.8	63.3	91.3	1.9	53.9	−0.10757	0.00066
Eritrea 1995	74.0	66.2	87.0	85.8	67.5	75.6	1.1	6.5	0.01420	0.00094
Ethiopia 2000	92.8	114.9	141.5	118.1	95.1	112.9	1.0	2.3	0.01745	0.00072
Gabon 2000	57.0	68.1	66.6	72.7	35.9	61.1	1.6	21.1	−0.03738	0.00198
Ghana 1993	77.5	94.6	82.8	64.2	45.8	74.7	1.7	31.7	−0.09289	0.00159
Ghana 1998	72.7	58.0	82.1	52.5	26.0	61.2	2.8	46.7	−0.10845	0.00250
Ghana 2003	61.5	63.8	73.5	66.0	57.7	64.7	1.1	3.8	0.00286	0.02313
Guinea 1999	118.9	127.9	113.5	91.4	70.2	106.6	1.7	48.7	−0.09207	0.00089
Kenya 1993	90.0	79.3	52.7	39.1	43.3	62.5	2.1	46.8	−0.17573	0.01842

(continued)

Table A1.3 (continued)

Region, country, and year of survey	Infant mortality rate (per 1,000 live births)						Ratio of poorest to wealthiest quintiles	Difference between poorest and wealthiest quintiles (absolute value)	Concentration index	
	Poorest quintile	2nd	3rd	4th	Wealthiest quintile	Population average			Value	Standard error
Kenya 1998	95.8	82.9	58.5	61.0	40.2	70.7	2.4	55.6	−0.15329	0.00103
Kenya 2003	95.8	75.2	81.9	53.1	62.2	75.5	1.5	33.6	−0.09794	0.02652
Madagascar 1997	119.1	118.3	103.2	76.2	57.5	99.3	2.1	61.6	−0.12211	0.00106
Malawi 1992	141.2	133.7	154.1	139.2	106.1	136.1	1.3	35.1	−0.03439	0.00092
Malawi 2000	131.5	110.7	117.4	109.1	86.4	112.5	1.5	45.1	−0.04368	0.00059
Mali 1995/96	151.4	146.9	138.9	129.0	93.2	133.5	1.6	58.2	−0.07526	0.00059
Mali 2001	137.2	125.2	140.6	128.7	89.9	126.2	1.5	47.3	−0.04922	0.00059
Mauritania 2000/01	60.8	59.4	78.0	72.8	62.3	66.8	1.0	1.5	0.02324	0.00093
Mozambique 1997	187.7	136.2	144.3	134.2	94.7	147.4	2.0	93.0	−0.11552	0.00085
Mozambique 2003	142.5	147.1	128.2	106.1	71.1	123.6	2.0	71.4	−0.10612	0.05125
Namibia 1992	63.6	63.0	48.4	72.2	57.3	61.5	1.1	6.3	−0.00278	0.00105
Namibia 2000	35.8	63.2	39.7	37.3	22.7	39.8	1.6	13.1	−0.09742	0.00227
Niger 1998	131.1	152.3	157.2	142.0	85.8	135.8	1.5	45.3	−0.05034	0.00110
Nigeria 1990	102.2	102.3	93.1	85.8	68.6	91.6	1.5	33.6	−0.07024	0.00058
Nigeria 2003	133.0	139.7	110.0	86.8	52.1	109.3	2.6	80.9	−0.14475	0.06225

Rwanda 2000	138.7	120.2	123.4	118.9	87.9	117.4	1.6	50.8	−0.06043	0.00068
Senegal 1997	84.5	81.6	69.6	58.8	44.9	69.4	1.9	39.6	−0.11254	0.00077
South Africa 1998	61.6	51.6	35.8	34.0	17.0	42.2	3.6	44.6	−0.19631	0.00155
Tanzania 1996	87.3	118.0	95.6	102.1	64.8	94.1	1.3	22.5	−0.04028	0.00115
Tanzania 1999	114.8	107.5	115.4	106.8	91.9	107.8	1.2	22.9	−0.03234	0.00101
Tanzania 2004	88.0	97.1	87.8	69.8	64.2	82.5	1.4	23.8	−0.06740	0.02675
Togo 1998	84.1	81.7	90.0	73.9	65.8	80.3	1.3	18.3	−0.03547	0.00063
Uganda 1995	109.0	79.5	90.4	84.5	63.2	86.1	1.7	45.8	−0.08126	0.00083
Uganda 2000/01	105.7	98.3	94.5	81.0	60.2	89.4	1.8	45.5	−0.09190	0.00077
Zambia 1996	123.6	131.5	105.1	104.1	69.8	107.7	1.8	53.8	−0.09519	0.00087
Zambia 2001	115.2	93.1	113.8	80.8	56.7	93.9	2.0	58.5	−0.10397	0.00112
Zimbabwe 1994	52.0	49.5	47.4	64.2	41.6	51.2	1.3	10.4	−0.00672	0.00128
Zimbabwe 1999	59.1	63.9	67.1	63.1	44.3	59.7	1.3	14.8	−0.03605	0.00144
All Countries	**86.9**	**76.2**	**70.7**	**55.9**	**41.2**	**68.9**	**2.1**	**45.7**	**−0.13513**	**0.03850**

Sources: Country data from Gwatkin and others (2007); regional and global population-based averages are author's calculations using 2001 estimates from World Bank World Development Indicators.
Note: — = not available.

Table A1.4 Adolescent Fertility Inequalities in Low- and Middle-Income Countries

Region, country, and year of survey	Adolescent fertility (births per 1,000 adolescent girls)						Ratio of poorest to wealthiest quintiles	Difference between poorest and wealthiest quintiles (absolute value)	Concentration index	
	Poorest quintile	2nd	3rd	4th	Wealthiest quintile	Population average			Value	Standard error
East Asia and Pacific	**81.2**	**56.9**	**46.9**	**36.3**	**18.4**	**45.0**	**4.4**	**62.7**	**−0.13513**	**0.03850**
Cambodia 2000	50.0	48.0	56.0	51.0	25.0	44.0	2.0	25.0	−0.11160	0.00174
Indonesia 1997	75.0	63.0	55.0	41.0	15.0	62.0	5.0	60.0	−0.25346	0.00125
Indonesia 2002/03	79.5	58.6	53.6	46.4	23.6	50.9	3.4	55.9	−0.15725	0.06145
Philippines 1998	130.0	90.0	32.0	29.0	12.0	46.0	10.8	118.0	−0.44261	0.00179
Philippines 2003	133.7	84.1	51.7	32.3	15.8	52.5	8.5	117.9	−0.39022	0.07255
Vietnam 1997	51.0	41.0	27.0	18.0	11.0	32.0	4.6	40.0	−0.26233	0.00373
Vietnam 2002	39.0	27.0	23.0	11.0	6.0	22.0	6.5	33.0	−0.32235	0.00399
Europe and Central Asia	**71.8**	**57.0**	**62.7**	**58.3**	**31.0**	**57.0**	**2.3**	**40.8**	**−0.11450**	**0.06382**
Armenia 2000	107.0	61.0	27.0	35.0	32.0	50.0	3.3	75.0	−0.25620	0.00341
Kazakhstan 1995	104.0	55.0	91.0	45.0	28.0	64.0	3.7	76.0	−0.21580	0.00522
Kazakhstan 1999	46.0	35.0	46.0	50.0	21.0	40.0	2.2	25.0	−0.22984	0.00499
Kyrgyz Republic 1997	120.0	81.0	61.0	91.0	29.0	75.0	4.1	91.0	−0.18031	0.00546
Turkey 1993	56.0	66.0	64.0	43.0	32.0	55.0	1.8	24.0	−0.03557	0.00096
Turkey 1998	81.0	63.0	65.0	56.0	28.0	60.0	2.9	53.0	−0.21264	0.00322
Turkmenistan 2000	28.0	26.0	30.0	35.0	33.0	30.0	0.8	5.0	—	
Uzbekistan 1996	56.0	54.0	77.0	70.0	45.0	61.0	1.2	11.0	−0.00623	0.00299

	171.1	115.0	78.9	61.2	31.2	88.5	5.5	139.9	−0.29183	0.06701
Latin America and the Caribbean										
Bolivia 1998	168.0	126.0	100.0	68.0	27.0	84.0	6.2	141.0	−0.30929	0.00233
Bolivia 2003	160.5	127.9	81.2	73.1	38.2	84.0	4.2	122.3	−0.25584	0.06072
Brazil 1996	176.0	109.0	70.0	57.0	28.0	86.0	6.3	148.0	−0.31361	0.00203
Colombia 1995	180.0	126.0	93.0	65.0	24.0	89.0	7.5	156.0	−0.31963	0.00266
Colombia 2000	155.0	133.0	90.0	45.0	34.0	85.0	4.6	121.0	−0.29987	0.00162
Colombia 2005	155.0	118.2	96.9	60.5	37.4	90.4	4.1	117.5	−0.25128	0.06309
Dominican Republic 1996	234.0	153.0	130.0	65.0	30.0	112.0	7.8	204.0	−0.34908	0.00280
Dominican Republic 2002	214.4	161.6	116.8	86.7	36.3	116.2	5.9	178.1	−0.28850	0.08043
Guatemala 1995	203.0	173.0	141.0	108.0	54.0	126.0	3.8	149.0	−0.23115	0.00173
Guatemala 1998/99	182.0	182.0	116.0	113.0	32.0	117.0	5.7	150.0	−0.26628	0.00389
Haiti 1994/95	105.0	99.0	92.0	93.0	25.0	76.0	4.2	80.0	−0.20190	0.00107
Haiti 2000	101.0	95.0	120.0	91.0	54.0	86.0	1.9	47.0	−0.12270	0.00172
Nicaragua 1997/98	213.0	176.0	147.0	90.0	58.0	130.0	3.7	155.0	−0.24193	0.00138
Nicaragua 2001	193.0	150.0	122.0	94.0	70.0	119.0	2.8	123.0	−0.19126	0.00106
Paraguay 1990	181.0	130.0	95.0	70.0	34.0	97.0	5.3	147.0	−0.29801	0.00283
Peru 1996	169.0	126.0	77.0	45.0	18.0	75.0	9.4	151.0	−0.38249	0.00143
Peru 2000	163.0	98.0	56.0	38.0	23.0	66.0	7.1	140.0	−0.36702	0.00120
Middle East and North Africa	**64.8**	**66.6**	**62.1**	**46.5**	**25.8**	**54.5**	**2.5**	**38.9**	**−0.14744**	**0.06832**
Egypt, Arab Rep. of 1995	93.0	73.0	69.0	37.0	25.0	61.0	3.7	68.0	−0.22625	0.00133

(continued)

37

Table A1.4 (continued)

Region, country, and year of survey	Adolescent fertility (births per 1,000 adolescent girls)						Ratio of poorest to wealthiest quintiles	Difference between poorest and wealthiest quintiles (absolute value)	Concentration index	
	Poorest quintile	2nd	3rd	4th	Wealthiest quintile	Population average			Value	Standard error
Egypt, Arab Rep. of 2000	57.0	71.0	55.0	44.0	16.0	51.0	3.6	41.0	−0.17843	0.00184
Jordan 1997	44.0	60.0	43.0	25.0	30.0	43.0	1.5	14.0	−0.12622	0.00164
Morocco 1992	52.0	51.0	48.0	30.0	21.0	40.0	2.5	31.0	−0.17090	0.00198
Morocco 2003/04	50.7	35.7	44.3	21.0	12.5	32.4	4.0	38.2	−0.22823	0.08463
Yemen, Rep. of 1997	121.0	100.0	121.0	101.0	82.0	105.0	1.5	39.0	0.00996	0.00042
South Asia	**135.0**	**128.0**	**103.9**	**82.8**	**42.3**	**106.5**	**3.2**	**92.7**	**−0.18757**	**0.06882**
Bangladesh 1996/97	187.0	171.0	170.0	133.0	91.0	147.0	2.1	96.0	−0.11861	0.00165
Bangladesh 1999/2000	207.0	177.0	160.0	112.0	78.0	144.0	2.7	129.0	−0.18343	0.00111
Bangladesh 2004	189.9	157.6	153.5	121.3	85.4	137.1	2.2	104.4	−0.12445	0.04567
India 1992/93	135.0	140.0	116.0	84.0	45.0	116.0	3.0	90.0	−0.19504	0.00051
India 1998/99	134.0	130.0	102.0	78.0	36.0	107.0	3.7	98.0	−0.21269	0.00079
Nepal 1996	143.0	149.0	132.0	128.0	90.0	127.0	1.6	53.0	−0.08416	0.00111
Nepal 2001	156.0	120.0	136.0	115.0	66.0	110.0	2.4	90.0	−0.13250	0.00171
Pakistan 1990/91	88.0	87.0	66.0	76.0	44.0	74.0	2.0	44.0	−0.11665	0.00164

Sub-Saharan Africa	167.1	157.5	148.0	118.1	69.7	126.9	2.4	97.3	−0.14181	0.05843
Benin 1996	178.0	175.0	143.0	113.0	33.0	119.0	5.4	145.0	−0.25183	0.00422
Benin 2001	176.0	151.0	155.0	90.0	35.0	109.0	5.0	141.0	−0.27568	0.00349
Burkina Faso 1992/93	186.1	139.2	173.7	191.5	97.4	148.9	1.9	88.8	−0.08760	0.06388
Burkina Faso 1998/99	168.0	129.0	148.0	148.0	90.0	131.0	1.9	78.0	−0.09258	0.00194
Burkina Faso 2003	142.3	161.9	138.7	132.6	61.1	119.2	2.3	81.2	−0.15814	0.07297
Cameroon 1991	208.0	207.0	184.0	150.0	101.0	164.0	2.1	107.0	−0.13871	0.00212
Cameroon 1998	202.0	198.0	162.0	100.0	63.0	137.0	3.2	139.0	−0.22666	0.00215
Cameroon 2004	203.8	190.4	158.4	114.6	70.3	137.7	2.9	133.5	−0.20329	0.04947
Central African Republic 1994/95	155.0	144.0	158.0	179.0	138.0	155.0	1.1	17.0	−0.00345	0.00123
Chad 1996/97	178.0	177.0	191.0	201.0	205.0	190.0	0.9	27.0	0.03331	0.00054
Chad 2004	138.8	220.2	223.5	191.9	164.1	187.3	0.8	25.3	0.00752	0.05671
Comoros 1996	65.0	102.0	69.0	42.0	25.0	59.0	2.6	40.0	−0.20741	0.00472
Côte d'Ivoire 1994	191.0	192.0	159.0	134.0	72.0	140.0	2.7	119.0	−0.18180	0.00182
Eritrea 1995	226.0	128.0	181.0	140.0	40.0	125.0	5.7	186.0	−0.25845	0.00458
Ethiopia 2000	84.0	113.0	131.0	119.0	67.0	100.0	1.3	17.0	−0.05675	0.00175
Gabon 2000	205.0	194.0	147.0	135.0	71.0	142.0	2.9	134.0	−0.19005	0.00205
Ghana 1993	149.0	149.0	119.0	115.0	72.0	116.0	2.1	77.0	−0.13217	0.00235
Ghana 1998	129.0	105.0	125.0	87.0	24.0	88.0	5.4	105.0	−0.23081	0.00512
Ghana 2003	132.7	113.4	113.2	50.1	16.3	73.7	8.2	116.4	−0.34044	0.11245
Guinea 1999	210.0	207.0	214.0	167.0	93.0	168.0	2.3	117.0	−0.15391	0.00218
Kenya 1993	156.5	109.6	120.3	122.1	66.8	110.4	2.3	89.7	−0.11731	0.06409

(continued)

Table A1.4 (continued)

| Region, country, and year of survey | Adolescent fertility (births per 1,000 adolescent girls) | | | | | | Ratio of poorest to wealthiest quintiles | Difference between poorest and wealthiest quintiles (absolute value) | Concentration index | |
	Poorest quintile	2nd	3rd	4th	Wealthiest quintile	Population average			Value	Standard error
Kenya 1998	163.0	143.0	108.0	103.0	63.0	111.0	2.6	100.0	−0.17796	0.00162
Kenya 2003	173.5	141.2	111.3	93.7	80.8	114.2	2.1	92.7	−0.15325	0.02741
Madagascar 1997	271.0	215.0	206.0	141.0	78.0	180.0	3.5	193.0	−0.21105	0.00232
Malawi 1992	143.0	171.0	196.0	162.0	131.0	161.0	1.1	12.0	−0.01925	0.00195
Malawi 2000	192.0	170.0	176.0	186.0	140.0	172.0	1.4	52.0	−0.02502	0.00043
Mali 1995/96	198.0	219.0	210.0	217.0	122.0	187.0	1.6	76.0	−0.08744	0.00174
Mali 2001	200.0	246.0	225.0	203.0	108.0	185.0	1.9	92.0	−0.12953	0.00163
Mauritania 2000/01	85.0	106.0	95.0	67.0	52.0	80.0	1.6	33.0	−0.11085	0.00186
Mozambique 1997	191.0	144.0	178.0	208.0	126.0	171.0	1.5	65.0	−0.04844	0.00177
Mozambique 2003	234.1	196.8	207.7	188.0	110.5	178.7	2.1	123.6	−0.13893	0.04649
Namibia 1992	105.0	119.0	106.0	118.0	99.0	109.0	1.1	6.0	−0.01307	0.00132
Namibia 2000	102.0	92.0	101.0	82.0	64.0	88.0	1.6	38.0	−0.07744	0.00166
Niger 1998	260.0	231.0	229.0	246.0	148.0	218.0	1.8	112.0	−0.07877	0.00160
Nigeria 1990	194.0	213.0	116.0	151.0	66.0	146.0	2.9	128.0	−0.18304	0.00226
Nigeria 2003	183.9	161.8	152.4	97.8	57.7	126.3	3.2	126.2	−0.20084	0.06232

Rwanda 2000	51.0	49.0	60.0	53.0	49.0	52.0	1.0	2.0	−0.00572	0.00047
Senegal 1997	189.0	147.0	109.0	83.0	36.0	103.0	5.3	153.0	−0.28480	0.00234
South Africa 1998	108.0	109.0	66.0	68.0	22.0	76.0	4.9	86.0	−0.21252	0.00251
Tanzania 1996	151.0	130.0	165.0	160.0	93.0	135.0	1.6	58.0	−0.07161	0.00180
Tanzania 1999	196.0	141.0	178.0	117.0	81.0	138.0	2.4	115.0	−0.15197	0.00301
Tanzania 2004	172.5	159.2	163.8	129.2	71.4	132.5	2.4	101.2	−0.15966	0.06114
Togo 1998	142.0	129.0	114.0	79.0	35.0	89.0	4.1	107.0	−0.25975	0.00237
Uganda 1995	222.0	206.0	223.0	208.0	171.0	204.0	1.3	51.0	−0.04309	0.00090
Uganda 2000/01	225.0	226.0	204.0	149.0	112.0	178.0	2.0	113.0	−0.14489	0.00130
Zambia 1996	210.0	172.0	179.0	161.0	86.0	158.0	2.4	124.0	−0.14472	0.00183
Zambia 2001	194.0	209.0	180.0	154.0	94.0	160.0	2.1	100.0	−0.13770	0.00163
Zimbabwe 1994	144.0	126.0	83.0	112.0	59.0	99.0	2.4	85.0	−0.15333	0.00214
Zimbabwe 1999	162.0	108.0	106.0	130.0	74.0	112.0	2.2	88.0	−0.10945	0.00233
All Countries	**132.1**	**117.1**	**98.7**	**78.5**	**42.1**	**95.9**	**3.1**	**90.0**	**−0.18650**	**0.06444**

Sources: Country data from Gwatkin and others (2007); regional and global population-based averages are author's calculations using 2001 estimates from World Bank World Development Indicators.
Note: — = not available.

41

Table A1.5 Severe Stunting Inequalities in Low- and Middle-Income Countries

Region, country, and year of survey	Severe stunting						Ratio of poorest to wealthiest quintiles	Difference between poorest and wealthiest quintiles (absolute value)	Concentration index	
	Poorest quintile	2nd	3rd	4th	Wealthiest quintile	Population average			Value	Standard error
East Asia and Pacific										
Cambodia 2000	25.7	22.0	19.5	15.4	14.0	20.2	1.8	11.7	−0.10459	0.01985
Indonesia 1997	—	—	—	—	—	—	—	—	—	—
Indonesia 2002/03	—	—	—	—	—	—	—	—	—	—
Philippines 1998	—	—	—	—	—	—	—	—	—	—
Philippines 2003	—	—	—	—	—	—	—	—	—	—
Vietnam 1997	—	—	—	—	—	—	—	—	—	—
Vietnam 2002	—	—	—	—	—	—	—	—	—	—
Europe and Central Asia	**12.8**	**7.3**	**6.1**	**4.3**	**4.1**	**7.2**	**3.1**	**8.7**	**−0.23559**	**0.04777**
Armenia 2000	3.3	4.3	1.8	1.2	1.4	2.5	2.4	1.9	−0.14299	0.08502
Kazakhstan 1995	3.5	5.8	2.6	2.0	1.2	3.1	2.9	2.3	−0.19318	0.10635
Kazakhstan 1999	2.1	1.4	3.9	2.0	3.8	2.5	0.6	1.7	−0.02309	0.14060
Kyrgyz Republic 1997	6.0	8.0	6.8	5.5	2.7	6.0	2.2	3.3	−0.13716	0.06830
Turkey 1993	14.7	8.1	3.6	2.0	0.5	6.3	29.4	14.2	−0.45626	0.04274
Turkey 1998	13.7	6.4	4.6	3.0	0.5	6.1	27.4	13.2	−0.43767	0.04778
Turkmenistan 2000	8.2	7.1	8.9	6.4	5.7	7.4	1.4	2.5	—	—
Uzbekistan 1996	20.1	13.4	11.2	9.1	14.5	14.0	1.4	5.6	−0.09351	0.04470

Latin America and the Caribbean	8.6	4.4	2.1	1.0	0.5	4.0	17.9	8.2	−0.47387	0.09115
Bolivia 1998	18.0	9.8	6.7	4.8	2.1	9.4	8.6	15.9	−0.33367	0.02341
Bolivia 2003	14.5	11.1	4.8	2.6	1.1	7.8	13.1	13.4	−0.35121	0.02137
Brazil 1996	6.3	2.1	0.5	0.5	0.4	2.5	15.8	5.9	−0.57537	0.06879
Colombia 1995	6.9	3.7	2.2	1.1	1.4	3.5	4.9	5.5	−0.34539	0.04837
Colombia 2000	4.6	3.8	2.4	1.5	0.5	2.8	9.2	4.1	−0.28761	0.05231
Colombia 2005	4.4	2.4	0.8	0.7	0.6	2.1	7.3	3.8	−0.51563	0.04586
Dominican Republic 1996	7.3	1.9	1.3	0.9	0.8	2.8	9.1	6.5	−0.61372	0.07137
Dominican Republic 2002	4.9	2.0	2.2	0.8	0.5	2.3	10.6	4.5	−0.34021	0.04156
Guatemala 1995	35.2	30.6	24.0	11.2	2.0	23.5	17.6	33.2	−0.25962	0.01135
Guatemala 1998/99	35.3	30.4	22.8	6.5	0.3	21.2	117.7	35.0	−0.22899	0.01671
Haiti 1994/95	25.4	17.1	12.4	9.0	4.3	14.9	5.9	21.1	−0.27512	0.02644
Haiti 2000	12.6	9.3	7.3	3.7	2.3	7.5	5.5	10.3	−0.27972	0.02729
Nicaragua 1997/98	15.5	9.9	7.7	4.4	2.7	9.2	5.7	12.8	−0.28103	0.02289
Nicaragua 2001	12.8	7.4	3.3	3.0	0.4	6.2	32.0	12.4	−0.40694	0.03109
Paraguay 1990	5.8	4.7	1.7	0.6	0.0	3.0	0.0	5.8	−0.46996	0.05335
Peru 1996	17.4	9.2	4.0	1.4	0.7	8.0	24.9	16.7	−0.50474	0.01716
Peru 2000	17.6	7.9	3.5	0.9	0.3	7.7	58.7	17.3	−0.49495	0.01960
Middle East and North Africa	**13.5**	**10.3**	**9.5**	**7.7**	**4.6**	**9.2**	**3.0**	**9.0**	**−0.17966**	**0.05709**
Egypt, Arab Rep. of 1995	19.8	14.4	11.7	10.1	9.6	13.4	2.1	10.2	−0.14516	0.01447

(continued)

Table A1.5 *(continued)*

Region, country, and year of survey	Severe stunting						Ratio of poorest to wealthiest quintiles	Difference between poorest and wealthiest quintiles (absolute value)	Concentration index	
	Poorest quintile	2nd	3rd	4th	Wealthiest quintile	Population average			Value	Standard error
Egypt, Arab Rep. of 2000	10.1	6.5	6.3	4.8	3.1	6.2	3.3	7.0	−0.20477	0.02296
Jordan 1997	3.4	1.5	1.5	0.5	0.5	1.6	6.8	2.9	−0.22578	0.03686
Morocco 1992	15.9	12.1	6.5	2.5	1.4	8.7	11.4	14.5	−0.37357	0.02788
Morocco 2003/04	12.1	7.0	4.6	3.4	3.4	6.5	3.5	8.6	−0.26650	0.03026
Yemen, Rep. of 1997	31.3	31.7	31.4	27.1	12.9	26.7	2.4	18.4	−0.15440	0.01030
South Asia	**32.6**	**28.5**	**24.3**	**17.2**	**9.8**	**23.1**	**3.3**	**22.8**	**−0.20259**	**0.06503**
Bangladesh 1996/97	33.0	35.1	31.1	23.9	13.1	28.1	2.5	19.9	−0.14184	0.01274
Bangladesh 1999/2000	—	—	—	—	—	—	—	—	—	—
Bangladesh 2004	25.4	19.0	15.2	12.8	6.4	16.7	4.0	19.0	−0.22918	0.01596
India 1992/93	36.7	35.6	30.2	24.1	14.0	28.8	2.6	22.7	−0.16591	0.00519
India 1998/99	33.1	28.5	24.1	16.3	9.3	23.0	3.6	23.8	−0.21131	0.00651
Nepal 1996	25.5	22.1	19.4	18.1	11.8	20.2	2.2	13.7	−0.12432	0.01806
Nepal 2001	28.8	23.1	20.2	17.8	11.2	21.3	2.6	17.6	−0.15782	0.01362
Pakistan 1990/91	35.9	38.1	35.3	27.4	16.1	29.8	2.2	19.8	−0.17768	0.01432

Sub-Saharan Africa	22.4	20.8	19.3	14.9	8.3	17.5	2.7	14.1	−0.15928	0.06469
Benin 1996	10.0	9.9	6.5	6.6	4.7	7.8	2.1	5.3	−0.14301	0.04314
Benin 2001	13.5	14.4	10.1	10.3	3.9	10.7	3.5	9.6	−0.16461	0.02489
Burkina Faso 1992/93	15.5	15.2	14.3	12.6	7.1	13.0	2.2	8.5	−0.16719	0.02129
Burkina Faso 1998/99	20.9	18.3	16.1	16.2	11.2	16.6	1.9	9.7	−0.11825	0.01989
Burkina Faso 2003	26.5	21.5	21.0	17.5	7.1	19.4	3.8	19.4	−0.16119	0.01257
Cameroon 1991	15.9	13.9	13.7	5.3	2.5	9.6	6.4	13.4	−0.32680	0.03497
Cameroon 1998	15.9	11.0	11.7	6.9	5.2	10.7	3.1	10.7	−0.21179	0.03842
Cameroon 2004	19.6	15.1	14.8	8.0	2.5	13.0	7.8	17.1	−0.26206	0.02621
Central African Republic 1994/95	20.2	17.3	12.0	11.6	9.6	14.3	2.1	10.6	−0.17556	0.02955
Chad 1996/97	24.2	22.1	21.5	21.0	12.3	20.4	2.0	11.9	−0.10970	0.01399
Chad 2004	31.0	23.7	25.0	21.1	15.1	23.2	2.0	15.8	−0.12327	0.01397
Comoros 1996	21.4	19.4	9.4	8.0	5.5	13.4	3.9	15.9	−0.28475	0.05082
Côte d'Ivoire 1994	12.9	10.5	8.4	5.6	2.5	8.4	5.2	10.4	−0.24213	0.03229
Eritrea 1995	24.8	21.5	16.9	13.9	9.0	18.3	2.8	15.8	−0.17900	0.02562
Ethiopia 2000	27.2	27.2	29.6	24.3	19.9	25.9	1.4	7.3	−0.08670	0.00954
Gabon 2000	12.1	9.2	5.1	2.8	2.7	6.7	4.5	9.4	−0.32728	0.03606
Ghana 1993	13.3	9.0	12.4	6.5	3.5	9.1	3.8	9.8	−0.19161	0.04061
Ghana 1998	14.5	9.9	9.8	7.1	1.1	9.3	13.2	13.4	−0.28593	0.03312
Ghana 2003	15.4	12.4	9.5	6.6	4.9	10.5	3.1	10.5	−0.19457	0.02898
Guinea 1999	13.6	15.1	10.5	7.8	4.1	10.1	3.3	9.5	−0.22311	0.03013
Kenya 1993	18.3	13.2	10.8	12.4	6.2	12.5	2.9	12.05	−0.15362	0.02180

(continued)

Table A1.5 *(continued)*

Region, country, and year of survey	Severe stunting Poorest quintile	2nd	3rd	4th	Wealthiest quintile	Population average	Ratio of poorest to wealthiest quintiles	Difference between poorest and wealthiest quintiles (absolute value)	Concentration index Value	Standard error
Kenya 1998	17.4	16.0	11.1	9.7	6.6	12.7	2.6	10.8	−0.18805	0.02403
Kenya 2003	13.8	11.2	11.1	10.3	6.1	10.8	2.3	7.7	−0.16284	0.02264
Madagascar 1997	24.6	19.2	21.1	23.6	17.3	21.6	1.4	7.3	−0.05775	0.01899
Malawi 1992	28.8	26.7	23.4	22.0	14.0	23.2	2.1	14.8	−0.14057	0.01664
Malawi 2000	32.0	26.9	27.1	21.6	10.9	24.4	2.9	21.1	−0.14468	0.00979
Mali 1995/96	18.0	17.7	15.1	13.8	7.2	14.5	2.5	10.8	−0.13600	0.01973
Mali 2001	25.1	23.8	21.4	15.7	7.5	19.1	3.3	17.6	−0.16810	0.01168
Mauritania 2000/01	20.6	18.5	16.9	17.6	8.7	16.5	2.4	11.9	−0.12723	0.02214
Mozambique 1997	25.4	18.5	14.7	13.9	7.4	15.7	3.4	18.0	−0.21865	0.02342
Mozambique 2003	24.3	21.0	20.3	12.7	5.8	17.9	4.2	18.5	−0.19237	0.01275
Namibia 1992	13.8	8.9	9.8	5.8	3.6	8.4	3.8	10.2	−0.22663	0.03839
Namibia 2000	8.3	7.1	7.0	6.7	6.2	7.2	1.3	2.1	−0.14861	0.03697
Niger 1998	20.7	22.7	19.4	21.3	11.4	19.5	1.8	9.3	−0.10688	0.01698
Nigeria 1990	26.3	25.5	26.2	18.7	12.9	21.9	2.0	13.4	−0.15322	0.01310
Nigeria 2003	26.9	27.2	22.9	15.2	5.3	19.6	5.1	21.6	−0.22362	0.01712

Rwanda 2000	22.4	21.5	19.5	19.5	11.2	18.7	2.0	11.2	−0.13243	0.01407
Senegal 1997	—	—	—	—	—	—	—	—	—	—
South Africa 1998	—	—	—	—	—	—	—	—	—	—
Tanzania 1996	22.6	20.3	19.2	16.1	9.3	17.8	2.4	13.3	−0.12999	0.01670
Tanzania 1999	21.0	21.9	17.1	12.0	7.1	16.5	3.0	13.9	−0.18550	0.02148
Tanzania 2004	17.2	14.7	12.5	10.3	3.7	12.3	4.7	13.6	−0.21505	0.01779
Togo 1998	10.0	10.1	5.5	5.8	0.9	7.0	11.1	9.1	−0.27069	0.03489
Uganda 1995	18.2	18.8	13.2	14.7	9.3	15.0	2.0	8.9	−0.14231	0.01868
Uganda 2000/01	18.2	15.8	16.9	13.4	7.1	14.8	2.6	11.1	−0.15722	0.01796
Zambia 1996	25.8	21.8	19.4	12.4	6.0	17.5	4.3	19.8	−0.21082	0.01614
Zambia 2001	27.2	26.1	24.2	16.7	12.1	22.1	2.2	15.1	−0.13959	0.01481
Zimbabwe 1994	6.3	7.0	6.0	6.6	4.3	6.1	1.5	2.0	−0.08284	0.04890
Zimbabwe 1999	13.5	9.8	10.2	7.4	5.5	9.4	2.5	8.0	−0.11769	0.03418
All Countries	**22.0**	**18.8**	**16.2**	**11.7**	**6.7**	**15.5**	**3.3**	**15.3**	**−0.20011**	**0.06358**

Sources: Country data from Gwatkin and others (2007); regional and global population-based averages are author's calculations using 2001 estimates from World Bank World Development Indicators.

Note: — = not available. Severe stunting (height-for-age) is the percentage of children with a height-for-age Z-score below −3 standard deviations of the median reference standard for their age.

Table A1.6 Full Immunization Inequalities in Low- and Middle-Income Countries

Region, country, and year of survey	Children fully immunized (percent)						Ratio of poorest to wealthiest quintiles	Difference between poorest and wealthiest quintiles (absolute value)	Concentration index	
	Poorest quintile	2nd	3rd	4th	Wealthiest quintile	Population average			Value	Standard error
East Asia and Pacific	**42.1**	**53.8**	**61.0**	**64.4**	**74.3**	**57.9**	**0.6**	**32.2**	**0.10147**	**0.02920**
Cambodia 2000	28.6	34.7	38.4	45.4	67.7	39.9	0.4	39.1	0.12895	0.01780
Indonesia 1997	42.9	47.2	56.5	58.0	72.1	54.8	0.6	29.2	0.10419	0.00813
Indonesia 2002/03	37.1	46.6	52.5	58.1	64.7	51.4	0.6	27.6	0.12733	0.00942
Philippines 1998	59.8	72.5	76.3	79.6	86.5	72.8	0.7	26.7	0.07122	0.00870
Philippines 2003	55.5	69.3	77.8	72.4	83.0	69.8	0.7	27.4	0.08139	0.00988
Vietnam 1997	42.2	50.7	48.2	56.3	60.0	50.2	0.7	17.8	0.06484	0.02290
Vietnam 2002	44.3	61.0	70.7	76.3	92.3	66.7	0.5	48.0	0.11756	0.01745
Europe and Central Asia	**48.6**	**35.2**	**42.2**	**64.6**	**52.0**	**59.0**	**0.9**	**3.5**	**0.06003**	**0.03427**
Armenia 2000	66.2	70.6	72.8	81.3	(68.0)	71.4	1.0	134.2	0.02240	0.02188
Kazakhstan 1995	21.3	19.0	21.6	25.6	(34.1)	23.4	0.6	55.4	0.08745	0.06594
Kazakhstan 1999	68.7	(77.4)	(79.3)	78.4	(62.3)	73.1	1.1	131.0	0.00800	0.02349
Kyrgyz Republic 1997	69.3	64.7	73.4	69.4	73.1	69.7	0.9	3.8	0.00065	0.01898
Turkey 1993	40.7	59.4	66.3	82.9	81.9	64.2	0.5	41.2	0.12651	0.01512
Turkey 1998	27.7	36.9	48.5	54.9	69.7	45.7	0.4	42.0	0.17137	0.02292
Turkmenistan 2000	85.0	92.3	86.4	81.2	77.5	84.8	1.1	7.5	—	—

Uzbekistan 1996	80.9	76.8	79.4	77.2	77.5	78.7	1.0	3.4	−0.01238	0.01428
Latin America and the Caribbean	**53.3**	**66.1**	**75.4**	**73.7**	**70.9**	**66.1**	**0.8**	**17.5**	**0.05028**	**0.02920**
Bolivia 1998	21.8	24.9	21.0	33.4	30.6	25.5	0.7	8.8	0.06075	0.02720
Bolivia 2003	47.5	49.4	43.8	59.2	57.9	50.6	0.8	10.4	0.04122	0.01310
Brazil 1996	56.6	74.0	84.9	83.1	73.8	72.5	0.8	17.2	0.09321	0.01226
Colombia 1995	57.7	69.7	68.8	75.2	77.3	68.3	0.7	19.6	0.06769	0.01248
Colombia 2000	50.0	59.7	69.7	72.8	65.4	62.2	0.8	15.4	0.07834	0.01473
Colombia 2005	48.2	56.0	66.8	61.8	73.5	59.3	0.7	25.4	0.06297	0.00928
Dominican Republic 1996	34.4	26.1	46.6	43.2	46.5	39.0	0.7	12.1	0.10963	0.02408
Dominican Republic 2002	28.2	33.1	41.5	42.4	37.9	36.3	0.7	9.7	0.10733	0.01682
Guatemala 1995	48.6	47.0	44.8	46.9	45.5	46.8	1.1	3.1	0.01059	0.01531
Guatemala 1998/99	66.3	66.3	67.7	58.4	56.0	63.8	1.2	10.3	0.00828	0.01435
Haiti 1994/95	18.8	20.1	35.3	37.9	44.1	30.2	0.4	25.3	0.17949	0.03620
Haiti 2000	25.4	30.3	41.1	31.7	42.3	33.5	0.6	16.9	0.11565	0.02437
Nicaragua 1997/98	61.0	74.6	75.3	85.7	73.1	72.6	0.8	12.1	0.07360	0.00936
Nicaragua 2001	63.6	77.2	78.0	71.4	71.0	71.6	0.9	7.4	0.04391	0.00996
Paraguay 1990	20.2	30.8	36.4	40.7	53.0	34.2	0.4	32.8	0.20225	0.02674
Peru 1996	55.3	63.8	63.5	71.7	66.0	63.0	0.8	10.7	0.05449	0.00764
Peru 2000	57.9	62.5	68.1	72.4	81.1	66.3	0.7	23.2	0.07663	0.00822
Middle East and North Africa	**73.1**	**76.3**	**78.0**	**83.2**	**84.7**	**78.8**	**0.9**	**11.6**	**0.03047**	**0.00498**
Egypt, Arab Rep. of 1995	65.1	72.8	81.0	86.6	92.5	79.1	0.7	27.4	0.08189	0.00640

(continued)

Table A1.6 *(continued)*

Region, country, and year of survey	Children fully immunized (percent)						Ratio of poorest to wealthiest quintiles	Difference between poorest and wealthiest quintiles (absolute value)	Concentration index	
	Poorest quintile	2nd	3rd	4th	Wealthiest quintile	Population average			Value	Standard error
Egypt, Arab Rep. of 2000	91.2	91.9	91.8	94.0	92.0	92.2	1.0	0.8	0.00515	0.00398
Jordan 1997	21.3	21.9	20.2	20.9	17.1	20.5	1.2	4.2	0.02759	0.03376
Morocco 1992	53.7	69.1	83.8	92.9	95.2	75.7	0.6	41.5	0.12240	0.00948
Morocco 2003/04	80.7	85.7	90.6	95.6	97.3	89.3	0.8	16.7	0.03556	0.00625
Yemen, Rep. of 1997	7.8	18.0	22.8	40.1	55.7	28.3	0.1	47.9	0.36167	0.01811
South Asia	**25.6**	**33.4**	**43.6**	**54.1**	**65.4**	**42.8**	**0.4**	**39.8**	**0.18065**	**0.03670**
Bangladesh 1996/97	47.4	43.8	60.8	58.8	66.6	54.2	0.7	19.2	0.07616	0.01632
Bangladesh 1999/2000	50.3	55.0	60.8	68.1	74.9	60.4	0.7	24.6	0.08515	0.01187
Bangladesh 2004	57.5	77.0	74.1	78.7	86.7	73.3	0.7	29.2	0.07957	0.00856
India 1992/93	17.1	21.7	34.7	48.2	65.0	35.4	0.3	47.9	0.30612	0.00685
India 1998/99	21.3	28.2	41.0	52.2	63.8	39.4	0.3	42.5	0.25456	0.00635
Nepal 1996	32.4	34.6	40.8	51.0	71.1	43.3	0.5	38.7	0.15944	0.01692
Nepal 2001	54.2	62.4	64.5	74.7	81.6	65.6	0.7	27.4	0.09290	0.01107
Pakistan 1990/91	22.5	25.6	30.2	41.1	54.7	35.1	0.4	32.2	0.20638	0.02326

Sub-Saharan Africa	25.3	30.3	34.3	39.1	52.9	35.5	0.5	27.6	0.14078	0.03304
Benin 1996	37.8	53.4	62.7	59.2	73.6	55.6	0.5	35.8	0.11361	0.01709
Benin 2001	52.6	57.2	59.9	67.9	79.5	62.8	0.7	26.9	0.08786	0.01424
Burkina Faso 1992/93	17.2	32.2	27.7	38.5	58.4	34.6	0.3	41.2	0.26457	0.02263
Burkina Faso 1998/99	21.4	24.3	21.7	32.1	52.1	29.3	0.4	30.7	0.21374	0.02776
Burkina Faso 2003	33.4	41.1	41.5	45.9	61.4	43.9	0.5	28.0	0.10289	0.01512
Cameroon 1991	27.4	27.3	29.9	46.5	63.5	40.0	0.4	36.1	0.22229	0.02790
Cameroon 1998	23.5	24.0	37.5	45.6	56.9	35.8	0.4	33.4	0.20711	0.02794
Cameroon 2004	39.4	45.5	46.9	51.7	66.3	48.6	0.6	26.9	0.10303	0.02073
Central African Republic 1994/95	18.1	25.3	28.9	45.0	64.0	36.6	0.3	45.9	0.25873	0.02512
Chad 1996/97	4.0	8.5	5.7	17.1	23.0	11.3	0.2	19.0	0.39042	0.04661
Chad 2004	1.1	7.1	12.4	12.4	23.6	11.3	—	22.5	0.39444	0.04793
Comoros 1996	39.8	49.5	52.7	60.5	82.0	54.5	0.5	42.2	0.12586	0.02419
Côte d'Ivoire 1994	15.7	27.1	32.7	52.6	64.2	37.4	0.2	48.5	0.26026	0.01992
Eritrea 1995	25.0	15.5	44.0	53.4	83.8	41.4	0.3	58.8	0.33564	0.02316
Ethiopia 2000	7.0	8.8	9.1	17.1	33.5	14.3	0.2	26.5	0.43044	0.03967
Gabon 2000	5.5	9.4	18.3	19.6	23.5	14.6	0.2	18.0	0.21052	0.04215
Ghana 1993	37.5	56.5	48.2	56.0	79.2	54.8	0.5	41.7	0.12643	0.01882
Ghana 1998	49.6	54.0	63.3	72.7	79.3	62.0	0.6	29.7	0.08675	0.01589
Ghana 2003	53.0	70.3	73.1	73.9	78.3	68.3	0.7	25.4	0.07548	0.01373
Guinea 1999	17.2	22.5	32.9	39.5	51.8	32.2	0.3	34.6	0.20721	0.02640
Kenya 1993	64.8	78.0	77.1	86.7	86.4	78.2	0.8	21.6	0.04870	0.00899

(continued)

Table A1.6 (continued)

Region, country, and year of survey	Children fully immunized (percent)						Ratio of poorest to wealthiest quintiles	Difference between poorest and wealthiest quintiles (absolute value)	Concentration index	
	Poorest quintile	2nd	3rd	4th	Wealthiest quintile	Population average			Value	Standard error
Kenya 1998	48.1	57.6	71.0	64.6	59.9	59.5	0.8	11.8	0.05775	0.01475
Kenya 2003	37.8	50.2	62.3	56.6	59.5	52.1	0.6	21.7	0.11143	0.01592
Madagascar 1997	22.0	25.2	27.1	54.7	66.0	36.2	0.3	44.0	0.24615	0.02049
Malawi 1992	73.0	78.8	80.3	87.1	89.3	81.8	0.8	16.3	0.03914	0.00920
Malawi 2000	65.4	65.0	69.1	72.5	81.4	70.1	0.8	16.0	0.04734	0.00800
Mali 1995/96	15.8	26.2	26.9	34.6	55.6	31.5	0.3	39.8	0.23803	0.02032
Mali 2001	19.5	20.2	18.7	31.9	56.0	28.7	0.3	36.5	0.22501	0.02101
Mauritania 2000/01	15.6	26.1	36.8	38.3	45.3	31.9	0.3	29.7	0.17006	0.02680
Mozambique 1997	19.7	30.8	35.6	69.5	85.3	47.3	0.2	65.6	0.25068	0.01489
Mozambique 2003	45.0	53.5	61.5	79.3	90.5	63.4	0.5	45.5	0.13988	0.00882
Namibia 1992	53.9	58.6	57.2	56.9	63.1	57.8	0.9	9.2	0.03640	0.01728
Namibia 2000	59.5	58.7	64.7	73.0	68.2	64.8	0.9	8.7	0.05431	0.01533
Niger 1998	4.6	9.7	9.0	19.8	50.9	18.4	0.1	46.3	0.53079	0.03308
Nigeria 1990	13.9	19.7	23.4	35.3	58.1	29.0	0.2	44.2	0.32663	0.02196
Nigeria 2003	3.4	3.9	9.0	10.9	40.2	13.0	0.1	36.8	0.42556	0.05472

52

Rwanda 2000	71.3	73.8	74.9	79.0	78.8	76.0	0.9	7.5	0.00951	0.00896
Senegal 1997	—	—	—	—	—	—	—	—	—	—
South Africa 1998	51.3	61.1	69.1	70.4	70.2	63.4	0.7	18.9	0.06158	0.01349
Tanzania 1996	57.3	68.8	66.9	79.3	82.5	70.5	0.7	25.2	0.06136	0.01068
Tanzania 1999	53.1	74.3	61.7	80.8	78.4	68.3	0.7	25.3	0.07866	0.01479
Tanzania 2004	26.6	30.3	29.6	31.7	29.3	29.4	0.9	2.7	−0.00493	0.02131
Togo 1998	22.2	26.0	32.2	30.3	52.0	30.8	0.4	29.8	0.16123	0.02578
Uganda 1995	34.2	46.0	49.3	47.0	63.1	47.4	0.5	28.9	0.10846	0.01519
Uganda 2000/01	26.5	38.0	39.6	39.5	42.6	36.7	0.6	16.1	0.08982	0.01904
Zambia 1996	71.3	77.3	80.0	79.8	86.4	78.3	0.8	15.1	0.03661	0.00853
Zambia 2001	63.9	65.7	66.2	78.8	80.0	70.0	0.8	16.1	0.05593	0.01066
Zimbabwe 1994	71.8	77.8	84.6	81.4	85.7	80.1	0.8	13.9	0.03061	0.01098
Zimbabwe 1999	63.9	69.2	67.9	56.6	64.1	64.0	1.0	0.2	−0.00927	0.01670
All Countries	**33.8**	**40.9**	**48.9**	**56.3**	**65.0**	**48.2**	**0.5**	**31.3**	**0.12724**	**0.02620**

Sources: Country data from Gwatkin and others (2007); regional and global population-based averages are author's calculations using 2001 estimates from World Bank World Development Indicators.

Note: — = not available. Full basic immunization coverage is the percentage of children who had received a dose of BCG vaccine, measles vaccine, and three doses of DPT and polio vaccines by the time of the survey, excluding polio vaccine given at birth.

Table A1.7 Antenatal Care (Three or More Visits) Inequalities in Low- and Middle-Income Countries

| Region, country, and year of survey | Antenatal care (percentage with three or more visits) | | | | | | Ratio of poorest to wealthiest quintiles | Difference between poorest and wealthiest quintiles (absolute value) | Concentration index | |
	Poorest quintile	2nd	3rd	4th	Wealthiest quintile	Population average			Value	Standard error
East Asia and Pacific	**63.3**	**76.6**	**81.0**	**85.2**	**92.9**	**78.9**	**0.7**	**29.6**	**0.06806**	**0.02105**
Cambodia 2000	9.4	12.8	14.1	21.5	56.9	20.1	0.2	47.5	0.31388	0.01537
Indonesia 1997	65.9	81.8	87.1	92.5	96.1	84.0	0.7	30.2	0.08080	0.00206
Indonesia 2002/03	74.8	87.9	90.9	94.2	98.0	88.7	0.8	23.2	0.05390	0.00168
Philippines 1998	64.1	74.0	83.9	89.1	92.8	79.0	0.7	28.7	0.07952	0.00397
Philippines 2003	71.1	79.6	84.7	91.4	93.3	82.8	0.8	22.2	0.05961	0.00366
Vietnam 1997	15.3	29.9	34.8	41.6	72.7	35.6	0.2	57.4	0.29185	0.01656
Vietnam 2002	34.0	54.1	62.1	65.7	85.2	58.6	0.4	51.2	0.17231	0.01197
Europe and Central Asia	**46.3**	**55.5**	**67.4**	**76.2**	**87.8**	**66.0**	**0.5**	**41.5**	**0.12465**	**0.02591**
Armenia 2000	46.8	67.1	83.6	84.2	91.1	73.6	0.5	44.3	0.12273	0.00956
Kazakhstan 1995	83.5	88.7	81.7	87.0	93.6	86.2	0.9	10.1	0.01286	0.00872
Kazakhstan 1999	71.4	71.4	74.2	73.5	78.4	73.5	0.9	7.0	0.00521	0.01079
Kyrgyz Republic 1997	83.2	82.0	87.0	84.2	84.4	84.1	1.0	1.2	0.00375	0.00715
Turkey 1993	19.2	33.2	48.1	68.1	84.2	49.3	0.2	65.0	0.26752	0.00896
Turkey 1998	22.6	37.7	58.4	72.3	90.9	55.4	0.2	68.3	0.25560	0.00788
Turkmenistan 2000	81.4	84.2	84.1	84.6	91.7	85.1	0.9	10.3	—	—
Uzbekistan 1996	82.4	82.8	79.3	84.5	84.4	82.5	1.0	2.0	0.00923	0.00784

Latin America and the Caribbean	64.4	80.6	89.1	93.5	96.0	83.1	0.7	31.5	0.07162	0.02569
Bolivia 1998	27.6	47.8	62.2	81.7	91.3	59.1	0.3	63.7	0.22573	0.00538
Bolivia 2003	44.6	60.7	71.0	80.7	93.4	68.1	0.5	48.9	0.12385	0.00406
Brazil 1996	64.0	82.9	91.5	95.6	96.7	84.3	0.7	32.7	0.09313	0.00428
Colombia 1995	56.2	78.3	87.9	93.4	96.2	81.3	0.6	40.0	0.10220	0.00441
Colombia 2000	68.7	83.0	90.8	94.4	93.7	85.4	0.7	25.0	0.06346	0.00431
Colombia 2005	75.9	86.8	92.1	94.4	96.3	88.4	0.8	20.5	0.05941	0.00226
Dominican Republic 1996	86.3	94.4	95.0	96.7	97.6	93.7	0.9	11.3	0.02990	0.00315
Dominican Republic 2002	92.4	95.3	96.5	97.3	97.5	95.8	0.9	5.1	0.01230	0.00147
Guatemala 1995	68.1	72.2	77.2	83.0	94.1	77.5	0.7	26.0	0.06379	0.00412
Guatemala 1998/99	65.4	76.1	84.9	85.8	95.7	80.7	0.7	30.3	0.08415	0.00535
Haiti 1994/95	26.4	38.5	52.7	68.8	81.6	51.6	0.3	55.2	0.21980	0.01018
Haiti 2000	41.0	52.0	62.5	70.3	82.0	61.1	0.5	41.0	0.13210	0.00668
Nicaragua 1997/98	55.3	71.7	78.8	84.5	91.3	74.5	0.6	36.0	0.10037	0.00419
Nicaragua 2001	57.7	76.4	83.0	89.6	92.5	78.5	0.6	34.8	0.09395	0.00428
Paraguay 1990	66.3	72.8	81.5	92.0	94.8	81.1	0.7	28.5	0.08110	0.00517
Peru 1996	28.7	54.9	71.5	81.8	93.7	62.3	0.3	65.0	0.21707	0.00326
Peru 2000	53.6	70.3	83.7	91.9	95.9	76.3	0.6	42.3	0.11735	0.00298

(continued)

Table A1.7 (continued)

Region, country, and year of survey	Antenatal care (percentage with three or more visits)						Ratio of poorest to wealthiest quintiles	Difference between poorest and wealthiest quintiles (absolute value)	Concentration index	
	Poorest quintile	2nd	3rd	4th	Wealthiest quintile	Population average			Value	Standard error
Middle East and North Africa	**19.9**	**30.1**	**41.8**	**54.7**	**72.3**	**43.4**	**0.3**	**52.4**	**0.23652**	**0.05222**
Egypt, Arab Rep. of 1995	11.1	15.6	31.7	45.6	75.3	34.9	0.1	64.2	0.35800	0.00742
Egypt, Arab Rep. of 2000	19.4	28.7	41.8	53.8	73.6	43.7	0.3	54.2	0.26140	0.00616
Jordan 1997	83.7	89.3	92.0	93.5	94.9	90.5	0.9	11.2	0.06744	0.00518
Morocco 1992	2.1	6.0	14.1	33.2	54.2	20.0	—	52.1	0.52148	0.01922
Morocco 2003/04	20.7	38.1	52.5	71.0	82.3	51.1	0.3	61.6	0.22628	0.00699
Yemen, Rep. of 1997	3.4	7.2	11.6	22.3	45.6	17.4	0.1	42.2	0.53113	0.01491
South Asia	**18.2**	**26.2**	**37.7**	**53.0**	**76.0**	**39.5**	**0.2**	**57.8**	**0.26971**	**0.00263**
Bangladesh 1996/97	5.5	5.9	7.0	11.6	41.1	13.0	0.1	35.6	0.46904	0.02705
Bangladesh 1999/2000	4.7	6.9	10.6	18.8	50.2	16.4	0.1	45.5	0.55342	0.01956
Bangladesh 2004	10.4	17.5	23.7	32.1	60.1	27.1	0.2	49.7	0.37335	0.01207
India 1992/93	21.6	30.4	42.8	56.9	81.4	44.1	0.3	59.8	0.28544	0.00295
India 1998/99	21.1	30.5	43.9	60.3	81.0	44.2	0.3	59.9	0.28457	0.00321

Nepal 1996	10.4	16.6	16.8	22.4	47.9	20.6	0.2	37.5	0.30984	0.01874
Nepal 2001	13.3	18.0	29.3	35.7	62.4	29.1	0.2	49.1	0.31384	0.01242
Pakistan 1990/91	5.5	3.9	7.3	22.0	56.6	18.3	0.1	51.1	0.60926	0.02116
Sub-Saharan Africa	**45.0**	**50.4**	**57.4**	**66.6**	**80.9**	**58.9**	**0.6**	**35.8**	**0.11703**	**0.00050**
Benin 1996	45.6	59.1	74.0	80.9	92.1	67.7	0.5	46.5	0.14230	0.00712
Benin 2001	59.3	69.3	77.7	87.7	92.4	76.3	0.6	33.1	0.09192	0.00517
Burkina Faso 1992/93	26.1	31.4	32.9	49.7	74.5	42.3	0.4	48.5	0.26486	0.00927
Burkina Faso 1998/99	35.5	38.0	39.7	48.0	71.4	45.4	0.5	35.9	0.16011	0.00950
Burkina Faso 2003	32.5	34.7	45.9	50.8	74.5	46.7	0.4	42.0	0.16937	0.00679
Cameroon 1991	39.5	54.5	63.4	78.0	89.1	65.4	0.4	49.6	0.16049	0.00807
Cameroon 1998	47.4	59.4	76.1	80.3	88.1	67.9	0.5	40.7	0.12804	0.00835
Cameroon 2004	53.9	64.4	80.3	88.6	91.7	74.5	0.6	37.8	0.10815	0.00448
Central African Republic 1994/95	33.8	47.7	60.6	72.6	78.6	58.0	0.4	44.8	0.17315	0.00885
Chad 1996/97	8.0	13.4	18.1	30.7	59.4	24.9	0.1	51.4	0.43944	0.01364
Chad 2004	4.9	19.8	27.4	37.5	64.4	30.5	0.1	59.4	0.41482	0.01075
Comoros 1996	41.4	61.2	74.3	81.8	87.9	67.3	0.5	46.5	0.14301	0.01237
Côte d'Ivoire 1994	26.0	43.6	45.7	62.5	75.0	48.7	0.3	49.0	0.19513	0.00899
Eritrea 1995	20.6	21.2	29.3	57.0	83.7	38.3	0.2	63.1	0.34190	0.01442
Ethiopia 2000	6.7	9.0	10.8	14.1	44.9	16.1	0.1	38.2	0.55577	0.01745
Gabon 2000	70.0	82.6	89.2	91.6	93.5	85.4	0.7	23.5	0.06250	0.00459
Ghana 1993	60.2	62.5	71.2	86.0	91.7	73.6	0.7	31.5	0.09093	0.00716
Ghana 1998	58.6	72.7	77.0	81.9	91.3	74.4	0.6	32.7	0.07937	0.00629

(continued)

Table A1.7 (continued)

Region, country, and year of survey	Antenatal care (percentage with three or more visits)						Ratio of poorest to wealthiest quintiles	Difference between poorest and wealthiest quintiles (absolute value)	Concentration index	
	Poorest quintile	2nd	3rd	4th	Wealthiest quintile	Population average			Value	Standard error
Ghana 2003	69.4	76.3	80.8	86.8	94.1	80.3	0.7	24.7	0.06166	0.00517
Guinea 1999	48.4	46.1	60.9	75.4	85.1	62.0	0.6	36.7	0.13195	0.00664
Kenya 1993	76.3	85.1	83.9	84.9	87.7	83.4	0.9	11.4	0.02475	0.00420
Kenya 1998	77.4	78.5	82.4	84.3	86.5	81.4	0.9	9.1	0.01879	0.00515
Kenya 2003	64.0	75.5	75.9	78.4	84.3	75.5	0.8	20.3	0.07126	0.00522
Madagascar 1997	55.2	58.1	61.5	72.3	82.6	63.9	0.7	27.4	0.09551	0.00708
Malawi 1992	73.6	75.8	82.8	89.8	88.8	82.0	0.8	15.2	0.04066	0.00510
Malawi 2000	76.9	78.3	78.4	82.2	85.7	80.0	0.9	8.8	0.02284	0.00316
Mali 1995/96	10.8	21.3	31.7	43.8	69.6	34.3	0.2	58.8	0.32089	0.00982
Mali 2001	24.7	29.3	30.8	45.8	73.8	40.0	0.3	49.1	0.22935	0.00758
Mauritania 2000/01	16.3	32.6	50.0	61.1	75.1	46.5	0.2	58.8	0.26528	0.00909
Mozambique 1997	30.0	49.0	47.3	72.3	75.1	52.7	0.4	45.1	0.17033	0.00833
Mozambique 2003	52.8	66.1	72.7	86.1	90.0	71.8	0.6	37.2	0.10496	0.00408
Namibia 1992	61.9	69.4	67.6	65.0	76.0	68.2	0.8	14.1	0.03911	0.00789
Namibia 2000	71.6	76.0	82.7	77.1	84.2	78.4	0.9	12.6	0.02639	0.00573
Niger 1998	13.5	15.1	16.5	27.4	63.7	25.7	0.2	50.2	0.39439	0.01508

Nigeria 1990	32.3	42.8	63.2	69.3	90.2	57.4	0.4	57.9	0.21842	0.00577
Nigeria 2003	30.7	33.5	52.0	72.5	90.8	53.8	0.3	60.2	0.21830	0.00742
Rwanda 2000	40.0	45.4	44.7	45.7	59.6	47.3	0.7	19.6	0.07459	0.00819
Senegal 1997	43.5	52.5	64.5	74.1	83.6	62.6	0.5	40.1	0.13619	0.00623
South Africa 1998	78.2	83.9	82.8	82.7	90.2	83.1	0.9	12.0	0.02309	0.00413
Tanzania 1996	81.0	88.2	89.5	88.7	90.5	87.5	0.9	9.5	0.01631	0.00345
Tanzania 1999	82.0	84.4	83.0	89.0	92.5	86.1	0.9	10.5	0.01406	0.00413
Tanzania 2004	80.2	85.5	85.3	88.3	91.3	86.0	0.9	11.1	0.02748	0.00310
Togo 1998	49.5	60.3	72.4	78.4	89.6	67.7	0.6	40.1	0.11194	0.00608
Uganda 1995	65.7	64.5	71.0	74.8	83.9	71.6	0.8	18.2	0.05684	0.00533
Uganda 2000/01	58.5	62.9	67.6	73.6	85.7	69.0	0.7	27.2	0.07981	0.00549
Zambia 1996	80.7	84.1	85.2	90.1	91.8	86.2	0.9	11.1	0.02606	0.00346
Zambia 2001	80.4	85.2	86.8	90.2	91.9	86.6	0.9	11.5	0.02807	0.00347
Zimbabwe 1994	83.0	86.1	85.3	89.0	90.9	86.7	0.9	7.9	0.01584	0.00482
Zimbabwe 1999	84.1	80.1	77.0	71.4	68.6	75.9	1.2	15.5	−0.04374	0.00612
All Countries	**35.7**	**44.9**	**54.3**	**65.3**	**81.7**	**54.5**	**0.4**	**45.9**	**0.15934**	**0.03206**

Sources: Country data from Gwatkin and others (2007); regional and global population-based averages are author's calculations using 2001 estimates from World Bank World Development Indicators.

Note: — = not available.

Table A1.8 *Contraception (Women) Inequalities in Low- and Middle-Income Countries*

| Region, country, and year of survey | Use of contraception by women (percent) | | | | | | Ratio of poorest to wealthiest quintiles | Difference between poorest and wealthiest quintiles (absolute value) | Concentration index | |
	Poorest quintile	2nd	3rd	4th	Wealthiest quintile	Population average			Value	Standard error
East Asia and Pacific	**44.2**	**51.5**	**53.2**	**53.3**	**51.0**	**50.6**	**0.9**	**6.8**	**0.02422**	**0.01900**
Cambodia 2000	12.5	15.4	20.1	19.9	25.4	18.8	0.5	12.9	0.16156	0.01204
Indonesia 1997	46.2	55.6	56.8	58.0	56.9	54.7	0.8	10.7	0.06029	0.00297
Indonesia 2002/03	48.6	57.9	60.0	59.3	58.1	56.7	0.8	9.6	0.03187	0.00285
Philippines 1998	19.6	26.2	33.0	33.0	29.4	28.2	0.7	9.8	0.11463	0.00968
Philippines 2003	23.8	33.8	35.7	37.9	35.2	33.4	0.7	11.4	0.07195	0.00861
Vietnam 1997	47.0	57.3	59.5	59.4	55.5	55.8	0.8	8.5	0.01431	0.00677
Vietnam 2002	57.9	57.9	58.1	58.0	51.6	56.7	1.1	6.3	−0.02528	0.00671
Europe and Central Asia	**33.0**	**40.3**	**43.9**	**45.0**	**49.6**	**43.0**	**0.7**	**16.6**	**0.07147**	**0.02307**
Armenia 2000	15.5	20.9	22.4	22.3	29.2	22.3	0.5	13.7	0.09426	0.01592
Kazakhstan 1995	43.8	49.1	40.6	45.8	49.6	46.1	0.9	5.8	0.00752	0.01183
Kazakhstan 1999	48.9	50.6	52.9	54.5	55.1	52.7	0.9	6.2	0.01747	0.00978
Kyrgyz Republic 1997	44.4	44.9	48.4	50.9	54.4	48.9	0.8	10.0	0.04022	0.01085
Turkey 1993	21.0	29.4	33.1	38.5	45.5	34.5	0.5	24.5	0.12191	0.00972
Turkey 1998	23.6	32.2	37.7	41.9	48.0	37.7	0.5	24.4	0.12904	0.00977

Turkmenistan 2000	50.9	56.7	53.1	55.4	49.9	53.1	1.0	1.0	—	—
Uzbekistan 1996	46.0	55.1	55.5	47.7	52.2	51.3	0.9	6.2	−0.00728	0.00985
Latin America and the Caribbean	**50.1**	**60.8**	**65.8**	**67.7**	**70.6**	**63.5**	**0.7**	**20.5**	**0.06077**	**0.02190**
Bolivia 1998	7.1	17.2	22.2	32.2	45.6	25.2	0.2	38.5	0.28389	0.01127
Bolivia 2003	22.5	27.7	31.5	41.8	49.3	34.9	0.5	26.8	0.14658	0.00774
Brazil 1996	55.8	68.9	73.6	73.8	76.8	70.3	0.7	21.0	0.05942	0.00444
Colombia 1995	42.2	59.6	62.7	64.2	65.7	59.3	0.6	23.5	0.06654	0.00611
Colombia 2000	53.8	61.6	67.2	70.1	66.4	64.0	0.8	12.6	0.04500	0.00551
Colombia 2005	60.4	66.6	69.3	71.7	71.8	68.2	0.8	11.4	0.04093	0.00306
Dominican Republic 1996	51.2	61.7	58.2	61.5	63.7	59.2	0.8	12.5	0.04534	0.00639
Dominican Republic 2002	58.8	64.6	68.0	66.9	69.6	65.8	0.8	10.7	0.03378	0.00372
Guatemala 1995	5.4	10.1	21.4	37.4	57.1	26.9	0.1	51.7	0.35895	0.01024
Guatemala 1998/99	5.4	11.9	24.5	45.0	59.7	30.9	0.1	54.3	0.35723	0.01243
Haiti 1994/95	4.9	7.4	12.7	20.4	20.9	13.2	0.2	16.0	0.29046	0.02584
Haiti 2000	17.4	22.2	25.7	24.2	24.2	22.8	0.7	6.8	0.10090	0.01386
Nicaragua 1997/98	40.2	55.5	60.3	65.4	64.2	57.4	0.6	24.0	0.09526	0.00559
Nicaragua 2001	50.2	65.8	71.2	71.1	71.0	66.1	0.7	20.8	0.06226	0.00507
Paraguay 1990	20.6	25.3	34.4	44.3	46.1	35.2	0.4	25.5	0.17938	0.01235
Peru 1996	24.0	37.5	45.2	48.9	50.3	41.3	0.5	26.3	0.13758	0.00486
Peru 2000	36.8	45.8	54.4	56.3	58.0	50.4	0.6	21.2	0.09177	0.00444

(continued)

61

Table A1.8 (continued)

Region, country, and year of survey	Use of contraception by women (percent)						Ratio of poorest to wealthiest quintiles	Difference between poorest and wealthiest quintiles (absolute value)	Concentration index	
	Poorest quintile	2nd	3rd	4th	Wealthiest quintile	Population average			Value	Standard error
Middle East and North Africa	**37.8**	**43.5**	**46.5**	**49.9**	**53.7**	**46.6**	**0.7**	**15.9**	**0.06600**	**0.01633**
Egypt, Arab Rep. of 1995	28.2	39.0	47.1	52.0	57.4	45.5	0.5	29.2	0.16077	0.00505
Egypt, Arab Rep. of 2000	42.6	49.9	54.2	58.1	60.8	53.7	0.7	18.2	0.07156	0.00443
Jordan 1997	27.5	35.7	35.4	42.1	46.8	37.7	0.6	19.3	0.17507	0.01149
Morocco 1992	17.9	30.0	37.8	43.1	48.3	35.5	0.4	30.4	0.17225	0.01020
Morocco 2003/04	51.4	55.2	55.4	54.8	56.8	54.8	0.9	5.4	0.01886	0.00562
Yemen, Rep. of 1997	1.4	3.5	6.8	13.8	24.1	9.8	0.1	22.7	0.52786	0.01875
South Asia	**27.7**	**32.8**	**40.7**	**45.1**	**50.8**	**39.5**	**0.5**	**23.1**	**0.11876**	**0.02511**
Bangladesh 1996/97	38.8	40.8	43.7	38.8	48.5	42.1	0.8	9.7	0.04452	0.00751
Bangladesh 1999/2000	37.4	43.7	44.8	43.5	50.2	44.0	0.7	12.8	0.05696	0.00646
Bangladesh 2004	44.7	47.7	46.6	47.4	50.0	47.3	0.9	5.3	0.02480	0.00580
India 1992/93	24.9	27.5	36.1	42.0	50.6	36.5	0.5	25.7	0.14456	0.00242
India 1998/99	29.3	34.9	44.9	49.7	54.6	42.8	0.5	25.3	0.12920	0.00222

Nepal 1996	15.7	21.2	23.2	26.6	44.9	26.0	0.3	29.2	0.20910	0.01084
Nepal 2001	23.8	28.7	31.7	38.9	55.2	35.4	0.4	31.4	0.17967	0.00814
Pakistan 1990/91	1.2	4.1	6.1	10.7	23.2	9.0	0.1	22.0	0.51205	0.02485
Sub-Saharan Africa	**8.8**	**11.1**	**14.3**	**18.5**	**30.5**	**16.6**	**0.3**	**21.7**	**0.24519**	**0.04642**
Benin 1996	1.3	1.4	1.7	4.6	9.0	3.4	0.1	7.7	0.38588	0.05442
Benin 2001	4.0	3.2	6.7	8.3	14.7	7.2	0.3	10.7	0.27534	0.03278
Burkina Faso 1992/93	0.8	0.3	1.0	2.5	16.4	4.2	—	15.7	0.91224	0.04923
Burkina Faso 1998/99	1.8	2.6	2.9	2.4	16.0	4.8	0.1	14.2	0.57474	0.04340
Burkina Faso 2003	1.8	4.5	6.2	6.9	26.8	8.8	0.1	25.0	0.48610	0.02230
Cameroon 1991	0.7	1.2	2.8	4.4	12.5	4.3	0.1	11.8	0.59516	0.05731
Cameroon 1998	1.4	2.2	6.1	10.5	16.6	7.1	0.1	15.2	0.45378	0.03608
Cameroon 2004	2.4	5.1	11.5	20.2	27.2	13.1	0.1	24.8	0.39885	0.01816
Central African Republic 1994/95	0.7	0.9	1.9	5.6	8.8	3.2	0.1	8.1	0.55563	0.05851
Chad 1996/97	0.1	0.2	0.1	1.0	4.8	1.2	—	4.7	0.94274	0.09954
Chad 2004	0.0	0.2	1.0	0.4	7.3	1.6	—	7.3	0.83194	0.08120
Comoros 1996	6.6	11.6	10.2	10.0	18.6	11.4	0.4	12.0	0.15895	0.03934
Côte d'Ivoire 1994	1.1	2.1	2.0	5.3	12.5	4.3	0.1	11.4	0.47567	0.04214
Eritrea 1995	0.3	0.7	1.0	2.6	18.9	4.0	—	18.6	0.84891	0.06552
Ethiopia 2000	2.7	2.7	2.0	3.6	22.9	6.3	0.1	20.2	0.78631	0.03104
Gabon 2000	5.6	8.3	11.8	13.4	18.2	11.8	0.3	12.6	0.19990	0.02680
Ghana 1993	5.4	5.5	7.8	11.8	19.1	10.1	0.3	13.7	0.25983	0.03190
Ghana 1998	7.5	11.5	13.6	16.7	17.9	13.3	0.4	10.4	0.17092	0.02415

(continued)

Table A1.8 (continued)

Region, country, and year of survey	Use of contraception by women (percent)						Ratio of poorest to wealthiest quintiles	Difference between poorest and wealthiest quintiles (absolute value)	Concentration index	
	Poorest quintile	2nd	3rd	4th	Wealthiest quintile	Population average			Value	Standard error
Ghana 2003	8.6	19.1	18.6	21.3	26.3	18.7	0.3	17.6	0.17986	0.01980
Guinea 1999	1.0	1.9	2.8	7.4	9.2	4.2	0.1	8.2	0.44846	0.04042
Kenya 1993	10.3	15.7	27.3	37.5	45.1	27.3	0.2	34.9	0.26378	0.01340
Kenya 1998	12.6	24.1	30.7	39.7	50.1	31.5	0.3	37.5	0.23115	0.01153
Kenya 2003	11.8	24.2	33.4	41.0	44.5	31.5	0.3	32.7	0.23325	0.01042
Madagascar 1997	2.3	3.0	7.3	12.4	23.8	9.7	0.1	21.5	0.49740	0.02754
Malawi 1992	3.9	3.6	5.6	6.9	17.2	7.4	0.2	13.3	0.41164	0.04027
Malawi 2000	19.9	23.4	22.9	25.8	39.6	26.1	0.5	19.7	0.14022	0.01003
Mali 1995/96	0.5	1.4	2.0	4.2	15.3	4.5	—	14.8	0.61241	0.03806
Mali 2001	4.2	3.6	3.4	7.3	17.9	7.0	0.2	13.7	0.34229	0.02502
Mauritania 2000/01	0.1	0.5	2.6	6.8	16.5	5.1	—	16.4	0.61491	0.04331
Mozambique 1997	0.9	1.8	3.1	5.3	16.9	5.1	0.1	16.0	0.74981	0.04425
Mozambique 2003	14.1	16.2	21.5	19.3	36.6	20.8	0.4	22.5	0.20537	0.01212
Namibia 1992	5.4	6.5	11.8	28.9	56.9	26.0	0.1	51.5	0.43759	0.01944
Namibia 2000	28.8	24.1	30.3	48.5	64.2	42.6	0.4	35.4	0.18596	0.01198
Niger 1998	0.8	1.6	2.2	2.9	18.1	4.6	—	17.3	0.70688	0.04287

Nigeria 1990	0.5	1.7	1.7	3.3	11.6	3.4	—	11.1	0.67519	0.04407
Nigeria 2003	3.6	2.9	6.7	9.2	20.5	8.2	0.2	16.9	0.38446	0.02867
Rwanda 2000	2.4	2.3	3.5	5.2	14.6	5.7	0.2	12.2	0.21090	0.06294
Senegal 1997	1.0	1.6	4.8	11.6	23.6	8.1	—	22.6	0.52113	0.02817
South Africa 1998	34.0	45.1	54.5	62.1	70.3	55.1	0.5	36.3	0.13618	0.00688
Tanzania 1996	4.9	7.2	10.0	14.1	28.9	13.3	0.2	24.0	0.33190	0.02078
Tanzania 1999	5.6	12.8	11.8	20.4	32.1	16.9	0.2	26.5	0.27361	0.02168
Tanzania 2004	10.7	12.8	15.6	24.1	36.0	20.0	0.3	25.3	0.18557	0.01358
Togo 1998	3.3	4.9	7.0	7.5	12.5	7.0	0.3	9.2	0.23834	0.02845
Uganda 1995	2.1	2.7	4.1	6.2	25.8	7.8	0.1	23.7	0.66008	0.03373
Uganda 2000/01	11.3	9.3	11.9	19.5	40.6	18.2	0.3	29.3	0.36349	0.01824
Zambia 1996	5.4	10.3	8.4	18.1	31.3	14.4	0.2	25.9	0.34414	0.02182
Zambia 2001	10.8	13.2	19.7	31.3	52.5	25.3	0.2	41.7	0.32306	0.01433
Zimbabwe 1994	31.2	32.7	38.0	49.9	55.8	42.2	0.6	24.6	0.12549	0.01127
Zimbabwe 1999	41.1	42.1	42.8	53.7	67.4	50.4	0.6	26.3	0.09751	0.00938
All Countries	**29.2**	**34.7**	**40.2**	**43.5**	**49.0**	**39.5**	**0.6**	**19.7**	**0.09824**	**0.02281**

Sources: Country data from Gwatkin and others (2007); regional and global population-based averages are author's calculations using 2001 estimates from World Bank World Development Indicators.

Note: — = not available. Contraceptive use is the percentage of married or in-union women ages 15–49 who used any modern means of contraception.

Table A1.9 Attended Delivery Inequalities in Low- and Middle-Income Countries

Region, country, and year of survey	Deliveries attended by trained personnel (percent)						Ratio of poorest to wealthiest quintiles	Difference between poorest and wealthiest quintiles (absolute value)	Concentration index	
	Poorest quintile	2nd	3rd	4th	Wealthiest quintile	Population average			Value	Standard error
East Asia and Pacific	**39.8**	**60.2**	**73.5**	**83.5**	**94.2**	**67.7**	**0.4**	**54.4**	**0.15059**	**0.04629**
Cambodia 2000	14.7	21.3	27.4	40.7	81.2	31.8	0.2	66.5	0.31138	0.00888
Indonesia 1997	21.3	34.8	48.1	64.4	89.2	49.1	0.2	67.9	0.28647	0.00315
Indonesia 2002/03	39.9	56.1	68.7	80.6	93.6	66.2	0.4	53.8	0.17487	0.00262
Philippines 1998	21.2	45.9	72.8	83.9	91.9	56.4	0.2	70.7	0.27632	0.00441
Philippines 2003	25.1	51.4	72.4	84.4	92.3	59.8	0.3	67.3	0.24967	0.00437
Vietnam 1997	49.0	78.4	84.2	93.6	99.2	77.0	0.5	50.2	0.13787	0.00681
Vietnam 2002	58.1	86.0	95.1	97.4	99.7	85.1	0.6	41.6	0.10092	0.00710
Europe and Central Asia	**71.3**	**87.0**	**93.1**	**96.9**	**98.7**	**88.1**	**0.7**	**27.4**	**0.05786**	**0.02216**
Armenia 2000	93.3	94.2	99.4	98.8	100.0	96.8	0.9	6.7	0.01628	0.00269
Kazakhstan 1995	99.4	100.0	98.8	100.0	100.0	99.6	1.0	0.6	0.00108	0.00108
Kazakhstan 1999	99.2	99.6	98.6	99.0	98.5	99.0	1.0	0.7	0.00111	0.00182
Kyrgyz Republic 1997	96.0	98.2	98.1	99.7	100.0	98.1	1.0	4.0	0.00445	0.00178
Turkey 1993	43.4	71.0	84.3	95.5	98.9	76.0	0.4	55.5	0.14212	0.00523
Turkey 1998	53.4	77.7	88.9	95.2	98.2	80.6	0.5	44.8	0.12310	0.00513

Turkmenistan 2000	96.8	97.7	96.2	97.3	98.3	97.2	1.0	1.5	—	—
Uzbekistan 1996	91.7	100.0	99.0	99.3	100.0	97.5	0.9	8.3	0.01501	0.00390
Latin America and the Caribbean	**61.0**	**78.0**	**87.3**	**92.8**	**96.7**	**80.0**	**0.6**	**35.7**	**0.08293**	**0.02811**
Bolivia 1998	19.8	44.8	67.7	87.9	97.9	56.7	0.2	78.1	0.29662	0.00413
Bolivia 2003	26.6	49.7	69.9	87.6	98.4	60.8	0.3	71.8	0.22564	0.00371
Brazil 1996	71.6	88.7	95.7	97.7	98.6	87.7	0.7	27.0	0.08182	0.00356
Colombia 1995	60.6	85.2	92.8	98.9	98.1	84.5	0.6	37.5	0.10278	0.00387
Colombia 2000	64.3	85.6	94.7	98.6	98.6	86.4	0.7	34.3	0.08616	0.00367
Colombia 2005	72.0	94.0	97.3	98.9	99.3	90.7	0.7	27.4	0.07520	0.00208
Dominican Republic 1996	88.9	97.1	97.5	98.4	97.8	95.5	0.9	8.9	0.03238	0.00273
Dominican Republic 2002	93.8	98.2	98.9	99.5	99.6	97.8	0.9	5.8	0.01904	0.00136
Guatemala 1995	9.3	16.1	31.1	62.8	91.5	34.8	0.1	82.2	0.36543	0.00766
Guatemala 1998/99	8.8	17.8	38.8	73.5	91.9	40.6	0.1	83.1	0.36103	0.00905
Haiti 1994/95	24.0	37.3	47.4	60.7	78.2	46.3	0.3	54.2	0.22404	0.00955
Haiti 2000	4.1	9.4	13.5	37.9	70.0	24.2	0.1	65.9	0.45698	0.01232
Nicaragua 1997/98	32.9	58.8	79.8	86.0	92.3	64.6	0.4	59.4	0.20938	0.00404
Nicaragua 2001	77.5	88.5	95.0	97.2	99.3	89.7	0.8	21.8	0.05667	0.00275
Paraguay 1990	41.2	49.9	69.0	87.9	98.1	66.0	0.4	56.9	0.19569	0.00526
Peru 1996	13.7	48.0	75.1	90.3	96.6	56.4	0.1	82.9	0.31919	0.00255
Peru 2000	13.0	34.3	62.2	74.8	87.5	46.9	0.1	74.5	0.31759	0.00433

(continued)

Table A1.9 *(continued)*

Region, country, and year of survey	Deliveries attended by trained personnel (percent)						Ratio of poorest to wealthiest quintiles	Difference between poorest and wealthiest quintiles (absolute value)	Concentration index	
	Poorest quintile	2nd	3rd	4th	Wealthiest quintile	Population average			Value	Standard error
Middle East and North Africa	**29.6**	**43.6**	**57.8**	**72.2**	**87.9**	**56.8**	**0.3**	**58.3**	**0.19942**	**0.04738**
Egypt, Arab Rep. of 1995	20.5	29.8	47.0	62.1	86.4	46.2	0.2	65.9	0.29115	0.00474
Egypt, Arab Rep. of 2000	31.4	45.5	61.1	76.2	94.2	60.9	0.3	62.8	0.21894	0.00355
Jordan 1997	91.2	97.5	98.4	98.0	99.3	96.6	0.9	8.1	0.04834	0.00268
Morocco 1992	5.1	13.6	28.3	55.1	77.9	30.8	0.1	72.8	0.47385	0.00988
Morocco 2003/04	29.4	49.4	70.3	86.1	95.4	62.6	0.3	65.9	0.21363	0.00464
Yemen, Rep. of 1997	6.8	13.2	15.6	28.7	49.7	21.7	0.1	42.9	0.41622	0.01058
South Asia	**13.6**	**21.3**	**34.4**	**51.3**	**76.1**	**36.4**	**0.2**	**62.5**	**0.31503**	**0.06295**
Bangladesh 1996/97	1.8	2.5	4.0	9.0	29.8	8.1	0.1	28.0	0.61348	0.03288
Bangladesh 1999/2000	3.5	4.9	6.5	14.0	42.1	12.1	0.1	38.6	0.61741	0.02359
Bangladesh 2004	3.3	4.3	10.2	17.0	39.4	13.2	0.1	36.1	0.56602	0.02048
India 1992/93	11.9	18.2	30.1	47.9	78.7	34.3	0.2	66.8	0.37935	0.00337
India 1998/99	16.4	25.9	42.0	60.6	84.4	42.4	0.2	68.0	0.32203	0.00308
Nepal 1996	2.9	5.2	6.4	9.1	33.7	9.6	0.1	30.8	0.51143	0.03395

Nepal 2001	3.6	4.9	9.9	14.3	45.1	12.9	0.1	41.5	0.51203	0.02170
Pakistan 1990/91	4.6	6.6	6.0	21.5	55.2	18.6	0.1	50.6	0.59890	0.01727
Sub-Saharan Africa	**22.2**	**29.5**	**36.6**	**53.0**	**77.9**	**41.4**	**0.3**	**55.7**	**0.24603**	**0.04197**
Benin 1996	34.4	53.1	66.1	87.6	97.5	63.9	0.4	63.1	0.20346	0.00665
Benin 2001	49.6	60.5	76.9	90.2	99.3	72.9	0.5	49.7	0.14361	0.00436
Burkina Faso 1992/93	26.0	26.8	29.9	46.5	86.1	41.4	0.3	60.1	0.32740	0.00753
Burkina Faso 1998/99	17.9	20.8	21.9	32.4	75.0	30.9	0.2	57.1	0.35381	0.01106
Burkina Faso 2003	18.7	24.3	31.8	45.3	84.5	37.8	0.2	65.7	0.29563	0.00664
Cameroon 1991	32.0	48.4	57.8	81.2	94.7	63.5	0.3	62.7	0.20890	0.00637
Cameroon 1998	27.9	43.4	63.5	84.3	89.2	58.2	0.3	61.3	0.23392	0.00884
Cameroon 2004	29.4	44.7	72.6	86.6	94.5	61.9	0.3	65.2	0.22521	0.00441
Central African Republic 1994/95	14.3	25.2	40.7	69.9	81.7	45.9	0.2	67.4	0.33053	0.00943
Chad 1996/97	2.6	5.6	6.7	15.5	47.4	15.0	0.1	44.8	0.66574	0.01796
Chad 2004	1.4	7.2	7.9	14.8	51.4	16.1	—	50.1	0.73107	0.01689
Comoros 1996	26.2	40.1	54.6	67.1	84.8	51.6	0.3	58.6	0.23542	0.01418
Côte d'Ivoire 1994	16.8	29.6	45.8	65.2	83.5	45.4	0.2	66.7	0.30454	0.00818
Eritrea 1995	5.0	6.9	7.2	31.7	74.3	20.6	0.1	69.3	0.63049	0.02343
Ethiopia 2000	0.9	1.5	2.0	3.3	25.3	5.6	—	24.4	1.24456	0.03943
Gabon 2000	67.2	85.7	91.5	93.9	97.1	86.7	0.7	29.9	0.07707	0.00381
Ghana 1993	25.3	24.1	31.6	62.3	85.3	43.7	0.3	60.0	0.28067	0.01284

(continued)

69

Table A1.9 (continued)

Region, country, and year of survey	Deliveries attended by trained personnel (percent)						Ratio of poorest to wealthiest quintiles	Difference between poorest and wealthiest quintiles (absolute value)	Concentration index	
	Poorest quintile	2nd	3rd	4th	Wealthiest quintile	Population average			Value	Standard error
Ghana 1998	17.9	31.0	48.1	65.0	86.1	44.3	0.2	68.2	0.29790	0.00895
Ghana 2003	20.6	31.9	43.3	73.0	90.4	47.1	0.2	69.8	0.29956	0.00768
Guinea 1999	12.1	16.0	26.9	54.5	81.5	34.8	0.1	69.4	0.40156	0.00905
Kenya 1993	23.1	33.1	45.7	56.7	76.5	45.1	0.3	53.4	0.22699	0.00762
Kenya 1998	23.2	33.3	41.9	56.1	79.6	44.4	0.3	56.4	0.24185	0.01037
Kenya 2003	17.0	32.8	38.1	55.0	75.4	41.6	0.2	58.4	0.29895	0.00720
Madagascar 1997	29.6	37.0	40.5	65.0	88.5	47.3	0.3	58.9	0.23823	0.00868
Malawi 1992	44.6	46.2	50.4	58.8	77.9	54.9	0.6	33.3	0.14389	0.00709
Malawi 2000	43.0	49.4	50.9	58.5	83.0	55.6	0.5	40.0	0.13377	0.00442
Mali 1995/96	11.1	22.8	34.1	51.5	80.6	38.7	0.1	69.5	0.34284	0.00802
Mali 2001	22.0	27.0	29.4	45.8	88.7	40.6	0.2	66.7	0.27690	0.00590
Mauritania 2000/01	14.7	36.3	56.8	73.0	92.8	53.3	0.2	78.1	0.29594	0.00582
Mozambique 1997	18.1	35.2	31.4	64.0	82.1	44.2	0.2	64.0	0.29598	0.00859
Mozambique 2003	24.7	33.4	42.5	68.4	88.7	47.7	0.3	63.9	0.27062	0.00501
Namibia 1992	50.9	58.8	65.0	74.4	91.2	68.2	0.6	40.3	0.11728	0.00580
Namibia 2000	55.4	64.4	77.4	86.2	97.1	75.5	0.6	41.7	0.11912	0.00504

Niger 1998	4.2	7.1	7.6	15.5	62.8	17.6	0.1	58.6	0.65349	0.01962
Nigeria 1990	12.2	19.7	27.3	43.4	70.0	33.0	0.2	57.8	0.36522	0.00814
Nigeria 2003	12.9	19.0	27.6	51.1	84.5	36.2	0.2	71.6	0.34666	0.00913
Rwanda 2000	17.3	16.0	17.8	22.8	59.6	26.7	0.3	42.3	0.35511	0.01105
Senegal 1997	20.3	25.4	45.3	69.3	86.2	46.5	0.2	65.9	0.27628	0.00663
South Africa 1998	67.8	81.2	88.5	94.9	98.1	84.4	0.7	30.3	0.08473	0.00358
Tanzania 1996	26.7	40.4	41.2	51.8	80.9	46.7	0.3	54.2	0.20061	0.00686
Tanzania 1999	28.9	35.0	33.3	48.4	82.8	43.8	0.3	53.9	0.21340	0.00970
Tanzania 2004	31.0	35.7	37.6	53.4	86.8	46.3	0.4	55.8	0.18845	0.00672
Togo 1998	25.1	34.7	52.5	71.7	91.2	50.5	0.3	66.1	0.26757	0.00726
Uganda 1995	22.6	28.3	32.6	39.3	70.4	37.8	0.3	47.8	0.27554	0.00915
Uganda 2000/01	19.7	27.6	31.9	46.4	77.3	38.2	0.3	57.6	0.29717	0.00802
Zambia 1996	19.3	24.6	36.7	67.7	90.5	46.5	0.2	71.2	0.31358	0.00596
Zambia 2001	19.7	22.6	34.2	68.7	91.1	43.4	0.2	71.4	0.31226	0.00705
Zimbabwe 1994	55.1	59.5	65.3	77.9	92.8	69.4	0.6	37.7	0.11069	0.00713
Zimbabwe 1999	56.7	67.3	64.8	79.7	93.5	72.4	0.6	36.8	0.09013	0.00539
All Countries	**27.0**	**37.9**	**49.2**	**63.2**	**82.5**	**49.3**	**0.3**	**55.6**	**0.20988**	**0.04379**

Sources: Country data from Gwatkin and others (2007); regional and global population-based averages are author's calculations using 2001 estimates from World Bank World Development Indicators.

Note: — = not available.

Annex 1.3 Benefit Incidence Analysis

Objectives of Benefit Incidence Analysis (BIA)

A common goal among policy makers is to ensure that the dollars they allocate to public health are spent on the poor. This is mainly due to the belief that public spending should target the poor because they are often the ones who need health services the most. However, sometimes the money spent on public programs is applied in such a way that it does not necessarily benefit the poor more than it does the rich. A benefit incidence analysis (BIA) is a four-step process that identifies which groups receive how much of public spending on health care.

Groups can be defined in several ways, such as geographical regions, ethnicity, and age. However, differences in public spending between groups of different economic status are often of greatest interest to policy makers and researchers. For example, recipients of public spending can be divided into five groups (quintiles), representing the poorest 20 percent, the next-poorest 20 percent, the middle 20 percent, and so on. A BIA traces the distribution of public spending on health care by these quintiles, thereby identifying which groups benefit the most from public health expenditures. The results of a BIA may suggest inequitable distribution of public spending, in which case appropriate structural and policy changes can be discussed and implemented to ensure that targeted groups benefit from public health expenditures.

Data Needs for Conducting a BIA

A BIA requires micro data from a health or multipurpose household survey. The survey should provide an appropriate measure for living standard, such as income per capita, consumption expenditure per capita, or an ordinal measure such as a wealth index. The survey should also distinguish between public and private health care. Because the main purpose of a BIA is to establish the distribution of public spending, only services that are subsidized by the state should be considered. If the private sector is small enough in the region, then the distinction may not be necessary. Last, the survey data for health care use should be such that recall bias is minimized. Health care services that are used more frequently, such as ambulatory care, should have a recall period of no more than two to four weeks. Inpatient care, however, should be longer, at about 12 months.

Four Steps for Calculating BIA

A BIA can be divided into four basic steps. First, recipients of public health services must be ranked and assigned to groups. Individuals should be ranked by an appropriate living standard measure as discussed above. Individuals, for example, can be categorized into groups that fall within specified poverty levels or certain castes and tribes.

Second, individuals must be linked to the amount of public health services that the individual used. The amount of public health service is measured differently depending on the type of service that was used. For example, for inpatient services, quantity of public health service used is measured by length of stay. For outpatient services, the number of visits is an appropriate measure of quantity.

The third step is to calculate the total amount of public health subsidies provided by the government to each individual. This is done by multiplying the net per unit cost of providing health care services by the number of units of publicly provided care used by each individual less the amount the individual may have paid for his or her health care services, also referred to as user fees.

To obtain the unit cost, divide total public expenditure for each service type within a region or facility by total units used. To estimate total public expenditure for each service type, total public recurrent expenditure on health care should be broken down by geographic region, then by type of facility, then by type of service. If available, a system of national health accounts (NHA) can provide sufficient information regarding expenditures at the region, facility, and service levels. If NHA data are unavailable, public expenditure on health care will have to be broken down based on various assumptions and approximations. The accuracy of these approximations should be checked through sensitivity analysis. The number of service units used can be estimated from survey data or administrative records.

Ideally, individual user fee data should be obtained from surveys because user fees often differ by an individual's ability to pay. For example, in some countries, there may be fee exemptions for the poor. If the survey does not provide user fee information, it can be estimated by dividing aggregate user fee revenue reported in official accounts by an estimate of total use. This resulting average payment would then be applied to all users. However, this method ignores individual variation in user fee payments.

The fourth and final step is to analyze the distribution of net government health spending among the groups of interest, such as income or expenditure quintiles. To do this, first sum the value of the health care subsidy received by individuals within their assigned living-standard groups. The distribution can be presented in two ways. One way is to look at cumulative shares of the subsidy received by each quintile. Second, the distribution can be described as a ratio of net government spending to the average income or average expenditure for each group.

Annex 1.4   Recommendations for Further Reading

Selected from Goldman and others (forthcoming).

Arokiasamy, P. 2004. "Regional Patterns of Sex Bias and Excess Female Child Mortality in India." *Population* **59 (6): 833–64.**
A cross-sectional analysis of child mortality in different regions of India exploring dynamics of gender bias and the effects of overall lower immunization rates resulting in excess female mortality. Child mortality sex differentials in India's northern states are among the highest ever recorded in demographic history. The data, including birth histories of mothers and information on child health care provision, came from the National Family Health Survey, 1992–93 (IIPS 1995).

Cuyler, A., and A. Wagstaff. 1993. "Equity and Equality in Health and Health Care." *Journal of Health Economics* **12 (4): 431–57.**
Explores definitions of equity in health care: equality of utilization, distribution according to need, equality of access, and equality of health. The authors evaluate the current literature on equity in health care and develop their own recommendations for defining equity in health. The authors reject the principle of "distribution according to need" as an equity principle because it does not necessarily result in health care equity, unless "needs" are defined in such a way as to ensure equality.

Gwatkin, D. 2000. "Critical Reflection: Health Inequalities and Health of the Poor: What Do We Know? What Can We Do?" *Bulletin of the World Health Organization* **78 (1): 3–18.**
Summarizes research on poverty- and equity-oriented approaches to health disparities and emphasizes the importance of transitioning from research to action. It focuses on (i) presenting initial findings from new research on health inequalities and (ii) stimulating movement for action to correct problems identified in the research.

————. 2005. "How Much Would Poor People Gain from Faster Progress Towards the Millennium Development Goals for Health?" *Lancet* 365 (9461): 813–17.
Highlights the fact that countries can successfully achieve health-related Millennium Development Goals (MDGs) without the benefits of this attainment reaching the poor. The author shows that benefits from MDG target progress will not automatically flow to the poor because the targets are population and societal averages, and greater improvement that will affect those averages can be made in richer segments of the population faster. Increased efforts are needed to reach the poor when working to achieve the MDGs under these conditions.

Hatt, L., and H. Waters. 2006. "Determinants of Child Morbidity in Latin America: A Pooled Analysis of Interactions between Parental Education and Economic Status." *Social Science and Medicine* 62 (2): 375–86.
Analyzes the interactions between parental education and economic status in predicting the risk of diarrhea and respiratory illness among children less than age five in Latin America and the Caribbean. Twelve Demographic and Health Surveys (DHS) and nine Living Standards Measurement Study (LSMS) surveys from Latin America and the Caribbean, conducted from 1993 to 2003, are pooled to create two large databases.

Ochoa, H., H. Sanchez, M. Ruiz, and M. Fuller. 1999. "Social Inequalities and Health in Rural Chiapas, Mexico: Agricultural Economy, Nutrition and Child Health in La Fraylesca Region." *Cuadernos de Saude Publica* 15 (2): 261–70.
A cross-sectional survey of 1,046 households (5,549 individuals) was conducted in La Fraylesca, Chiapas, to explore the association between farmers' socioeconomic conditions and their children's health. Specifically, health outcomes for preschool children include childhood morbidity (intestinal parasites and the like), mortality, and nutritional status. Inequality is measured by comparing the health outcomes of preschoolers from poor households with those from wealthy households. Study participants are divided into socioeconomic agriculture groups using land tenure data and volume of maize production per year.

Pitchforth, E., E. van Teijlingen, W. Graham, and A. Fitzmaurice. 2007. "Development of a Proxy Wealth Index for Women Utilizing Emergency Obstetric Care in Bangladesh." *Health Policy and Planning* 22 (5): 311–19.
Evaluates the effectiveness of a facility-level proxy wealth index for assessing women's socioeconomic status with data from 638 women admitted to

the obstetrics ward of selected hospitals in the Dhaka Division of Bangladesh. Specifically, the proxy wealth index is used to compare the socioeconomic status of women using emergency obstetric care with that of women in the wider population.

Victora, C., J. Vaughan, F. Barros, A. Silva, and E. Tomasi. 2000. "Explaining Trends in Inequities: Evidence from Brazilian Child Health Studies." *Lancet* **356 (9235): 1093–98.**
Assesses surveillance data from the Americas and two cohort studies in Brazil for time trends in child-health inequities in Brazil (reviewing trends in coverage, morbidity, and mortality). Authors present the "inverse equity hypothesis," a logical corollary of Tudor Hart's "inverse care law," whereby inequities in health status between the wealthy and the poor usually widen before narrowing with new public health interventions. The phenomenon occurs because interventions reach groups of higher socioeconomic status first and affect poor groups later on.

Notes

1. The compendium of data for 56 low- and middle-income countries was published in September 2007, but the first set of poverty fact sheets, covering 44 countries, was made available in 2000. The data compendium covers the years 1991–2005. The average infant mortality rate (number of deaths before age one per 1,000 live births) was 87 in the poorest quintile and 41 in the wealthiest quintile. On average, 21.5 percent of the children in the poorest quintile were severely stunted, versus 6.5 percent in the wealthiest quintile. The average number of births per 1,000 adolescent girls was 132 in the poorest quintile and 42 in the wealthiest.

2. On average across the 56 countries, 77 percent of babies were delivered at home in the poorest quintile and 24 percent in the wealthiest quintile; 27 percent of deliveries were attended by a trained professional in the poorest quintile and 82 percent in the wealthiest quintile; the rate of full basic immunization was 34 percent in the poorest quintile and 65 percent in the wealthiest quintile; and the rate of use of contraception by women was 29 percent in the poorest quintile and 49 percent in the wealthiest quintile.

3. Filmer and Pritchett (2001) describe the asset-score approach now commonly used to measure distribution of health outcomes and health sector outputs.

4. Early analysis of inequality that led to Gwatkin and others (2007).

5. For example, for India, Pande and Yazbeck (2003), Gaudin and Yazbeck (2006).

6. More details on how to undertake a benefit incidence study are found in annex 1.3 of this chapter.

7. More details on BIA are found in chapter 3. It focuses on how BIA may be used in tracking public spending choices.

8. The example here uses data from quintiles (20 percent of the population), but the same can be done for deciles (10 percent of the population) or other percentage breakdowns.

2

Approaching a Complex and Persistent Problem

Chapter 1 highlighted some of the empirical aspects of measuring inequality and painted a disturbing picture of large and persistent inequalities in important outcomes, such as mortality and nutrition. It also revealed disappointing levels of inequality in the use of publicly financed preventive and simple curative health services. Before one can attack the problem of low use of health services by the poor, one must examine the nature of poverty as it relates to health—what are the factors determining the poor's health outcomes? And from the other side, one must examine the health sector itself—what are its operational and financial handicaps in meeting the health needs of the poor? Answers to these questions, the subject of this chapter, bring us closer to achieving the goal of this book, which is to improve the health sector's performance in reaching and serving the poor and vulnerable.

Pathways to Good Health

In October 1999, the International Monetary Fund (IMF) and the World Bank launched a new program, the Poverty Reduction Strategy Papers (PRSP), that changed the way those institutions support low-income countries. At the heart of the change was a renewed appreciation for the multidimensional nature of poverty. To support countries in their struggle to address inequality and poverty, the PRSP project issued a sourcebook of

Figure 2.1 *Determinants of Health Outcomes: The PRSP Pathways Framework*

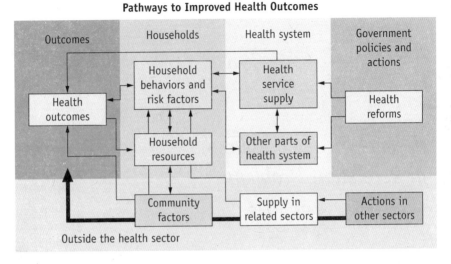

Pathways to Improved Health Outcomes

Sources: Adapted from World Bank (2003) and Campbell White, Merrick, and Yazbeck (2006).

analytical tools covering most sectors (World Bank 2003). The sourcebook included the health sector because health outcomes—specifically, ill health, malnutrition, and high fertility—were recognized both as elements of poverty and as causes of low income.

The health chapter of the PRSP sourcebook included a pathways framework (figure 2.1) to examine both the determinants of negative health outcomes and the impoverishing effect of the high price of care (Claeson and others 2003). The pathways framework presents a useful way of thinking through how health is produced and how the poor interact with the health sector and with related sectors.

The starting point of the framework, as with this book, is the ability to measure health outcomes for the poor. Once those outcomes are identified, the diagnostic journey (illustrated by moving from left to right in figure 2.1) continues by analyzing household behaviors and resources that influence health outcomes. The third segment examines household interactions with the health system and with community factors, such as education, roads, and water, and the final segment highlights the role of policy making in the health sector and in other sectors.

The pathways framework puts considerable emphasis on factors within households and communities because poverty is primarily a household characteristic that in many cases reflects the physical and cultural conditions of the community. The framework recognizes that households are not only consumers of health services but are also the primary producers of their health status. The health of individuals is influenced by their diet; the extent and nature of their physical activity; the extent to which they engage in risky behaviors, such as smoking, drinking, or unprotected sex; and the extent to which they seek health services. Such household-level determinants of health are often largely controlled by the availability of resources, such as education, financial assets, and income, and can be strongly influenced by cultural factors. Additional determinants of health outcomes include transportation and agriculture; although those sectors are not typically recognized as being within the health sector, their influence on health, and on the use of health services, is significant. Exploration of the influence of all sectors on the health of the poor is useful in attempting to reduce inequality in the use of health services.

The Binding Constraints Faced by the Poor

Poor households face a complex set of constraints and living conditions that impede good health. These factors limit their ability or willingness to use critical health services and expose them to additional risks not typically faced by the better-off. This complex set of interactions and intersections is best illustrated through an example. Box 2.1 presents a summary selection of interview transcripts concerning a Bangladeshi woman, Safar Banu, who died in childbirth.[1] The summary reveals the complexity that surrounded her death—factors from inside and outside the health sector, from within the household, and from the wider culture.

Household and Cultural Factors

The pathways framework identifies household behaviors, household resources, and cultural factors in explaining the determinants of health outcomes. In the Safar Banu case, these items include the following factors:

Household Behaviors and Risk Factors

- Household decision not to use contraception
- Household decision not to seek care from a qualified provider

- Decisions about priority feeding when food is limited
- Decision not to seek prenatal care

Household Resources

- Limited financial resources delayed health-seeking behavior and transport
- Limited knowledge affected appropriate actions
- Limited women's empowerment

Cultural Factors

- Religious factor in household decision on contraception
- Gender relations and the lack of voice within the household
- Acceptance of traditional healers

Box 2.1 *Why Did Safar Banu Die?*

Safar Banu, age 43, never attended an antenatal clinic. She said she had already given birth to nine children without the help of a clinic. Why should she need antenatal checkups now? She was too busy and had no time for such visits. While several months pregnant, she worked in the fields shredding jute fibers. Such work is usually performed only by the poorest women. Safar Banu did not use contraceptives. She wished to, but her husband forbade her and threatened to divorce her if she did. According to her mother, when Safar became pregnant for the 10th time, she was sorry and cried. The pregnancy itself did not present special problems, but during the last month, Safar complained of swollen feet and dizziness. A week before giving birth, she felt very weak and told her mother she feared she would not survive this birth. At the time, her anemic condition, which later became obvious, was not recognized by her family, and especially by her husband.

The husband held a great deal of faith in Gopal Daktar (the local healer). Daktar was called at the onset of labor and gave two tablets to increase labor contractions. After the birth, he again gave medicine to reduce the pain. All of these tablets were just aspirin, which Daktar admitted when later interviewed. In the delivery hut, Safar's mother was present with the dai (traditional birth attendant). The birth was difficult because Safar was so weak. After the birth, she was unable to get up for 10 hours. The dai and Safar's mother knew that something was seriously wrong. The husband did not realize that his wife's condition had deteriorated. He became alarmed only on the fifth day, when Safar's entire body became swollen.

Box 2.1 *(continued)*

The women in her village explained Safar's headaches by the blood that had risen from her womb to her head. They see this blood as polluted and thus extremely harmful. Also, blood that circulates in the lower limbs may kill if it goes to the head. It seems that Safar lost a considerable amount of blood after giving birth. This did not cause as much concern because she was considered not to have bled long enough. Thus, she did not completely eliminate the polluted and harmful blood that was believed to be the cause of her swelling.

On the fifth day, Safar had a sensation of burning in her limbs and asked for water to be poured over her head for the entire day. She was sweating profusely; however, she registered no fever. Two days before she died, a midwife from the maternal and child health (MCH) clinic was called. She recommended that Safar be transferred immediately to the district hospital. She diagnosed a case of extreme anemia and thought that a blood transfusion was necessary and urgent. The husband did not listen to the midwife. He had more confidence in Gopal Daktar, who tried various medications and injections but to no avail. Daktar later claimed that he gave no "good" (meaning expensive) medicines because the family was too poor to pay. Daktar was annoyed with them for wasting his time.

On the seventh day, Safar Banu became unconscious. Her mother had her carried to the MCH clinic to get treatment from the midwife. Safar's condition had deteriorated considerably, and it was feared that she would not survive the night. Her pulse was extremely low and she had difficulty breathing. The clinic offered to pay for medicines, but transport to a hospital was to be the family's responsibility according to the official policy. At this point, the elder son and a cousin took charge of the affair. They organized and paid for transport to the district hospital. Safar's mother felt that it was probably too late and of little use. She attempted to discourage her grandson. Half a "kani" of land had to be sold to pay for these costs, and the husband is still bitter with the clinic for not having provided any financial help. The son gave his own blood to save his mother but it was of no avail. The husband, a sick man himself, never went to the hospital. Safar Banu died the following day.

Safar Banu's mother confirmed how late the husband became aware of his wife's critical state. Mention was also made of how hard Safar worked and how little she ate after her husband and sons had been fed. She drank water when there was no rice. When she was ill in the past, she had returned to her mother, a poor woman herself, to get help and treatment. The husband thought only of his own illness and did not see his wife's problems. Safar Banu knew how to bear her sorrows in silence. Her husband praised her because she was uncomplaining.

Note: This summary is based on interviews with the persons mentioned above, except Safar Banu.

Medical, Health System, and Community Factors

The above elements were not the only influences in Safar Banu's death. Medical factors and the health system also played a role, and poverty exacerbated their effects by limiting the family's access to good services and even basic information. The medical and health system factors included no regulation of less-qualified private health care providers, limited outreach, and limited availability of health information.

Complications with other sectors, namely education and transportation, also had an effect. Again, the health determinants originating in other sectors are not the main focus of this book, but their influence on the health of the poor and vulnerable is especially important. A summary of critical factors in other sectors (transportation, education, water and sanitation, the environment, and nutrition) affecting health outcomes for the poor is in annex 2.1.

The Blind Spots of the Health Sector

The pathways framework helps identify the ways in which poor households are disadvantaged as they attempt to achieve good health. They have limited resources, low levels of health-related knowledge, and low levels of education; they suffer from more risk factors than the better-off, and are more heavily affected by environmental factors like water and sanitation. Arguably, the health sector, especially when publicly financed, should play an equalizing role.

The evidence presented in chapter 1 shows, however, that the health sector often increases inequality by providing critical services disproportionately to the better-off. If that unfortunate empirical fact is to change, its causes must be understood, policies must be devised and implemented to tackle the blind spots of the sector, and the sector must be monitored to ensure that policies produce the needed outcomes. The tools available for analysis, policy making, and monitoring will be covered in detail in the remainder of this book (analysis in chapter 3, policies in chapter 4, country examples in chapters 5–18, and monitoring in chapter 19).

The task, then, is to think systematically about inequalities in the use of health services, and the diagnostic tool briefly described below—a simple list of possible bottlenecks faced by the poor in accessing and using health services—can help us do so (figure 2.2). The list can yield insights into causes, help identify the potential blind spots in the health sector that contribute to inequality in health service, and provide a focus for monitoring.

Figure 2.2 *Eight Steps to Effective Use of Health Services by the Poor*

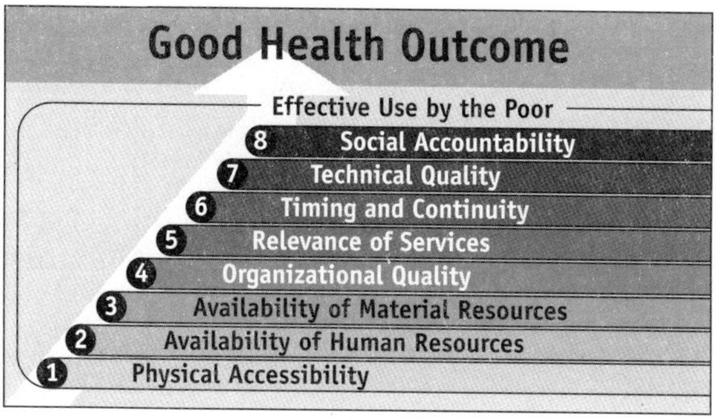

Sources: Adapted from Claeson and others 2003.

The diagnostic tool is presented here to address this dimension of health services use, although it has implications for the poor beyond the issue of health services.

The diagnostic tool—*eight steps to effective use by the poor*—takes a linear approach to disentangling the fairly complex, interactive, and nonlinear constraints that the poor face. This simple approach is effective because it identifies the types of constraints and uses analytical tools and data to prioritize the most difficult and urgent problems. The order of the eight steps is logical, but the interactive nature of the constraints makes the order less important than the need to explore all eight steps and the interactions across them.

The first step is to consider whether services at health facilities and elsewhere are available and sufficiently accessible to the poor. Distance is clearly an important factor, and travel time regardless of distance can become a significant factor depending on the availability of roads and public transportation. In areas of Africa, South Asia, and many other regions, seasonal variation in accessibility is important. The physical infrastructure of facilities is also significant—a lack of ramps may impede the access of persons with physical impairments.

The second step in the diagnostic tool considers the availability of human resources. Services may be geographically accessible, but trained staff may be unavailable or in short supply part of the time. In low- and middle-income countries, the problem of staff shortages in rural areas is fairly widespread. The lack or inappropriate use of trained staff can often be attributed to weak deployment practices; to an absence of financial incentives for health staff to work in poor, remote areas; to inadequate staff training; and to skills profiles poorly matched to service needs.

The third step in the diagnostic tool examines the availability of essential medicines and supplies at public and private facilities or outreach programs serving the poor. Unfortunately, it is often the case that facilities exist and staff is present but the necessary drugs and supplies are absent. Facilities and programs serving the poor typically face two major problems: (i) shortages of drugs and supplies and (ii) poor quality of drugs, which are often counterfeit. The problem of shortages of essential drugs is often attributed to inadequate supply logistics and drug management but could also be due to pilferage. Shortages are much more likely to take place in rural areas or in areas where the poor live. In many countries, a predominance of supply-side financing leads to rationing.

The fourth step examines the organizational quality of service delivery mechanisms. The organization of health services that serve poor populations may deter, rather than attract, poor patients. The literature on inequality in the use of health services identifies several factors related to organizational quality that have been found to limit access by the poor. Among them are (i) hours of operation that are incompatible with the ability of the working poor to leave work and seek services; (ii) long waits at facilities, which increase the loss of wages incurred by the poor; (iii) a perception of low quality of care, which may be due to the condition of the facilities or the way the poor and socially marginalized are treated; (iv) providers of the sex opposite to the patient's when it is culturally necessary that providers and patients be of the same sex; and (v) corruption in the form of required under-the-table payments to providers, which tend to have a larger financial impact on the poor.

The fifth step examines the degree to which the health sector provides services that are relevant to the diseases that affect the population, especially the poor. Although a core package of interventions may be defined, it may not be delivered in practice. Examining the mix of services is critical in judging whether priority is really given to the most relevant. In many cases, however, need and demand are not the same. As such, even if a package of services is well designed and serves the needs of the poor, it may not be what the poor demand. Careful consideration of this gap between need and demand is especially important given the low levels of education and minimal knowledge of life-saving services among the poor.

Step six in the diagnostic tool relates to the timing and continuity of services. Some key health services, such as emergency obstetric care and epidemic control measures, must be delivered in a timely manner. For other services, such as the completion of tuberculosis treatment or childhood immunizations, continuity is an essential determinant of efficacy and the improvement of outcomes. A question that is typically asked in the inequality literature is, do the poor benefit from timely and continuous services? The failure to provide such services typically results from lack of norms, inadequate application of norms that do exist, inadequate training, and poor supervision.

The seventh step, technical quality, comprises several issues. Are the services used by the poor of lower technical quality compared with those provided to the better-off population? Is a basic service of reasonable quality available to all? The term "technical quality" is meant to capture the variations across providers or patients regarding the effect of a particular service on health status. Health facilities in low- and middle-income countries, especially those serving the rural poor, are often plagued by low levels of training and competence.

The last step, social accountability, is a dimension that is essential, yet difficult to measure. To what extent are health systems and service providers accountable to their clients and communities, and in particular, to their poor clients? The literature on inequality of use in the health sector, as well as in other sectors, finds that the "social distance"—for example, the extent of differences in caste, class, education, and income—between service providers and poor or socially vulnerable populations is an important determinant of the latter's low demand for and use of services.

As noted earlier, the eight-step tool is a simplified linear representation of the complex nonlinear problem of inequality in service use. However, it is essential to break down the complex nature of the problem into pieces that are both relevant to the problem and amenable to analytical work. The idea of the tool is to explore the different dimensions of the problem—the steps of the tool—to identify the most binding constraints in a country or a region. Such prioritizing of constraints is critical to effective policy development, which must address the complex nature of the problem without overwhelming weak systems with answers that may be too complex to implement.

Health Sector Finance and the Poor

An important factor in the organization of the health sector is the way it is financed. Health financing—the collection and disbursement of funds to pay for health care—can be broken down into three functions: (i) resource mobilization, (ii) pooling of resources, and (iii) provider payment. The first function refers to mobilizing revenues from a variety of sources, such as direct and indirect general taxation, earmarked taxation for health, and out-of-pocket spending. The second function pertains to how resources are combined, or pooled, once mobilized. And the third relates to the variety of approaches to paying for health care provided by both institutions and individuals. As in the case of the eight-step diagnostic tool for service delivery and use, the three functions of finance in the health sector mask a fairly complex set of interactions; nevertheless, it is a useful systematic approach with which to explore the effect of finance policies on inequality in health service use.

Resource Mobilization

Of the three financing functions, resource mobilization is probably the most debated in the public domain and the least amenable to policy change. The main difference in resource mobilization across countries lies in how funds are collected from the population. A dominant form of financing is general revenue taxation, which comes in the form of direct taxes such as corporate profit taxes, property taxes, and wealth taxes. General taxes also include indirect taxes like sales, value added, excise, import, and export taxes. Most countries collect both direct and indirect general revenue taxes.

Another important source of financing for the health sector, especially for middle- and high-income countries, is social health insurance. Social insurance typically involves a law that compels both employers and employees (via employer withholding) to contribute a certain percentage of each employee's wages into a "social insurance fund." The employer's and employee's contributions are earmarked for health and cannot be used for any other purpose. Social insurance funds can be managed publicly or privately and can be monopolies or competitively run.

Private voluntary health insurance is the dominant form of health financing in a few industrial countries, mainly the United States. A relatively new form of private insurance in low-income countries is community-based microinsurance. Community-based funds offer a specified package of services for which members voluntarily prepay a set amount each year. In some cases, governments subsidize the poor if they cannot pay the insurance premium. Typically, the community organizes and operates primary care clinics at the village level and contracts for secondary services. Management by the community, rather than the government, is an important feature of this system and fosters strong accountability to paying members. The governmental role is usually to initiate, train, support, monitor, and regulate the microinsurance schemes. The case of Rwanda Community-Based Health Insurance (chapter 17) is instructive in this regard.

The dominant form of revenue generation in the health sectors of low- and middle-income countries is out-of-pocket payments to providers. In India, out-of-pocket spending accounts for an estimated four-fifths of all health sector expenditures. One of the more controversial out-of-pocket approaches to resource mobilization for health is user fees (or cost recovery) at public sector clinics. Many countries chose user fees to raise additional heath care revenue in the belief that consumers use services more effectively when they pay directly for them. Although user fees are opportunities for generating badly needed resources at the facility level, experience has shown them to be difficult and expensive to design and implement without inhibiting service use by the poor. A well-designed user fee system ensures that mechanisms exist to aid the poor who cannot afford to pay the fees. It also ensures that the better-off in society are not unintentionally subsidized.

Most countries use a mixture of approaches for generating revenue for health. Some rely more heavily on tax revenues while others rely on out-of-pocket spending. Many factors influence the mixture of approaches used in a country, including cultural and historic factors, the capacity of government to collect taxes, the level of employment in the formal (tax-paying) sector, and the effect of the system on efficiency and equity throughout the country. In attacking inequality in health service use, the main questions that need to be asked regarding a resource-generating option are, will it be likely to

- increase or decrease the financial access of low-income groups?
- create incentives or disincentives for the poor in seeking care?
- increase or decrease the financial burden on the poor?
- increase the level of poverty (head count and depth)?
- provide a cross-subsidy from the rich to the poor or vice versa?
- improve the quality of services at facilities where the poor seek care (retention and recycling)?[2]

Pooling Resources

Pooling describes methods of combining, sharing, and organizing funds raised for the health sector. As economies grow and health systems develop, the tendency is to use pooling to finance health services. Pooling (i) creates a *risk pool*, in which the healthy help pay for the sick, and (ii) provides a *subsidy to the poor*, by which the better-off help pay for the poor.

Traditional sources of resource pooling in the health sector include

- the budgets of the ministry of health or other ministries that finance health care (such as the armed forces, which provide health care to enlisted personnel, veterans, and their families; or the education ministry, which in many cases manages medical schools housed in large hospitals);
- social security systems (especially in Latin America); and
- private insurance plans (mostly in selected high- and middle-income countries).

Newer reform trends in pooling include community-based insurance plans; decentralized district health funds, such as block grants and basket funds; and combinations of insurance and subsidy pools.

A critical question for understanding the relationship between pooling arrangements and the poor is, who is covered by a pooling arrangement for health financing? Pooling arrangements are likely to first develop around communities in the formal sector and middle- to high-income groupings in urban settings. This typical development is inequitable in that low-income groups are not likely to be in the formal employment sector or have access to resources for insurance premiums. Policy can address this issue directly in the development of pooling arrangements. As shown in later chapters, Colombia, Mexico, and Rwanda illustrate the expansion of pooling arrangements in nontraditional and nonformal settings.

Another critical question when addressing inequality in pooling is, what is covered by an insurance mechanism? An important concern for the poor is the extent to which health expenditures lead to increasing numbers of people in poverty or the deepening of poverty for those already below the poverty line. Policies that reduce these effects can play an important role in addressing inequality. When economically vulnerable populations have access to subsidized curative care, a significant financial barrier to seeking care is eliminated, and the risk of deepening poverty levels is decreased. The reforms in Colombia and Mexico discussed in later chapters provide good examples of such pro-poor health sector policies.

It can also be argued that insurance mechanisms that provide access to lower-cost primary health care can produce a lasting reduction in inequality. The experiences in Rwanda and countries in West Africa show that the poor are not likely to seek primary care, including preventive care, unless the problem of financial access is addressed. The community-based microinsurance schemes discussed in the preceding section have been shown, mainly in Rwanda, to drastically increase access by both better-off and poorer segments of society and by doing so, increase the use of health care by vulnerable groups.

In designing or assessing resource pooling arrangements for the health sector, there are three key questions: are the arrangements likely to

- increase the number and percentage of the poor that are covered under pooling arrangements?
- decrease the risk of catastrophic payments for the poor?
- increase the use of preventive and simple curative care through pooling?

Provider Payment

The third function of health financing is provider payment—the means by which money is exchanged between parties. A functional way to approach provider payment is to ask three questions: How much is being paid (or the unit of payment)? When are payments made (before or after the service is completed)? What are the performance criteria or other conditions governing payment? These three seemingly simple questions can produce a variety of answers and combinations of answers that have critical implications for the incentives faced by both payers and providers.

The literature on payment methods covers payments for facilities (such as hospitals, clinics, and diagnostic centers) and individual providers (including physicians and nurses). For facilities, the most familiar payment mechanism is line items, such as salaries, capital investments, equipment, medicines, and maintenance, in the budgets of public sector providers. Line-item amounts are based on norms, such as number of beds, number of staff, bed occupancy rates, and historic trends. Budget allocations are usually prospective—set up at the beginning of a fiscal or calendar year to cover services to be provided during that period.

Another traditional form of payment to facilities is through grants to nongovernmental organizations (NGOs). The grants are usually provided to increase access to services in geographic regions with limited public sector facilities. Such grants take various forms and can be linked to the number of beds, staff availability, or the need for drugs or supplies. These grants are also typically prospective and are sometimes linked to expected provision of services to underserved and vulnerable communities. While in most cases the payer is a government, in some countries donors provide direct support to NGOs without going through the government budget.

Other traditional tools for hospital reimbursement of inpatient care are retrospective payments per diem (payment determined by the number of days the patient is in the hospital) or per admission (fixed payment for patient admission regardless of length of stay). Clearly, per diem and per admission criteria create different incentives for providers with regard to length of stay. At the same time, these criteria create different cost conditions for payers.

Newer trends in provider payments to facilities include features that attempt to link performance to payment or budgeting; to adjust payment according to case severity; and to provide more autonomy to decentralized structures. One type of reform is to link allocations to past performance. Performance-based budgeting identifies performance criteria for facilities and bases allocation on the ability of facilities to improve how they deliver services or achieve outcomes. A companion reform in payment to public facilities is a move away from item-specific allocations to mechanisms such as block grants, which allow facility managers to make decisions on input mix. A term used to describe such block approaches to payment is "capitation."

Another new facet of the performance-based allocation approach to provider payment is contractual agreements with nongovernmental providers that link payment to performance. Contracting is growing in the health sector, and the evidence regarding the positive effect of linking outputs to payments is encouraging, as we will see in the Cambodia experience (chapter 6; Loevinsohn and Harding 2005). Finally, one reform effort in a number of high-income countries, and increasingly in middle-income countries, is reimbursement based on the severity of the patient's condition. Developed first in the United States, Diagnosis-Related Groups (DRGs) take the more traditional per case method of payment further by defining a long list of health conditions and possible complications. Facilities or individual providers are then paid on the basis of the category to which patients are medically assigned.

Payments to individual providers follow approaches similar to those for facilities. Traditional approaches include salaries or fee for service, and newer approaches include linking payment to performance, severity (DRGs), or block-budgeting based on the expected population to be served a given package of services (capitation).

Mechanisms to reimburse providers are potent instruments that mold incentives for facility managers and individual providers. In assessing the effect of different payment methods on inequality, some important questions to answer are, is the mechanism likely to

- change the incentives to facilities or providers to seek and serve poor or vulnerable populations?
- increase usage rates for the poor?
- improve the quality of care the poor receive?
- link productivity to payment in serving the poor?

Moving Forward

The first two chapters looked at the wider inequality picture by examining health, fertility, and nutrition outcomes and their determinants. The focus from this point forward will be on inequality in health service use. The first chapter defined the problem of inequality and explored tools for measuring inequality in the health sector. This chapter laid out a road map for addressing the health needs of the poor and improving the equality of health services provision. The remainder of the book takes on the difficult tasks of analyzing (chapter 3), then attacking, the causes of inequality in service use (chapters 4–18).

Annex 2.1 Summary of the Multisectoral Determinants of Health

Multisectoral actions are essential to achieving health outcomes, such as the health MDGs, because health outcomes depend not only on health care but also on a variety of factors beyond care. Some of these factors are obstacles to accessing care, including financial and physical barriers, such as distance from a health facility and the costs of reaching a facility and obtaining care. Other factors, such as lack of medicines, poor provider performance, and inappropriate treatment, undermine the effectiveness of care.

Improvement of health outcomes, particularly for the poor, requires that a range of factors be understood and addressed. The contribution of these factors to such improvements will vary by setting and the health outcome in question. The choice of a mode of action to address them will depend on the institutional and organizational realities of the country or locality where improvements are being sought. For this reason, there is no single formula or template for multisectoral action; rather, a range of interventions should be considered depending on conditions and the particular outcome in question.

Identifying Potential Multisectoral Actions

Identification of the ways in which actions in sectors beyond care affect health outcomes is a key requirement for the design of multisectoral actions. A recent World Bank assessment of progress toward the Millennium Development Goals identified significant potential for multisectoral synergies in a range of sectors, including roads and transport, water, hygiene and sanitation, indoor air pollution, and agriculture, as noted in table A2.1. Research and sectoral assessments can help identify actions in these sectors (Wagstaff and Claeson 2004).

Roads and Transport   Delays in reaching a treatment facility pose life-threatening obstacles for poor women who experience obstetric emergencies. Such delays can be the result of physical accessibility factors, such as distance to a facility, the availability and cost of transport, and the condition of roads, all of which affect the time required to get a mother to a facility once the decision to seek care has been made. In Zimbabwe, unavailability of transport is reported to have been a factor in 28 percent of deaths in a rural area that was studied. In the case of hemorrhage, 50 percent of deaths were attributable to transport-related delays.

Table A2.1 *Potential for Multisectoral Synergies to Achieve the Millennium Development Goals for Health and Nutrition*

MDG	Target	Multisectoral inputs	Importance for poor people
Reduce maternal mortality	Improve access to emergency obstetric care	Availability of transport and referral facilities	Care facilities are generally located longer distances away from where poor women live, and transport is often too costly.
	Reduce indoor air pollution	Improved cooking practices, fuel, and ventilation	Poor women rely more heavily on biomass fuels, their homes are poorly ventilated, and the costs of alternative stoves and fuels are beyond their reach.
Reduce child mortality	Reduce diarrheal diseases in children through hand-washing, use of latrines, and proper disposal of young children's stools	Improved hand-washing practices, using soap and plenty of water	The poor have the least access to safe water and cannot afford soap. Poor households are least likely to have safe sanitation facilities, so poor children are at greatest risk of waterborne infections.
	Reduce indoor air pollution	Improved fuel, ventilation, and child play practices	Poor children spend more time with their mothers in poorly ventilated spaces polluted by smoke from biomass fuel.
Reduce hunger and improve nutrition	Regulate food prices, raise women's income, and promote dietary diversity and food security at the household level	Improved agricultural practices, tariffs, and trade; reduced women's workload; better gender relations and household decision making	Undernutrition among poor women and children is a leading risk factor for the higher maternal and child mortality rates that contribute to large rich-poor differences in these rates in poor countries.

Source: Wagstaff and Claeson 2004.

Research on health-seeking behavioral responses to cost recovery showed that poor people in Tanzania traveled an average of more than 60 kilometers for care, whereas the nonpoor traveled only 15 kilometers. There were several possible explanations, including the likelihood that the nonpoor have their own transport and that the poor travel farther to attend facilities where fees would be waived. In their review of obstacles to health care, Ensor and Cooper (2004) found studies that reported that transport accounted for 28 percent of total patient costs in Burkina Faso, 25 percent in northeast Brazil, and 27 percent in the United Kingdom. In Bangladesh, transport was reported to be the second most expensive item for poor patients after medicines. To quote from one of the focus groups in that study, "The hospital is far away and it costs a lot to travel there. We can easily buy medicines from the village doctors with this money. We spend money to go to the hospital but we don't even get medicines there, so why should we go to the hospital?" (CIET-Canada 2001, 38).

Country-level poverty analyses conducted by the World Bank have shown that the quality of rural road networks is a factor in the social and economic isolation of the rural poor. Research on the impact of improved rural road networks has focused mainly on travel time. For example, a poverty assessment for Guatemala found that road closures were a major constraint to access to schools, jobs, and markets, and that households in the poorest income quintile were much more affected (45 percent versus 12 percent) than the richest. Villagers identified "giving birth" as a risk because mothers could not reach health centers as a result of inadequate road access, particularly during the rainy season.

Education   Education affects health outcomes directly (through health and hygiene educational content as well as school health and feeding programs) and indirectly through improved capacity to practice healthy behaviors. Education of women influences health outcomes through a variety of channels, including childbearing attitudes, health-seeking behaviors, and earning opportunities. Early gains in female literacy played an important role in maternal mortality declines in Malaysia and Sri Lanka. In her review of the links between women's education, autonomy, and reproductive behavior, Jejeebhoy (1995) notes that education enhances women's knowledge about the outside world and makes them more aware than uneducated women of the importance of family health and hygiene as well as of the treatment and prevention of illness. Another consequence she notes is greater decision-making autonomy within the home. At the same time, she cautions that contextual factors influence the impact of education on women's participation in household decision making, so that this participation is likely to be weaker in a society characterized by a high degree of gender stratification.

Education is closely linked to gender status and the ways in which gender stratification affects access to household resources and use of health care services. In their work on intrahousehold bargaining power in Indonesia, Beegle, Frankenberg, and Thomas (2001) found that women who were more educated than their husbands were more likely to obtain prenatal care and, generally, that education enables a woman to make decisions regarding her reproductive health care. Education is also linked to several other factors that may enhance or limit access to life-saving interventions. Research on the impact of cost recovery on use of services has shown that educated women are more likely to understand and use exemption schemes, and the transport literature also highlights the links between education and access to and use of transport to get to health facilities.

Water and Sanitation   Provision of safe water has contributed to declines of mortality in developed countries. Poor sanitation and unsafe water, along with poor personal hygiene, are known to be major factors in the prevalence of parasitic diseases in poor countries. Waterborne diseases can undermine the health of pregnant women because they cause anemia, a risk factor for mothers as well as their newborns. Unsafe water supply and pollutants from fuels used in cooking are risk factors in the high maternal mortality ratios observed in several African countries. The link between water supply and the health of mothers and children involves both household and community factors. A household's consumption of water may be constrained by prices, income, and other household variables even if water is supplied at the community level. Jalan and Ravallion (2001) observe that health gains largely bypassed poor children when piped water was available in their community, particularly when the mother was poorly educated.

The Bank's MDG assessment noted that better hygiene (hand washing) and sanitation (use of latrines, safe disposal of children's stools) are at least as important as drinking water quality for health outcomes, especially the reduction in diarrhea and associated child mortality. Increased quantity of water has been shown to have a greater impact than improved quality of water, possibly because an adequate supply of water increases the feasibility of adopting safe hygiene behaviors and reduces the length of time that water must be stored and thus may become contaminated by handling.

Environmental Factors   Reduction of indoor air pollution (IAP) in developing countries is another area of potential multisectoral action. IAP is caused by the use of low-cost, traditional energy sources, such as coal and biomass (wood, cow dung, crop residues), in primitive stoves for cooking and heating—the main source of energy for billions of people. The health burden from IAP is greatest in high-altitude rural areas among poor families who use biomass in primitive stoves without proper ventilation. IAP is a major risk factor for pneumonia and associated deaths in children and for lung cancer in women who are at risk of exposure during cooking. Eventually, most developing countries will move up the energy ladder, but this move is delayed by low income and limited access to high-quality fuel. Improved biomass stoves have been effective in improving health outcomes in India and elsewhere. Large community-based intervention trials are documenting the affordability, cost effectiveness, feasibility, and sustainability of multisectoral interventions. Studies in China, Guatemala, and India are under way to improve access to efficient and affordable energy sources through local design, manufacturing, and dissemination of low-cost technologies, modern fuel alternatives, and renewable energy solutions.

Nutrition and Food Policy   Poor nutrition is another key cofactor affecting maternal and child health. Poor nutrition among pregnant women in a number of the very high maternal and neonatal mortality countries contributes to those high rates. In India, anemia is reported as an indirect factor in 64.4 percent of maternal deaths. Gender stratification and attitudes also contribute through household behaviors that deprive poor women of adequate nutrition, not only during pregnancy but also during their childhood and adolescence, which leads to small stature and higher risk of delivery complications.

Agricultural policies and practices that affect food prices, farm incomes, diet diversity and quality, and household food security also require government leadership to achieve better health outcomes. Agricultural policies that focus on women's access to resources (land, training, agricultural inputs), their role in production, and their income from agriculture are likely to have a greater impact on nutrition than policies that do not focus on women, particularly if combined with other strategies, such as strategies for improving women's education and effecting behavior-change communication.

Conclusion

Factors beyond care play an important role in achieving better health outcomes for the poor. Multisectoral actions are important in addressing these factors for all population groups, but are critically important in the poor segments of the population, for whom the health risks associated with limited access to care, low educational attainment, higher exposure to air and water pollution, and poor nutrition are consistently high. The design of multisectoral actions needs to ensure that such actions benefit the poor, while the monitoring and evaluation of such actions should determine whether, in fact, they do so.

Additional Resources for Multisectoral Action

Canadian Public Health Association. 1997. "The Canadian Experience of Intersectoral Collaboration for Health Gains." Ottawa, Canadian Public Health Association.

Claeson, M., C. Griffin, T. Johnston, A. Soucat, A. Wagstaff, and A. Yazbeck. 2003. "Health, Nutrition, and Population." In *A Sourcebook for Poverty Reduction Strategies Vol. II: Macroeconomic and Sectoral Approaches*, ed. Jeni Klugman. Washington, DC: World Bank.

Ensor, T., and S. Cooper. 2004. "Overcoming Barriers to Health Service Access: Influencing the Demand Side." *Health Policy and Planning* 19 (2): 69–79.

Health Canada. 2000. "Intersectoral Action Toolkit." Health Canada Northwest Territories Region, Edmonton, Alberta.

Schmeer, K. 2000. "Stakeholder Analysis Guidelines." In "Policy Toolkit for Strengthening Health Sector Reform," 2-1–2-43. Partners for Health Reform, Washington, DC.

Wagstaff, A., and M. Claeson. 2004. *The Millennium Development Goals for Health: Rising to the Challenges.* Washington, DC: World Bank.

World Health Organization. 1997. "Multisectoral Action for Health: Report of the Multinational Conference." Halifax, Nova Scotia, Canada, April 20–23, 1997.

Annex 2.2 Recommendations for Further Reading

Selected from Goldman and others (forthcoming).

Chowdhury, M., C. Ronsmans, J. Killewo, I. Anwar, K. Gausia, S. Das-Gupta, L. Blum, G. Dieltiens, T. Marshall, S. Saha, and J. Borghi. 2006. "Equity in Use of Home-Based or Facility-Based Skilled Obstetric Care in Rural Bangladesh: An Observational Study." *Lancet* 367 (9507): 327–32.

Uses advanced statistical techniques to look at whether socioeconomic status is related to differences in the use of free professional midwife services at home and in basic obstetric facilities in rural areas of Matlab, Bangladesh. Specifically, the authors look at whether a home-based approach results in more equitable provision of services than does a facility-based approach.

Gakidou, E., and E. Vayena. 2007. "Added Use of Modern Contraception by the Poor Is Falling Behind." *PLoS Medicine* **4 (2): 381–88.**
Based on 20 years of data (1985–2003) from the Demographic and Health Surveys in more than 55 developing countries in Latin America and the Caribbean, Sub-Saharan Africa, and South and Southeast Asia, this study explores the macro-level determinants of the use of modern contraceptives and whether the general rise in the use of modern contraceptives has translated to greater access and use among the poorest. A wealth index based on information about age, education, sex of the household head, urban or rural location, and household's ownership of durable goods and Gini index for 1990 and 2000 are used to evaluate economic status.

Houweling, T., C. Ronsmans, O. Campbell, and A. Kunst. 2007. "Huge Poor-Rich Inequalities in Maternity Care: An International Comparative Study of Maternity and Child Care in Developing Countries." *Bulletin of the World Health Organization* **85 (10): 733–820.**
Inequalities in maternity and child health care between the wealthy and poor, including professional delivery attendance, are explored in data from Demographic and Health Surveys conducted between 1990 and 1998 in 45 developing countries. Inequality is measured using the rate ratio of health care use by wealth group and the absolute rate difference in health care use between wealth groups. The wealth index used to divide the sample into groups is based on household ownership of durable goods, housing, and water and sanitation facilities.

Khe, N., N. Toan, L. Xuan, B. Eriksson, B. Höjer, and V. Diwan. 2002. "Primary Health Concept Revisited: Where Do People Seek Health Care in a Rural Area of Vietnam?" *Health Policy* **61 (1): 95–109.**
A cross-sectional study of health-seeking behavior and of health care access, use, and expenditure in northern Vietnam by socioeconomic status (determined by income). The study population consists of a random sample of 1,075 households (4,769 individuals) in the Bavi district of northern Vietnam (located 60 kilometers northwest of Hanoi).

Magadi, M., E. Zulu, and M. Brockerhoff. 2003. "The Inequality of Maternal Health Care in Urban Sub-Saharan Africa in the 1990s." *Population Studies: A Journal of Demography* **57 (3): 349–68.**

Descriptive and multivariate analyses, including binomial logistic regression models, are used to predict the odds of unplanned births, inadequate antenatal care, and nonprofessional delivery among the urban poor, urban nonpoor, and women in rural areas in 23 Sub-Saharan African countries. Multilevel regression models were also used to determine the magnitude and pattern of variations in the inequalities and whether health care inequalities are generalizable across countries in Sub-Saharan Africa.

Schellenberg, J., C. Victora, A. Mushi, D. de Savigny, D. Schellenberg, H. Mshinda, and J. Bryce. 2003. "Inequities among the Very Poor: Health Care for Children in Rural Southern Tanzania." *Lancet* **361 (9357): 561–66.**
Health care status and care-seeking behavior are measured in this baseline household survey for the Integrated Management of Childhood Illness strategy, a public health campaign promoting basic guidelines for prevention and treatment of common childhood illness. To explore inequalities in care-seeking behavior by sex and socioeconomic status in households with children less than five years of age in four rural districts of southern Tanzania, the investigators constructed an asset index, or relative wealth index, compiled using information about, for example, income sources, education of household head, and household assets.

Uzochukwu, B., O. Onwujekwe, and B. Eriksson. 2004. "Inequity in the Bamako Initiative Programme—Implications for the Treatment of Malaria in South-East Nigeria." *International Journal of Health Planning and Management* **19 (S1): S107–16.**
This exploratory study examined use of malaria treatment services in the Bamako Initiative (a strategy adopted by Nigeria in 1988 for strengthening primary health care at the community and local government levels). Authors describe equity in terms of community financing in rural Nigeria. They use indicators of use, exemption awareness, and exemption practices to study the importance of user fees for total cost recovery of malaria treatment.

Notes

1. A more detailed treatment of the Safar Banu case can be found in Campbell White, Merrick, and Yazbeck (2006).

2. "Retention and recycling" refers to regulations allowing facilities that collect fees to retain the resources and use them to improve quality.

3

The Importance of "Listening"

This chapter explores the causes of health inequality and the analytical approaches that can be used to deepen our understanding of the obstacles faced by poor households. Developing and sustaining policies that attack inequality in the use of critical health services requires usable information about the constraints faced by the poor. If policy design and implementation are not based on a deep understanding of the critical constraints faced by the poor, they are likely to fail. As the saying goes, "If you do not know where you are going, any road will take you there." Knowing the underlying causes of inequality in service use is also essential to tracking the degree to which policies are resolving those causes.

The Views of Leaders from Low- and Middle-Income Countries

Since 2002, participants in courses delivered by the health team at the World Bank Institute have been presented with some of the statistics on inequality summarized in chapter 1.[1] The participants were mainly government officials and key representatives of civil society from low- and middle-income countries. They were asked to state their understanding of reasons for the large and persistent gaps in health service use between the poor and better-off. The answers they gave can be grouped into two categories, demand side and supply side, and they echo the answers given in the literature on the problem. Within each of the two categories, it is easy to group the participants' answers into the boxes of the pathways framework described in chapter 2, as follows.[2]

Possible Supply-Side Causes

Service-Delivery Factors

- Inconvenient location of health facilities (urban bias, and within urban settings a focus on more-affluent localities). Location of facilities may lead to longer travel times and higher travel costs, which in turn decrease the likelihood of health care use by the poor.
- Long waits at facilities in poor areas. The poor can least afford to forgo wages to seek care. A related factor is the facilities' hours of operation, which typically coincide with peak working hours and thus make the decision to seek care more difficult.
- Perception of low quality of care in facilities serving the poor, including lack of drugs, absenteeism of providers, lack of functional equipment, and the inferior overall conditions of the facilities. A related issue is the extent to which the poor feel that they are not well treated, or even that they are discriminated against, by providers who may come from a different segment of society (the problem of "social distance").

Financing Factors

- Resource allocation that channels significant funding to curative care at tertiary hospitals rather than to basic care at primary health facilities, the latter of which are more likely to serve the poor.
- Resource allocation that moves resources away from programs that address the diseases of the poor.
- Cost recovery systems that do not protect the poor.
- Unofficial ("under the table") payments required by gatekeepers and providers.

Possible Demand-Side Causes

Resource Factors

- The out-of-pocket cost of traveling to health facilities, particularly for the poor living in dispersed rural settings.
- The opportunity cost of time taken to travel to a facility and wait for treatment—that is, the income lost by not working during that time.
- Limited knowledge about health services. Getting care, especially preventive care, is not likely if household heads are not aware of available services or are not convinced of the benefits of such services.

The poor historically have less access to such information than the better-off.

Behavioral or Risk Factors

- Preference for traditional (or nonqualified) healers over more qualified providers. This preference decreases the demand for preventive services and significantly affects the quality of care being provided to the poor.
- More value given to curative care than to preventive care. This preference is not unique to the poor but tends to be stronger in poor families and may be influenced by a lack of resources or knowledge.
- Preference for home-based births over delivery in facilities.

Cultural or Religious Factors

- Cultural norms or religious beliefs may discourage the seeking of health care. This factor disproportionately affects the poor and has especially strong implications for women. Also, such influences have sometimes undermined participation, especially of the poor, in immunization campaigns.
- Cultural norms or religious beliefs may discourage the use of contraceptives, even in families that desire a relatively small number of children.

The preceding list, by no means comprehensive, repeats themes in the literature on why the poor use health sector services much less than do the better-off. And it supports the view that attacking inequality is a daunting exercise that exposes the health sector's weakness in addressing the problem. Unfortunately, the preceding list cannot, on its own, lead us to effective policies to raise the level of health care use by the poor. Many of these supply and demand factors interact with each other to create further complexity. Moreover, because poverty is contextual, varying in cause and effect by setting, the dominant causes in one country, or even one part of a country, may be less important in another. Put another way, the factors in the above list are at the same time too numerous for any policy to address and too general.

The Dilemmas Posed by the Long List of Causes

As noted, the oft-repeated list of the causes of inequality in the use of health services has two significant characteristics, and each creates its own operational dilemma. The first characteristic is the large number, and inter-related nature, of the potential causes; the second is the local, contextual nature of the causes that are most binding on a given population.

The first dilemma involves the fact that attacking complex problems with complicated programs usually fails. Such programs are sometimes referred to as "Christmas trees," in recognition of the many disconnected features that often adorn them. Simpler policy alternatives are generally preferred, especially when financial and institutional resources are limited. Hence, the dilemma—a complex problem that needs to be resolved in an institutionally constrained environment.

The problem of recovering health care costs incurred in public facilities is an excellent example of the inadequacy of simplistic and ideological answers in resolving this operational dilemma. The imposition of user fees at public facilities has been seen as a simple way to make complex gains on both the supply side and the demand side—on the supply side by gathering financial resources for drugs, supplies, and incentives for providers; on the demand side by reducing the unnecessary use of facilities and increasing the perceived value of services. The results of the user-fee experiments, however, have generally been negative. The programs included failed or corrupted exemption mechanisms for the poor, high administrative costs that eroded financial gains, and a failure to retain and recycle resources within the facilities. At the other end of the policy spectrum, opponents of user fees have been advocating their abolition, even in places where the results were somewhat positive. Driving the abolishment movement is the fear that failed exemption mechanisms will punish the poor by increasing the financial barrier to seeking care. Yet simply abolishing user fees without appropriate action to address the resource needs of public facilities leads back to large supply problems. The supply problems, in turn, cause ineffi-ciency at facilities serving the poor and, ultimately, increased inequality. Simplistic and ideological answers, which inevitably ignore the complexity of the problem and cultural and institutional realities, are likely to fail.

The second dilemma stems from the local, contextual nature of the many reasons the poor make relatively little use of health care services. That con-textual nature makes it operationally essential to first understand which combination of possible factors represents the most binding constraint for the poor in a given country or locality within a country. Universal policies that are not tailored in design and implementation to tackle the critical local constraints are likely to fail in addressing inequality. Success requires cus-tomization of service delivery or financing arrangements, experimentation with different approaches, monitoring for results, and patience that allows redesign and midcourse adjustments (Gwatkin, Wagstaff, and Yazbeck 2005).

The World Bank's *World Development Report 1993: Investing in Health* advocated a basic package of health services that emphasized prevention and cost-effective services. Recognizing that local conditions should dictate feasibility, the report did not advocate a specific delivery mechanism. Geographically challenging localities, like mountainous regions or lowlands, would prevent the poor from consistently reaching fixed-point facilities. Similarly, government-managed delivery of the basic package would not make sense in countries with weak delivery structures. Countries that have successfully implemented a package of services and were able to reach and serve the poor did a lot more than define a package.

The remainder of this chapter focuses on a menu of analytical tools that are sensitive to the causes of inequality and are able to focus policy discussion and design. The two analytical tools discussed in the previous chapter, the eight steps and the three-function analysis of health financing, will be elaborated upon here because they can help organize thinking. But a basic framework that captures or organizes all the available analytical tools does not exist. Moreover, given the importance of local context, the lack of a universal framework is not the problem. We do not need to identify *all* of the supply or demand constraints facing the poor—only the most binding ones. Doing so requires listening to the poor themselves to discover the most important factors limiting their use of health care in the context of a given place and time.

Listening Is Critical

The question to be answered is why poor households do not seek care or do so much less frequently compared with the better-off. It is a simple question that is not easy to answer: Is it that the poor do not know about the services or that they do not value them? Is it that they cannot afford taking off from work to get them or that they do not feel that the providers respect and welcome them? That they cannot physically reach the facilities because of geography or transportation problems or that they feel that the facilities provide low-quality service? That the fees are too high? Or that they are not sure how much under-the-table payment is needed? Or is it some combination of the above plus a dozen other possible causes? Moreover, the answer is likely to vary by group asked. The only way that a policy designed to attack inequality can be truly effective is if the targeted population is involved in the basic design of the policies intended to help them. Such participation can be accomplished through the seemingly simple act of *listening*. The question of how to listen, however, raises some operational difficulties.

Active and Passive Listening

At the heart of those operational difficulties is a trade-off between getting answers that may be representative of the target population but superficial, and getting answers that are sufficiently deep but may represent only the views of a small subset of the population. Representative, statistically significant answers can be captured through quantitative methods such as population-based surveys. These surveys tend to be passive forms of listening and have two limitations: First, the same questions are asked of all the participants of a large, representative sample of households, so the method lacks the flexibility of free-flowing follow-up questioning. Second, the method limits participants to a preselected, closed list of possible answers, so problems not included in the survey design are not likely to surface.

The alternative method employs qualitative techniques, or active listening, through focus group discussions or interviews of key informants. Active listening, when done well, allows conversations to deepen the interviewer's understanding of why the poor do not seek care, but it comes at a price. The open-ended nature of the questions, which is the main avenue to acquiring a deeper understanding of the underlying problems, does not easily lend itself to tabulation for statistical significance through large-sample surveys of the population.

Chapters 5 through 18 summarize programs that have had success in attacking the inequality in use of health services in low- and middle-income countries. One of the shared characteristics of these programs is that they listened to the poor and then incorporated the findings into policy. The analytical tools used by these programs included both active (qualitative) and passive (quantitative) listening and covered the following types of data sources.[3]

Household Survey Data

Existing household surveys are excellent sources of information on health sector performance—including the use of health services by quintiles of wealth—and on the determinants of health-related behavior and outcomes.

The data on behaviors and outcomes can be used to quantify the determinants for the population as a whole and for specific groups, such as the poor.[4] Household surveys may include the following types of data:

- *Income and consumption.* Household data can be linked to census data to produce poverty maps, which can be useful in identifying poor districts and neighborhoods. Sometimes, neither income nor consumption data are available in a survey. In this case, proxies (such as the type of flooring material in the house) can be useful, especially for examining the differences in behavior determinants between poor and nonpoor households.
- *Education and knowledge.* Household surveys often contain information on educational attainment and literacy of household members. Many surveys also contain some information on health-specific knowledge, such as knowledge of HIV/AIDS issues. These data for women and girls are especially important.
- *Intrahousehold inequalities in control over resources.* Some household surveys, such as the Demographic and Health Surveys (DHS), ask about women's control over their earnings from the labor market and their involvement in family planning decisions.
- *Accessibility of health services.* Household surveys often ask respondents about the distance or travel time to local health facilities. Tabulations by household income can be revealing.
- *Insurance coverage and entitlement to fee waiving.* Some surveys ask about household health insurance coverage, copayments, and access to fee exemptions.

Government Statistics and Facility Surveys

Unlike household surveys, facility-based surveys and government statistics are typically not easily linked to socioeconomic status. However, they offer certain advantages in capturing supply-side factors that are not easily captured in household surveys. They offer the following types of data:

- *Availability of services.*[5] Availability of services can be very broadly defined by facilities—for example, a hospital; or more narrowly defined by interventions or packages of interventions—for example, a program for acute respiratory infections. In the case of a facilities definition, availability can be measured, for example, as the number of hospitals or hospital beds per 1,000 population; for interventions, as the number of facilities offering a particular intervention or package of interventions per 1,000 population. Data on service availability, from public and private providers, at a national level as well as for targeted areas within the country, are necessary to determine how well the poor fare. Targeted tracking can be achieved through the use of a poverty map. Alternatively, one can link availability data to household survey data to see how the poor fare with regard to the availability of services in their geographic area.

- *Quality.* Information on quality is more difficult to obtain. Official statistics often present crude measures of quality and often paint a rosier picture of quality than is warranted, for example, by reporting what is supposed to be available rather than what is actually available. Nonetheless, facility surveys often reveal troublesome gaps between poor rural areas and better-off urban areas, particularly in the proportions of facilities with immunization and growth-monitoring programs. More sophisticated instruments for assessing quality via facility surveys are available for some health outcomes. The World Health Organization's "Topical List of Priority Indicators for IMCI at Health-Facility Level" (WHO 2008, 6) provides a useful instrument for assessing quality in the management of childhood illness. Surveys done with that instrument suggest huge variations in quality across countries; the data could be linked to a poverty map or to a household survey to get a sense of how the poor fare compared with the better-off.

- *Prices.* As with quality, government statistics can, in principle, provide data on the prices charged for different services. They should also provide the categories for which fee waivers exist, if any. In practice, facility surveys provide more accurate information on both service charges and fee waiver categories. This reality exists in large part because fee waiver programs are often intended to be subject to local interpretation and implementation.

Community Surveys

Community surveys capture a community's key features, such as infrastructure, geographic or environmental characteristics, and available health and education facilities. They can often shed light on the extent of social capital within a community. Community surveys can also often help in the quantification of environmental influences on health-related behaviors and outcomes (such as altitude, tendency to drought and flooding, and cultural factors). The respondents in these surveys are usually leaders in the community—village elders, school teachers, health service officials or providers, and so on.

Focus Groups, Consultation Exercises, and In-Depth Interviews

Surveys are an important element in understanding why the poor do not seek care as much as the better-off, but they typically produce superficial answers to important questions. Active listening tools, such as in-depth interviews and focus group consultations, are invaluable ways of identifying the most binding constraints faced by the poor.[6]

Combining Active and Passive Listening: Immunization in India

The household survey data on immunization in India provide a working example of how supplementing the information with the household perspective—captured through active and passive listening—can guide more strategic and effective policy development. The resulting focused analysis can steer policy development by pointing to the policy levers likely to improve household behaviors and outcomes.[7]

The overall level of immunization coverage in India in 1992–93 appeared to be very low, but the level of inequality (table 3.1) was even more stark: the third row of the table shows that children of the wealthiest 20 percent of households were three times as likely to have received all routine vaccinations as the poorest children; and the fourth row shows that the wealthiest were four times as likely as the poorest to have received some vaccinations.

Table 3.1 Immunization Coverage of Children in India, by Wealth Quintile, 1992–93 (percent)

Immunization type	1st quintile (poorest)	2nd quintile	3rd quintile	4th quintile	5th quintile (wealthiest)
Measles	27.0	31.0	40.9	54.9	66.1
DPT 3	33.7	41.1	51.8	64.6	76.7
All vaccinations	20.2	25.1	34.1	46.9	59.8
No vaccinations	44.7	38.9	28.8	18.8	11.5

Source: Gwatkin and others 2007.
Note: DPT = diphtheria, pertussis, and tetanus.

The critical factor in determining whether a child is immunized is whether the decision makers of the household seek a health care provider. For the household action to occur, the following interrelated conditions should exist:

- Decision makers in the household must be aware of immunization availability and believe that it is important for child survival and well-being.
- Financial resources must be available. Money is needed for transportation, productive time lost in seeking the provider, and payments for the provider (official or unofficial).
- The household must have physical access to, and some element of trust in, a provider.

Listening to Vulnerable Families

To help determine the relative importance of those three conditions in India, a 1998 household survey asked households with unimmunized children why they did not seek this life-saving preventive service. All three conditions listed above were mentioned, but two specific answers accounted for more than 63 percent of responses: 33 percent were not aware of the time and place the immunizations were to be provided, and 30 percent of respondents were not aware of the need.

Once it is established that the information gap is an important determining factor, it is essential to find out how to reach the poor and socially vulnerable with information that will lead to a change in behavior. The 1998 household survey in India provided a *partial* answer: it found that the most likely point of contact between the health system and the poor and socially vulnerable groups was the auxiliary nurse midwife (ANM). Thus, ANMs would be the appropriate service delivery mechanism for delivering immunizations and information.

A fuller answer would give more insight into the determinants and constraints regarding immunization among the poor. At a minimum, it would have to provide a strategy for enlisting the ANMs and shaping the message they would deliver. Hence, passive forms of listening to the poor, through household and other surveys, must be supplemented with more active forms, such as qualitative data collection. Social or beneficiary assessment work is useful in the exploration of knowledge dissemination to target clients. Listening to the targeted clients can inform the design of a communication strategy to address the information gap and increase the probability that poor households seek immunization for their children.

The Role of Participants in the Health System

The idea of delivering both information and immunization to families in rural India through ANMs assumed that the government dominates the delivery of health services. Simple market analyses (a different form of listening) can shed light on the current roles of the private and public sectors and on possible future partnerships.

National and state surveys show that almost three-fourths of curative care spending in India is in the private sector, whereas the private sector accounts for no more than one-fourth (and in some states only one-twentieth) of immunization expenses. Moreover, most private sector delivery is focused in the urban sector. Market analysis showed that private providers were reluctant to supply immunization services, especially to the rural poor, largely because of the cost of buying and maintaining cold storage equipment and the low returns from limited demand.

The short-term strategy should then focus on making the public sector more effective in service delivery while using both private and public sector actors to address the information gaps largely responsible for the low demand for life-saving services.

Advanced Analytical Techniques

Many household surveys, including the World Bank–sponsored Living Standards Measurement Study (LSMS) surveys, ask interviewees about the reasons behind particular choices and behavior patterns.[8] Surveys include informative questions regarding the non-use of health services in the event of illness and the non-use of available immunization services. The Indian case study, reported in the previous section, is an excellent illustration of the usefulness of these questions. Cross-tabulations of responses by some measure of household resources can provide insights into whether certain factors underlying behavior, for example, knowledge, are more important among the poor than the nonpoor. More advanced statistical techniques, such as regression analysis, can also be used to take advantage of the wealth of information in surveys.

By using regression analysis[9] on household survey data, it is possible to look at the impact of one determinant on health behaviors, holding other determinants constant. This technique also allows for predictions about the size of the impact on health-related behaviors given changes in a particular determinant.

In Cebu, the Philippines, regression results suggest that a one-year increase in maternal education is associated with *reductions* in the probability of exclusive breast-feeding and any breast-feeding by 36 percent and 5 percent, respectively. The analysis also suggests an *increase* in the number of calories consumed by 7 percent, the use of preventive health services by 4 percent, the use of soap by 2 percent, and a reduction in the probability of poor disposal practices for excreta by 9 percent. These findings can then be coupled with estimates of the impact of these modified behaviors on health outcomes to assess the impact of maternal education on these outcomes. In the Cebu case, it was estimated that the changes described above would bring about a 3.2 percent reduction in the probability of diarrhea at age six months owing to a combination of a 5.2 percent reduction resulting from increased calories, preventive care use, and better excreta disposal, offset by a 2.0 percent increase resulting from reduced breast-feeding.

Regression analysis has been used in a number of developing countries to quantify the impact on health-related behaviors and outcomes of a variety of different determinants. The following examples illustrate the usefulness of regression analysis and reveal how estimated effects can vary across and within countries:

- *The effect of health service availability.* In Nigeria, total facility expenditure per capita in the population served (in effect, a measure of availability) was found to significantly influence the choice of facility as well as the choice of whether to seek care. In Malaysia, the number of nurses per capita was found to have a significantly positive effect on the use of prenatal care services. Opting for an institutional delivery was found to be significantly related to the availability of maternal and child health services and to the availability of private hospitals and clinics. In Ghana, the availability of child health services was found to have a significant influence on child survival and weight-for-height. In Indian communities, the presence of a family planning program, a hospital, and a dispensary all were found to reduce child mortality. However, in the same study other health facilities were found to *raise* child mortality. The findings from these studies would enable simulations of the effect of increased availability on service usage as well as on child survival and malnutrition.
- *The effect of health service accessibility.* In Ghana, simulations suggest that a reduction of 50 percent in the distance to public facilities would lead to a doubling in the use of public facilities. In Kenya, it was estimated that a 20 percent reduction in distance to public facilities would increase use of public facilities by nearly 2 percent. Households choose facilities based on their accessibility. In Ghana, it was

estimated that a reduction of 50 percent in the distance to public facilities would lead to a reduction of 15 percent in the use of *private* facilities, and that a 50 percent reduction in distance to private facilities would lead to a similar reduction in the use of *public* facilities. It was also found that distance to health facilities was significantly and inversely associated with weight-for-height, though *not* with height-for-age or with survival (indeed, the coefficients suggested a beneficial effect on survival of distance). In Côte d'Ivoire, by contrast, distance to the nearest health facility was found to be significantly and positively related to child mortality.

- *The effect of health service quality.* In Ghana, it was estimated that if the percentage of public facilities with drugs available increased from 66 percent to 100 percent, the use of these facilities would increase by 44 percent. In Sri Lanka, it was estimated that households are more likely to bypass local facilities for a more distant facility if the bypassed facility has inferior drug availability, is open for fewer hours per week, and has a poor appearance. In Ghana, it was found that drug availability in rural areas had a significant positive effect on height-for-age, though not on child survival.

- *The effect of the prices of health services.* In Kenya, it was estimated that an increase in public fees from nothing to 10 Kenya shillings would result in a reduction in the use of public facilities by 18 percent. In Ghana, a 50 percent increase in public sector user fees was estimated to reduce demand in public clinics by 6 percent. Also in Ghana, health service fees were found to have a significant and negative effect on height-for-age and weight-for-age in rural areas, but not in urban areas or on child survival.

- *The effect of availability of water and sanitation facilities.* A regression analysis in Nicaragua found that the presence of sewers in the community reduced the duration of breast-feeding, holding constant other determinants of breast-feeding duration. The availability of tap water was found to significantly reduce child mortality in India. In Ghana, poor sanitation and poor water quality within the household's community were found to significantly reduce the survival prospects of children.

- *The effect of food prices.* Some regression studies have found that higher food prices had a significant, harmful effect on child survival and child malnutrition. Two studies conducted in Ghana confirm this finding, whereas in Côte d'Ivoire and the Bicol region of the Philippines, an increase in food prices had a surprising opposite effect on these health outcomes.

- *The effect of accessibility of food.* In Ghana, it was found that the distance to local markets had a significantly positive impact on child mortality.

Eight Steps to Effective Use by the Poor

As described in chapter 2, the eight-step diagnostic tool serves as a simple checklist to help analyze system bottlenecks faced by the poor.[10] The operational value of each step in the tool will be illustrated throughout this section with examples from African countries.

Physical Accessibility (Step 1), the Capacity of the Sector to Ensure Physical Access to Essential Health Interventions for the Poor   There are several approaches to measuring accessibility. The first, measuring the service supply relative to the population served, is limited in that it does not account for the distribution of services with respect to the poor. This approach is more useful if it is broken down by region or district, which allows rural and urban, or poor and less-poor, district comparisons.

The second approach is to measure the proportion of the population living within a given distance of a particular type of health facility or intervention site, preferably broken down by income level or by poorer regions.

The third approach, related to the second, measures the time it takes a client to reach a facility or service delivery point; doing so takes account of obstacles and transportation options not revealed by the second approach.

To be meaningful, accessibility indicators need to take into account the density of population in the area. Variations in population density mean that accessibility may be a major constraint for the poor in some countries and regions but a relatively minor one in others. In addition, the distribution of public and private health facilities may be inefficient in some areas. For example, inadequate coordination can result in government facilities located within several kilometers of comparable nongovernmental organization (NGO) facilities.

Data Collection and Analysis

- A first step is to develop a map that shows the *geographical distribution* of essential services. If possible, the map should specify the location of fixed facilities, outreach points, mobile clinics, outreach workers for public and nongovernmental services, as well as major roads and natural barriers, such as rivers. This could be done manually or electronically using Geographic Information Systems. Many countries have developed or are in the process of developing health facility inventory and planning maps. The key step is to integrate the health maps with poverty maps by linking accessibility data to household survey data. It is then possible to see how poor and less-poor areas fare in availability of health services in their geographic areas.

- Information from household surveys can be used to calculate the *percentage of the poor with access to services*, and to determine the extent to which limited physical access is a major constraint for the poor. The DHS and LSMS, for example, include questions on household assets as well as availability of essential services in the community. As a result, it is possible to tabulate accessibility by income or asset levels. Because poverty is unevenly distributed, it is useful to assemble data on availability at regional and national levels. These quantitative methods may be complemented by beneficiary surveys or participatory assessment approaches in poor communities to assess whether physical access is perceived as a major problem.

An example of identifying physical access as a binding constraint for the poor is presented in figure 3.1. In Mauritania, a large country with low population density, a correlation between the poverty level of a province and the level of access to primary care centers is evident. Physical access, measured in this case as the percentage of the population living within 5 kilometers of a primary care facility, is considerably higher in districts of the country with very low levels of poverty. Conversely, access is limited in districts with a high percentage below the poverty line.

Availability of Essential Inputs (Human Resources and Consumables—Steps 2 and 3), the Capacity of the Sector to Ensure Continuous Availability of Essential Inputs, Particularly at the Periphery   In the poorest countries, a shortage of supplies is one of the most critical hurdles that health sectors have to face. Health facilities may be present and physically accessible in an area, yet essential resources for intervention (staff, drugs, or equipment) may be lacking or frequently unavailable. In remote areas, shortages of qualified health staff often hamper the provision of health services. The development of indicators that track the availability of critical inputs by level of service delivery can be very useful in problem assessment. In addition, maps showing the distribution of qualified staff, as well as drug and vaccine availability, could be drawn and linked to poverty maps to identify whether shortages are rampant in poorer or remote areas.

Figure 3.1 *Physical Access and Regional Poverty Levels, Mauritania, 1999*

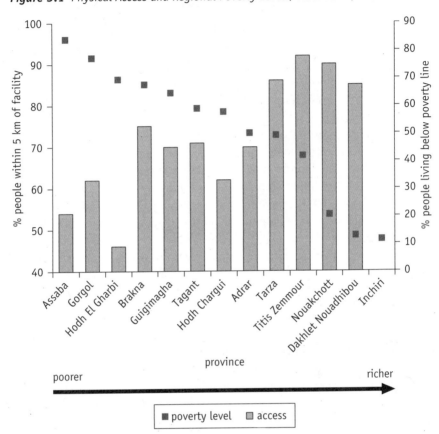

Source: Soucat, A., PRSP presentation, 2001.
Note: Access data for Inchiri not available.

Data Collection and Analysis   Central health information systems may have data on availability and distribution of personnel, equipment, drugs, vehicles, and other inputs. Unfortunately, these data are often incomplete or unreliable. Sample surveys of facilities can provide more detailed and reliable information on the availability of key inputs. Specific methodologies have been developed for this purpose, including essential drugs surveys. District or provincial officials could also be asked to tabulate the availability of staff and other key inputs in their areas. In addition, qualitative surveys can be used to determine if the absence of drugs or staff is viewed as a major

Figure 3.2 *Regional Drug Affordability, Cameroon*

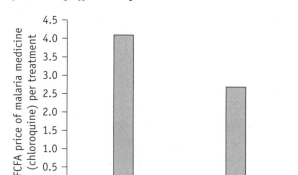

Source: Soucat, A., PRSP presentation, 2001.
Note: FCFA = Francs, Coopération financière en Afrique centrale.

impediment. If drug or staff shortages are identified as significant problems, the more difficult challenge lies in understanding why these problems persist. Inadequate funding for inputs may be part of the problem, but is rarely the only reason.

The example in figure 3.2 illustrates how markets for essential inputs, such as medicines, do not function well in areas where the poor live. In Cameroon, the price of medicine is higher in poor regions than in wealthier regions. It may seem counterintuitive that the poor would pay more for the same input. Market prices reflect both supply and demand conditions and, in this case, they seem to reflect market failures on the supply side.

Organizational Quality and Consumer Responsiveness (Step 4), the Extent to Which Public, Private, or NGO Services Are Responsive to Poor-Consumer Concerns and Are Delivered in a Way That Encourages Appropriate Use of Relevant Interventions   A number of factors influence the "user friendliness" of services. Some of these factors include the attitude of health staff, hours of operation, space, cleanliness and comfort of the waiting area and of the wards, waiting time, gender of the service provider, modes of payment, and efficiency of referral. These factors strongly affect the perception of quality by consumers and are important determinants of whether services are used—particularly because consumers are often not good judges of clinical quality. Organizational quality is likely to vary among public, private, and NGO providers. It is also likely to vary by geographic location (are they worse in poor areas?) and possibly by the type and level of service (clinics versus district hospitals or antenatal care versus treatment of sexually transmitted infections). Organizational quality can be measured objectively through average wait times or time spent with providers. It can also be measured qualitatively by asking the poor how they perceive the quality of different types of services.

Data Collection and Analysis   Measurement of organizational quality relies primarily on a mix of qualitative and quantitative tools. This type of information is rarely available through routine health information systems.

- Qualitative surveys, focus groups, or exit interviews with the poor can be illuminating. Because concerns differ, discussions with men and women, and possibly adolescents and adults, should be conducted separately. For example, in many countries women report being treated rudely or even abusively during delivery at government clinics. Often, women or adolescents avoid seeking care for sexually transmitted infections at public providers because of privacy concerns.
- Exit interviews provide useful information on provider-client interactions but do not reach the poor who are not using the services. Community-based approaches are therefore also useful to capture the opinions of the complete segment of the population.
- On-site assessment of various aspects of service organizations can be compared with the problems identified by the users. In this case, the challenge is to compare consumer perceptions with service-based "objective" measurements (average wait times, observations of provider behavior, cleanliness of facilities). Information collected could be used to build scales and indexes of quality, which allow comparisons between different types of services. Findings from such assessments can then be compared between facilities that serve the poor or are located in poor areas and facilities serving more affluent populations.

The family planning field has developed situation analysis methodologies that collect information from a sample of facilities and communities regarding the availability of inputs, provider behavior, process quality indicators, and perception of community members. The situation analysis approach can be adapted for other services.

Figure 3.3 *Perception of Quality, Cameroon*

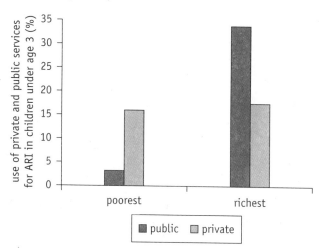

Source: Soucat, A., PRSP presentation, 2001.
Note: ARI = acute respiratory infection.

An indirect way of measuring perceived quality of care is to examine the use of the private sector. In some countries, choice of health care providers is significantly influenced by the perception that private health care provides a higher quality of service. In Cameroon, perceptions of service quality, particularly regarding wait times and provider empathy, cause the poor to rely more heavily on private services even though they are more expensive than public services (figure 3.3).

Relevance of Services (Step 5)   The next dimension examines whether the sector provides services that are relevant to the diseases affecting the population, especially the poor. Although a core package of interventions may be defined, these interventions may not be the ones that are provided in practice. It is, therefore, critical to examine the case mix of service units and assess whether priority is really given to the most relevant. Two problems are typically found when analyzing the extent to which services address the needs of the poor. First, there is sometimes little correlation between the burden of disease faced by the poor and the types of services provided. The second problem relating to service mix is disproportionate availability of cost-ineffective curative services relative to the more cost-effective preventive services.

Figure 3.4 *Relevance of Services by Age, Mauritania and Benin, 1998*

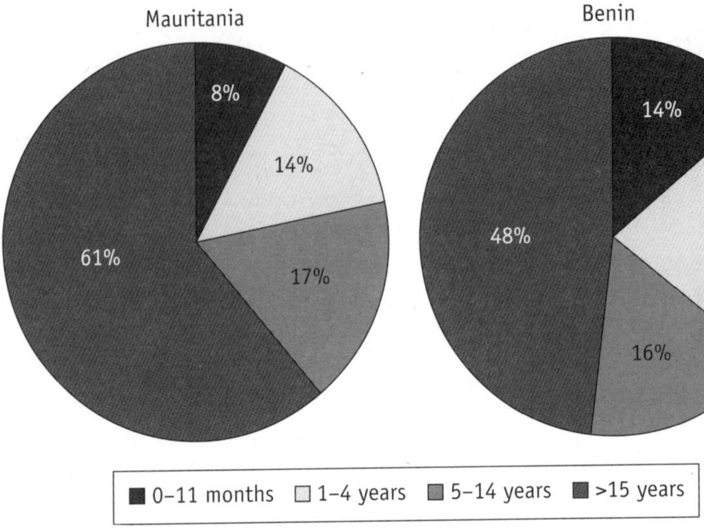

Source: Soucat, A., PRSP presentation, 2001.

Data Collection and Analysis   Health sector performance in raising or maintaining high use of essential interventions can be measured by assessing the quantity of services produced in specific areas relative to the income level of the area's population. Most countries define a package of essential health services for all, including the poor. Typically, a portion of the services are subsidized. However, the mix of services provided may be to a greater or lesser extent in line with the standard mix defined by the package.

Figure 3.4, comparing the primary care consultations mix of Benin and Mauritania, illustrates this latter point. Benin and Mauritania have similar core packages of health services. In addition, their epidemiological and demographic patterns are similar. However, the analysis of the case mix shows that the Benin primary health care system is more heavily oriented toward providing care to children less than five years of age than the Mauritanian services. In Mauritania, more than 60 percent of visits were adult consultations, while in Benin, this figure was less than 50 percent. In Benin, visits by children less than five years of age constitute 36 percent of total visits, compared with only 22 percent in Mauritania. It is, therefore, relatively clear that of the two countries, the primary health care system in Benin is more oriented toward serving children and reducing the under-five mortality rate. Ultimately, Benin is more in line with the intended goal of poverty reduction.

Timing and Continuity (Step 6), Whether Poor Consumers Receive the Requisite Number of Contacts for Services that Require Repeated Interventions; and Whether Time-Sensitive Services Are Delivered in a Timely Manner In the health sector, some interventions must be repeated at regular intervals to be effective. Examples of repeated interventions include antenatal care visits or BCG vaccinations for tuberculosis. The timing factor for some interventions, such as for emergency obstetric care, is absolutely critical. Too often intervention provision is incomplete or ill timed. Service continuity presents a significant organizational challenge because it requires the ability to track and follow up with consumers. As such, continuity of service is an important indicator of system effectiveness.

Data Collection and Analysis By using a combination of facility data and household surveys, continuity can be assessed by looking at dropout rates and other indicators of follow-up care. Key interventions and indicators include the following: BCG coverage of children with a full course of immunization, the number and timing of antenatal visits (percentage in the first trimester and percentage with more than three visits), and compliance with tuberculosis treatment.

Poor groups may also benefit less from appropriate continuous care. Often, the poor do not take advantage of the continuous services available or do not use them consistently or in a timely manner, thereby diminishing their effectiveness. In Mozambique, for example, the poorest group's DPT3 coverage is lower overall than the wealthiest group's. Yet the gap is less important for DPT1. The dropout rate between DPT1 and DPT3 accounts for the largest part of the wealthy-poor gap in the proportion of children fully immunized. Whereas 60 percent of the poorest 20 percent of the population do use immunization services, fewer than 30 percent complete a full course (figure 3.5).

Technical Quality (Step 7), the Likelihood That the Service, If Used, Will Lead to Improved Health Outcomes The capacity of the sector to provide the appropriate combination of technology and empathy at a given level of use is key to ensuring that interventions are translated into effective outcomes. Technical quality is determined by effective provider training and supervision, the existence of appropriate treatment protocols, and the adequacy of critical inputs, as well as factors such as provider workload. It is an unfortunate

Figure 3.5 *Continuity of Immunizations, Mozambique, 1997*

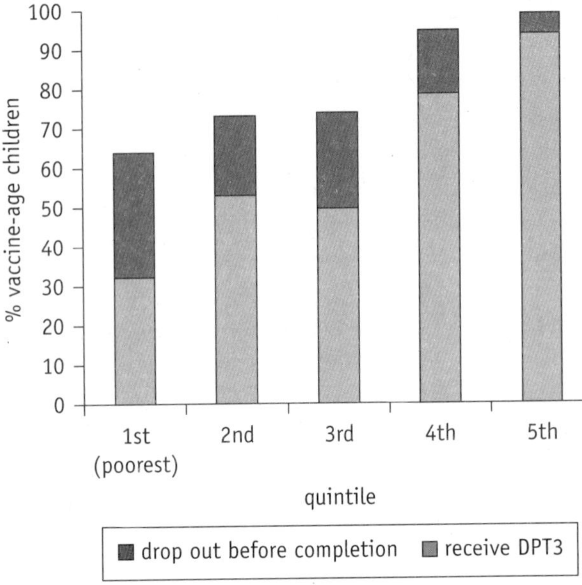

Source: Soucat, A., PRSP presentation, 2001.

reality that even when consumers express satisfaction with health services, the technical quality may be poor. Unwarranted consumer satisfaction can be a particular problem in the poorly regulated private sector. If a substantial portion of the poor use the private sector for priority interventions, it would be useful to assess the technical quality of private and public services.

Data Collection and Analysis   Assessing the capacity of the health sector to produce outputs of good technical quality usually requires direct observation of provider behavior in comparison with standard protocols. In addition, there are a number of indicators that are particularly sensitive to technical quality. These include perinatal mortality rates, malaria fatality rates, tuberculosis cure rates, and maternal mortality. Follow-up studies of maternal or perinatal deaths can help shed light on the contribution of clinical quality shortcomings. More sophisticated instruments for assessing quality via facility surveys are available for some health outcomes. The WHO's "Topical List of Priority Indicators for IMCI at Health-Facility Level" (WHO 2008) provides a useful instrument for assessing quality in the management of childhood illness. Surveys undertaken using this instrument suggest significant variations in quality across countries. These data could be linked to a poverty map or to a household survey to get a sense of how the poor fare compared with the better-off.

Social Accountability (Step 8)   Health systems or particular health services are more likely to be responsive to the poor if the poor are able to exert influence, or "voice," over health systems and providers. Health care providers in government-run clinics are often unresponsive to the poor because they are not directly accountable to them. There are several potential avenues for participation by the poor. First would be the direct management of local clinical services through community health centers or revolving drug funds. The second avenue would involve engaging the targeted population in monitoring the performance of facilities or providers through representation on a district or facility board or committee; through an effective grievance system; or through intermediaries, such as local political leaders, religious organizations, or NGOs. Some countries have also developed and publicized a "patient's bill of rights," to strengthen consumers' ability to demand quality care. A third avenue is community mobilization for health promotion activities, such as malaria prevention or improved water supply. Even when formal mechanisms for participation exist, health providers often will dominate by virtue of greater education and expertise. Women or certain ethnic groups may be excluded from decision making.

Data Collection and Analysis   The first step is to assess the extent to which mechanisms exist to exert influence on general and specific health services. The next step is to determine whether those mechanisms actually influence the quality of services provided to the poor. One approach is to assess the extent of participation by level and type of service according to the following categories: information sharing, consultation, and collaboration and shared decision making. In the case of private services, the poor exert varying degrees of influence through their roles as consumers. Assessment of voice and participation in health services could be incorporated into an overall participatory assessment for policy development. Information could then be collected through visits to a sample of communities and facilities, possibly by an NGO in collaboration with communities. Relevant questions might include the following: What percentage of health facilities have some sort of community committee or board associated with them? Do they meet regularly? Are they perceived as representative of the community and of the poor in particular, or are they dominated by local elites? Is there any measurable difference between the consumer-responsiveness of services for which the poor have some representation compared with those where they do not? What factors explain the differences? Are local political leaders responsive to the poor? Is the quality of health services an issue of concern for local leaders? If the poor have relatively little influence, are there existing traditional or modern institutional structures that could be developed to strengthen their voice?

The level of education and economic power of households influence the degree to which service providers are accountable to users and the population as a whole. In Mauritania, accountability was measured as the proportion of village health committees holding regular meetings. Although this may appear to be a rather weak indicator for such an important and broad dimension, it exemplifies an attempt to quantitatively define the participation level of some broad population's representatives in health-related issues. Data showed an overall low level of participation in Mauritania (figure 3.6). The poorer regions of the country exhibited the lowest levels of participation. These findings confirm the need for an enhanced level of support to build involvement of communities and households in poorer regions.

Figure 3.6 *Participation by Region, Mauritania, 2000*

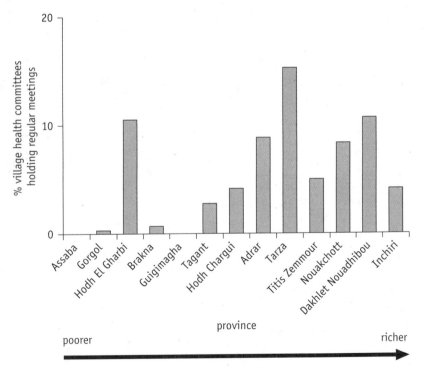

Source: Soucat, A., PRSP presentation, 2001.

Following the Money: Tools for Analyzing the Role of Resource Allocations and Financing in Inequality

Resource allocation and financing choices strongly influence the efficiency and patterns of use of health systems. Discerning the role of these factors in the inequality of health service use requires an analysis of (i) government allocations of health resources and (ii) the three functions of health finance introduced in chapter 2: resource mobilization, resource pooling, and provider payment mechanisms.

A Public Expenditure Review (PER) is a set of analytical tools used for analyzing the above four health financing topics: government allocations, resource mobilization, resource pooling, and provider payment mechanisms. PERs have been used for a number of years to examine overall public sector management of the economy. Within the health sector, PERs can be used to examine technical and allocation efficiency, inequity and inequality, budget development and execution, costs, and a number of other issues that are important to policy makers and health reform advocates. The elements of PERs that analyze the influence of government allocations on inequality are covered in the following section.

Analyzing Government Allocations

The most obvious link between inequality and health financing is government allocation of health sector budgets. Benefit incidence analysis (BIA), a tool used in PERs, was described and used in chapter 1 as a tool for identifying the extent to which the public subsidy to the health sector is pro-poor or pro-wealthy. BIA combines unit costs to government for different types of health care provision at different levels of delivery with the use rates of services by different socioeconomic groups to aggregate upward to a national level. The India BIA (summarized in box 1.3) was used to illustrate the health sector's pro-wealthy bias at the national level. In the overwhelming majority of India's large states, the analysis revealed the health subsidy to be pro-wealthy. Figure 3.7 from the India BIA summarizes the big inequality picture, showing that the poorest 20 percent of the population captured only about 10 percent of the total net public subsidy. The wealthiest quintile benefited three times more than the poorest.

As in the case of India, the overall findings of BIAs are politically powerful when presented at the aggregate level. However, they are mainly useful as advocacy and monitoring tools. From an analytical point of view, the factors underlying the overall findings are the most interesting. It is instructive

Figure 3.7 *Share of Public Subsidy for Curative Care by Income Group*

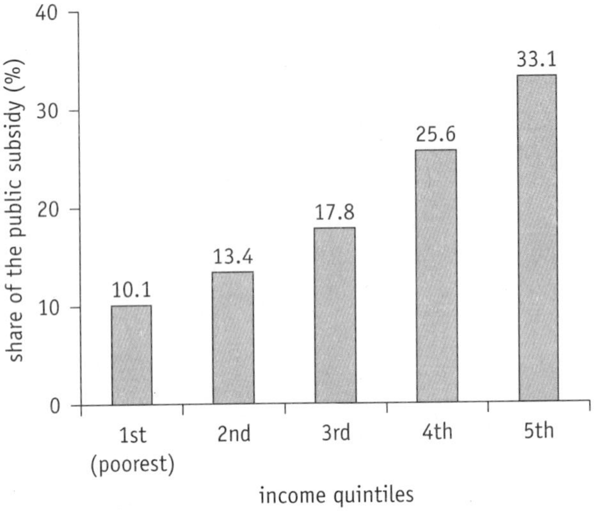

Source: Based on data from Peters and others (2002).

to disaggregate the overall findings to help identify which elements of the sector are the key drivers of inequality. In box 1.3 the disaggregated BIA data for the 16 largest states showed tremendous heterogeneity across states. Some displayed pro-poor public expenditure profiles while others revealed a pro-wealthy benefit by a factor between 5 and 10. By identifying successful and unsuccessful subnational regions, BIA allows the federal government to begin identifying what works in attacking inequality and what does not. BIA can also be disaggregated in different ways.

Two factors contribute to the pro-wealthy orientation of public spending. First, overall use of public services is skewed toward the wealthy because individuals from higher income groups are more likely to seek health care services. The second factor involves the type and level of services sought by the different income groups, especially because some levels of care cost considerably more than others. The data on India show that the wealthy are much more likely to use inpatient and outpatient hospital-based services (figure 3.8). However, outpatient care statistics from primary health care facilities revealed a slight pro-poor distribution. The concentration curves depicted in figure 3.8 show the cumulative benefits by income groups, starting from the poorest to the wealthiest. A concentration curve below the diagonal line indicates a pro-wealthy bias, and above the diagonal indicates a

Figure 3.8 *Subsidy Benefits Concentration Curve by Type of Care*

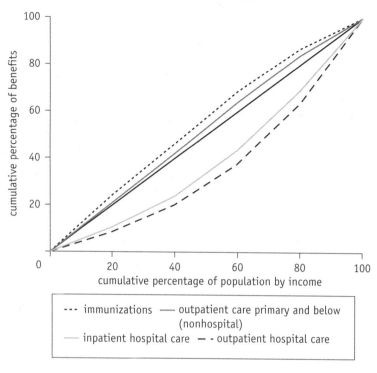

Source: Based on data from Mahal and others (2002).

pro-poor bias.[11] The main driver of the overall inequality in the use of health services in India is the hospital segment of the health sector.

The BIA analysis for India further segmented the data to explore the degree of inequality in subsidy benefits by gender and between urban and rural residence. Women benefit more from curative services than men. Cumulatively, women received 54 percent of total benefits while men received 47 percent, even though men represented a higher percentage of the sample population. Curative care services did not include any services related to pregnancies. At the national level, it appears that there is no clear implication of gender discrimination in the use of curative care.

Segmenting the data by residence reveals a higher level of inequality in subsidy benefits for the rural population. Figure 3.9 shows that the urban public subsidy concentration curve is almost the same as the diagonal, whereas the concentration curve for the rural population shows pro-wealthy

Figure 3.9 *Subsidy Benefits Concentration Curve for Curative Care by Residence*

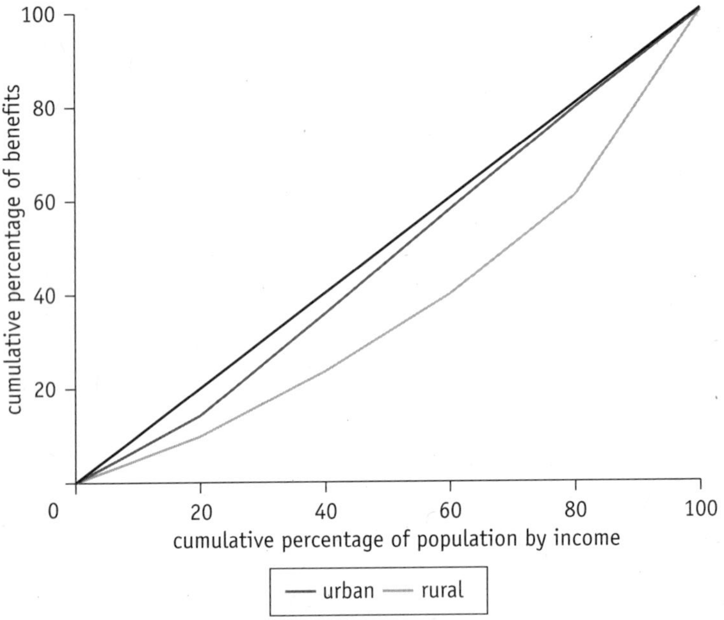

Source: Based on data from Peters and others (2002).

benefits. The urban-rural difference may be partly explained by increased accessibility to public hospitals for urban residents. Because hospitalization is the major contributor to subsidy benefits, increasing usage at rural public hospitals would help government health subsidies to be more pro-poor. In addition to the distributional differences for the rural and urban samples, there is inequality between the average use rates. While the rural population of India represented more than 75 percent of the national total, they captured only 67.6 percent of the net benefits from curative care. The 25 percent of the population in urban areas captured 32.4 percent of the benefits.

The India BIA work raises a number of possible policy actions that may impact inequality. The large variations across states and the fact that some states have achieved, or nearly achieved, equitable distribution sends an encouraging message of the state governments' ability to reverse inequality. These positive examples should encourage the federal authorities to better understand the causes of success and failure. The overwhelming number of states, however, failing to equitably distribute the government subsidy confirms that addressing the underlying causes of inequality is no easy task. Some general policy conclusions may be drawn from the BIA work.

Resource Allocation   A number of resource allocation decisions may be considered by states and the central government:

- Given the dominant use of tertiary hospitals by the wealthiest, the public sector may want to consider reallocating portions of the budget to primary and secondary facilities.
- Because preventive care services appear to be good investments on both equity and efficiency grounds, the public sector may want to consider reallocating portions of the budget to preventive care.
- The urban-rural differences suggest the need to increase resource allocation to rural areas.

Facility Placement and Access for the Poor   An important determinant of health service use, especially for poor families, is the location of facilities. The equity differences in facility use for urban and rural settings may be explained by the ease of physical access in cities. The variability in the states may be examined, using poverty density maps and facility locations, to confirm this conclusion.

Setting Targets and Monitoring Outcomes   The BIA study presents an opportunity for policy makers to set equity-specific targets for resource use of inputs and outputs. For example, resource allocation targets could be established for geographic coverage, focusing on areas with high levels of poverty. Service-level budgeting could be more strategically allocated among tertiary, secondary, and primary facilities. Output targets may include annual distributional reviews of service use in random locations. Such mechanisms could be used to assess performance and link it to incentives in the form of performance-related budgeting.

Documenting and Explaining Good Practice   Another possible use of the variations in inequality of performance is to motivate and drive an evaluation and knowledge-sharing function of the government. Evaluation efforts can document good practice and, more important, explore the causes of both good and bad practice. As mentioned earlier, empirical analysis can point to areas of strength or weakness but cannot provide in-depth results. Qualitative analysis can be used to explore the extent to which different supply and demand factors achieve good equity outcomes in several states.

As highlighted in the India example, public expenditure review tools such as BIA can be used to analyze the possible causes of inequality in health service use. Careful decomposition of the data can reveal ways in which health spending is misdirected and effectively motivate public action. BIA is also an excellent tool for monitoring the impact of policy changes on resource allocation inequality.

Financing Functions and Inequality

As noted in chapter 2, the three functions of financing—resource generation, pooling, and provider payment methods—can increase or decrease inequality. Box 3.1 repeats the questions that can be used to determine if or

---

Box 3.1 *Determining How Health-Financing Policy Choices Affect Inequality in Service Use*

In exploring the impact of different resource-generation approaches (tax financing, social health insurance, private health insurance, and user fees), questions to be considered are, will a resource-generating option be likely to

- increase or decrease the financial access of low-income groups?
- create incentives or disincentives for the poor in seeking care?
- increase or decrease the financial burden on the poor?
- increase the level of poverty (head count and depth)?
- provide a cross-subsidy from the wealthy to the poor or vice versa?
- improve the quality of services at facilities serving the poor (retention and recycling)?[a]

In designing or assessing different resource pooling arrangements in the health sector, it is important to ask if they are likely to

- increase the number and percentage of the poor that are covered under pooling arrangements?
- decrease the risk of catastrophic payments for the poor?
- increase access to preventive and simple curative care through pooling?

In looking at the impact of different provider payment methods on inequality, it is important to ask whether a mechanism is likely to

- change the incentives to facilities or providers to seek and serve poor or vulnerable populations?
- increase usage rates for the poor?
- improve the quality of care the poor receive?
- link productivity to payment in serving the poor?

a. "Retention and recycling" refers to policies that allow facilities that collect fees to keep them (instead of sending them to the Treasury) and to use them to improve quality of care.

how policy choices in health financing affect inequality in health service use. Basic public expenditure reviews may be used to analyze the potential for large health financing reforms to radically change the way in which a country finances health care. Such reviews can also be used to identify smaller reforms or changes that can, within existing arrangements, ameliorate inequality in health service use.

Who Pays? Chapter 2 detailed four broad means of resource mobilization: general revenue taxation, contributions to social health insurance, private health insurance premiums, and out-of-pocket payments. Of those, the two that dominate in low- and middle-income countries are general revenue taxes and out-of-pocket payments. Public and private insurance mechanisms are considerably less developed, especially in countries in which large segments of the labor force are either informal or unemployed. BIA captures who benefits from health sector spending by the public sector but does not touch on the equally important question of who pays for the services. Regardless of the source of financing, the ultimate payer tends to be the general population. The proportion of payment incidence by income group is different for each mechanism.

Two issues arise when examining who actually pays for health care. The first issue is fairness; the second is incentives.

Regarding fairness, should payment be proportional or progressive? Do we want health sector spending to be a tool for wealth redistribution? The alternative is to link payment to use. Many countries firmly believe that sectors like health and education should be vehicles for the redistribution of resources. In fact, the government often validates health and education spending as investments that are meant to serve the needs of the poor. Despite such lofty aspirations, the evidence in chapter 1 indicates that redistribution is not likely to happen as long as those who are better-off continue to capture the majority of public subsidies.

Measuring the extent to which redistribution takes place requires capturing not only the benefit incidence but also the payment incidence. Doing so for out-of-pocket payments of fees and insurance premiums is done relatively easily through household surveys. For other sources, like taxes, capturing payment incidence in low- and middle-income countries is considerably more difficult. The main reason for the difficulty is that, in those countries, indirect taxes (such as sales taxes and import or export tariffs) are the dominant method of taxation. That fact, combined with the difficulty in identifying the income groups, makes calculating tax incidence very difficult.

Figure 3.10 *Benefit and Tax Incidence for the Health Sector in Canada*

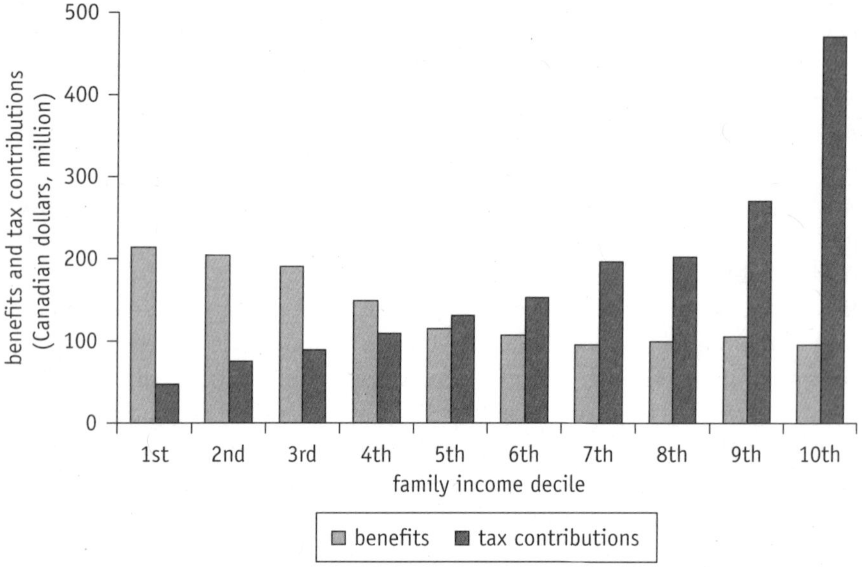

Sources: Mustard and others 1997; Evans 2002.

The following example illustrates the power of tools to calculate payment or tax incidence and suggests that efforts to estimate such incidence in lower-income countries can make an enormous difference in the policy debate. Both health sector benefit and general revenue tax incidence were calculated for the Canadian health care system, which is financed mainly through taxes. Figure 3.10 summarizes the redistributive effect of the pro-poor Canadian health system—the poor capture a large share of the benefits while the wealthy pay a larger share of taxes.

The available evidence on benefit incidence in most low- and middle-income countries, and the anecdotal evidence on the incidence of payments, point to a balance that is pro-wealthy rather than, as in the Canadian example, pro-poor—all the more reason that all countries would do well to develop the analytical tools and data to monitor the incidence of payments and benefits.

Evidence on fairness can carry a great deal of political weight, but the more relevant issue for inequality in health service use is the extent to which resource generation creates an incentive or disincentive for the poor to seek health care. The question of incentives turns on the link between payment for service and use of service. In out-of-pocket fee payment systems this link is direct and highly tangible. In health systems that are financed through general revenue taxes, the link is almost nonexistent. Social health insurance and private health insurance fall in the middle of this spectrum. The payment-use link is strengthened if facility-based copayments are used. A strong link between payment and use is likely to create a disincentive to seeking care, but not in all cases or for all potential users of health services.

A number of factors determine a strong or weak link between payment and use of health services. The most obvious is the financial barrier payments represent because of their direct impact on those with limited resources. In general, any system that has a direct link between payment and use, such as fee for service or copayment at the facility level, is more likely to negatively impact service use by the poor. Mitigating factors, however, do exist. Visible, targeted usage of fee-generated resources is an example of one such mitigating factor. Evidence suggests that fees may actually increase usage if payments are used to improve the quality of care in a way that the poor value. Therefore, it is absolutely imperative to analyze the impact of payments on the poor before jumping to the conclusion that they should be completely eliminated.

Another important and potentially mitigating factor is the extent to which exemption strategies exist and function to protect the poor. A well-designed and well-implemented exemption policy can secure resources for health facilities while protecting the poor from additional financial barriers. It should be noted, however, that well-designed and well-implemented exemption policies are rare in health and other service sectors in low- and middle-income countries. A summary of what constitutes a well-designed user-fee system with effective exemption mechanisms is provided in chapter 4.

To analyze the existing bottlenecks that revenue generation for health present to the poor, two levels of questions can be asked. The first level, and the simpler of the two, focuses on the degree to which there is a direct link between payment through fees or copayment at the facility and health service use. The stronger the payment-use link, the greater the likelihood that health service use will decrease. Basic analysis of health system financing sources, combined with household survey data, may provide answers to questions of service use and payment.

The second level of questions relates to the potential mitigating factors to the payment-use link disincentive. Are payments being used to improve the quality and effectiveness of the services for the poor? Do functional, effective exemption mechanisms that eliminate or mitigate financial barriers exist? Such questions are best answered through a combination of quantitative and qualitative data collection efforts that capture how the poor feel about the existing system and what they consider to be the most binding constraint.

Who Is Covered?   Pooling mechanisms such as public or private health insurance spread the financial risk of health services payment across the sick and healthy. Furthermore, they minimize the likelihood of catastrophic expenditures resulting from health care use. Pooling mechanisms also weaken the payment-use link, decreasing the potential financial barrier to the use of health services. Based on these two positive implications of pooling, universal health insurance coverage would most likely benefit the poor. Universal health insurance coverage is an admirable policy objective but is far from the reality of most low- and middle-income countries. Even some high-income countries, such as the United States, are far from achieving universal health insurance coverage. It is estimated that over 45 million Americans are covered by neither a social insurance mechanism like Medicare or Medicaid nor private health insurance.

Household surveys that include questions about health coverage and contain identifiers of relative household wealth provide a relatively simple way to capture who is covered by health insurance. Understanding the reasons for lack of coverage for the poor involves a more complex analytical process and typically requires both qualitative and quantitative tools. Possible causes include the following:

- Social insurance mechanisms in low- and middle-income countries typically provide coverage to a small proportion of the population and are linked to formal sector employment (public or private).
- Most insurance mechanisms prosper in formal sector employment clusters, which are typically in urban settings and cover better-off households, and sometimes cover only the contributor, not the whole family.
- Insurance markets are usually not well developed in low- and middle-income countries.
- Private health insurance mechanisms suffer from a number of market failures (moral hazard, adverse selection) that are difficult for governments to address even in high-income countries with strong government regulatory capacity.

What Is Covered? Asking who is covered by pooling mechanisms is a good first question because lack of insurance coverage typically leads to lower use of health services by the poor. But insurance coverage rates may mask some important issues with implications for inequality in the use of health services for those covered. The critical follow-up question is what these arrangements cover. Insurance coverage most likely includes a limited number of services that may vary according to household wealth and, ultimately, increase inequality. Other characteristics of insurance contracts that impact inequality include caps on financial coverage and the size of copayments at facilities.

Analyzing the details of coverage by different insurance programs and policies is fairly easy, but tedious, work. The more demanding component is identifying who is covered by the different policies and analyzing how the different characteristics of the policies impact demand for and use of health services. Issues to be explored include the following:

- Do insurance plans cover high cost curative care services as well as less expensive preventive care services? Catastrophic payments for expensive services play an important role in increasing poverty head counts and deepening poverty for those already below the poverty line. Policies that mitigate the poverty impact of catastrophic payments through expensive curative care coverage for economically vulnerable populations are one way of addressing inequality. Insurance mechanisms that address access to less expensive primary health care services can also have a lasting impact on decreasing inequality. Community-based microinsurance schemes, mainly in Rwanda, have been shown to drastically increase access by both better-off and poorer segments of society and by doing so, increase use by vulnerable groups.
- Undercoverage of health care insurance, especially in market-based, voluntary health insurance schemes, occurs in different ways. Low caps on the total annual financial coverage of an insurance policy can decrease demand for expensive services. Other potential barriers include high deductible minimums and high copayments at the facility level.

The User-Provider Payment Link As discussed in chapter 2, payment methods to providers, hospitals, and individuals have a significant influence on their behavior. Different payment mechanisms create incentives that motivate provider behaviors. Likewise, the link between consumer payment and service use influences the probability that consumers demand or use a particular service. A similar payment-to-use relationship exists in the link between provider payment methods and the services providers deliver. In this case, however, it is the behavior of the provider in delivering services to the poor that is at issue (that is, the supply of the services to the poor). Analysis should focus on the way in which different methods of compensation change provider incentives to serve the poor. However, the impact of payment mechanisms on inequality should not be the only factor influencing the selection of payment methods. Other factors to be considered include efficiency, cost containment, quality of care, and practical issues relating to capacity of the system to implement and monitor complex mechanisms.

The health financing dimensions described in chapter 2 can help frame the analytical questions necessary to determine the extent to which provider payment mechanisms are bottlenecks for the poor and how reforming them can make service delivery pro-poor. Three questions were identified to increase understanding of incentives: How much is being paid (or what is the unit of payment)? When are payments made (before or after the service is completed)? What are the conditions of payment (or the performance criteria)? Each of these simple questions can then be applied to the various provider payment methods to determine the incentives created to serve the poor.

In the spectrum of provider payment methods, the range begins with a zero use-provider payment link, in which providers are compensated regardless of productivity, to a heavy use-provider payment link whereby providers are paid only if they see patients and provide services. At one end of the spectrum, hospitals can be paid through annual input-based budgets that are not tied to productivity measures. At the other end, hospitals can be paid on a fee-for-service basis only after services are delivered. When considering the impact on inequality of provider payment mechanisms, the provision of health services to the poor should be measured and linked to provider payment.

A combination of qualitative and quantitative tools can be used to tease out how providers are likely to respond to different payment mechanisms. In countries where payment method experiments are conducted, the impact can be measured through household and facility surveys and supplemented with provider surveys and key informant interviews. In countries with little or no experimentation, the potential impact of reform can be estimated through intensive qualitative work and augmented by reviewing the international literature.

An Analytical Checklist

The complex nature of the inequality problem, and the fact that cultural and institutional context matters and varies by location and region, make it critical to base policy on analysis. Few countries have the resources and patience required to undertake all the analytical tools described in this chapter. The good news, however, is that most countries have considerably more useful data—in particular, household surveys—than are being exploited. Marginal Budgeting for Bottlenecks (MBB), developed by UNICEF and the World Bank, is an example of a packaged tool that includes an analytical component condensing the eight-step framework into five areas of focus. The focus areas use existing data to help the user systematically review and identify the most binding of the constraints.

To help navigate the long list of analytical tools reviewed in this chapter, a quick checklist of basic issues to be addressed in attacking inequality is provided below:

1. Identify the poor and vulnerable
2. Identify the gap in use of services between the different income groups
3. Identify the gaps in the different types of services (the largest inequalities)
4. Understand the different underlying causes of the gaps in service use
5. Prioritize the most binding constraints the poor face, both on the supply side of service delivery and on the demand side of seeking care
6. Identify pro-wealthy and pro-poor resource allocation choices by the public sector
7. Analyze the impact of the dominant resource mobilization choices on the use of health services by the poor
8. Analyze the gaps in resource pooling mechanisms and their impact on the poor
9. Analyze the incentives generated by the dominant provider payment mechanisms for serving the poor

Policy design or reform that does not address most of the issues in the checklist is not likely to result in positive change, even if well intentioned. However, refraining from any policy work before all the possible answers have been identified delays the implementation of sometimes obvious changes that can have a quick and positive impact. A pragmatic, moderate process combining continuous learning and action is necessary. A pragmatic approach is also essential to recognizing the institutional realities related to limited capacity and flexibility of health sectors in low- and middle-income countries. A policy that can successfully attack inequality in the health sector combines measurements of the size and nature of inequality, prioritized and actionable analysis of bottlenecks faced by the poor, realistic understanding of the institutional constraints in health care, and humility about the potential for policy action to produce quick and measurable results.

Annex 3.1 Data Sources and Their Limitations

Household Surveys and Other Nonroutine Data

Household surveys are implemented on a regular basis in many countries, and are probably the most important source of data for health equity analysis.[12] Some household surveys are designed as multipurpose surveys, with a focus on a broad set of demographic and socioeconomic issues, while other surveys focus explicitly on health. Surveys sample from population and are representative, or can be made representative, of the population as a whole (or whatever target population is defined for the survey). They have the advantage of permitting more detailed data collection than is feasible in a comprehensive census. Although many surveys are conducted on an ad hoc basis, there are an increasing number of multiround integrated survey programs. These include the Living Standards Measurement Study (World Bank), the Demographic and Health Surveys (ORC Macro), the Multiple Indicator Cluster Surveys (UNICEF), and the World Health Surveys (WHO). The Living Standards Measurement Study is different from the other surveys in that it collects detailed expenditure or income data. In that sense, LSMS surveys are a form of Household Budget Surveys. Many countries implement Household Budget Surveys in some form on a semi-regular basis. A core objective of these surveys is to capture the essential elements of household income and expenditure patterns. In some countries, the surveys focus exclusively on this objective, and hence are of limited use for health equity analysis. However, it is also common for Household Budget Surveys to include additional modules, for example, on health and nutrition, making them ideal for detailed analysis of the relationship between economic status and health variables.

Aside from large-scale household surveys, there is often a wealth of other nonroutine data that can be used for health equity analysis. This may include small-scale, ad hoc household surveys and special studies. It may also be possible to analyze data from facility-based surveys of users (exit polls) from an equity perspective. Relative to household surveys, exit polls are cheap to implement (particularly if they are carried out as a component of a health facility survey), and are an efficient means of collecting data on health service use and perceptions. With exit polls it is also easier to associate outcomes of health-seeking behavior (for example, client perceptions of quality, payments, receipt of drugs) with a particular provider and care-seeking episode. This is often difficult in general household surveys, where specific providers are typically not identified, and where recall periods of up to four weeks can result in considerable measurement error. However, unlike a household survey, an exit poll only provides information about users of health services.

While survey data can be of considerable value for health equity analysis, it is important to be aware of the limitations. For one, large-scale surveys are expensive to conduct. As a result, they tend to be implemented only periodically. Moreover, the scope, focus, and measurement approaches can vary across surveys and over time, limiting the scope for comparisons. Another challenge concerns the way the survey sample is selected, and what this implies for making inferences from the data. It is important for analysts to be aware of the "representativeness" of the survey data, and to take this into account when drawing conclusions about the wider population.[13]

Routine Data: Health Information Systems and Censuses

Some forms of routine data may be suitable for health equity analysis. Health information systems (HIS) collect a combination of health data through ongoing data collection systems. These data include administrative health service statistics (for example, from hospital records or patient registration), epidemiological and surveillance data, and vital events data (registering births, deaths, marriages, and the like). HIS data are primarily used for management purposes, such as planning, needs assessments, resource allocation, and quality assessments. However, in some contexts, HIS data include demographic or socioeconomic variables that permit equity analysis. This is the case in Britain, where mortality data, based on death certificates, have been used for tabulations of mortality rates by occupational groups since the 19th century. Similar analysis has been undertaken in other countries by ethnic group or educational level. Although many HIS do not routinely record socioeconomic or demographic characteristics, this may change in the future with greater recognition of the importance of monitoring health system equity.

Periodic population and housing censuses are another form of routine data. Censuses are an important source of data for planning and monitoring of population issues and socioeconomic and environmental trends, both in developed and developing countries. National population and housing censuses also provide valuable statistics and indicators for assessing the situation of various special population groups, such as those affected by gender issues, children, youth, the elderly, persons with a disability, and the migrant population. Population censuses have been conducted in most countries in recent years. Census data often contain only limited information on health and living standards, but have sometimes been used to study health inequalities by linking it to HIS data. For example, socioeconomic differences in disease incidence and hospitalization have been studied by linking cause-of-death or hospital discharge records with census data. In the United States, there have also been efforts to link public health surveillance data with area-based socioeconomic measures based on geocoding. While poor data quality and availability may currently preclude such linking in low-income countries, census data may be used to study equity issues by constructing needs indicators for geographic areas based on demographic and socioeconomic profiles of the population.

Notwithstanding the potential for using routine data for health equity analysis, it is important to be aware of the common weaknesses of such data. In particular, coverage is often incomplete and data quality may be poor. For example, because of spatial differences in the coverage of health facility infrastructure, routine data are likely to be more complete and representative in urban than in rural areas. Similarly, better-off individuals are more likely to seek and obtain medical care, and hence, to be recorded in the HIS. Moreover, where routine data is used for management purposes, incentives may exist for staff to record information inaccurately. Data sources and their limitations are summarized in table A3.1.

Examples of Survey Data

Demographic and Health Surveys (DHS and DHS+)   The DHS have been an important source of individual and household-level health data since 1984.[14] The design of the DHS drew on the experiences of the World Fertility Surveys[15] and the Contraceptive Prevalence Surveys, but included an expanded set of indicators in the areas of population, health, and nutrition. DHS are nationally representative, with sample sizes typically ranging from 5,000 to 30,000 households.

The standard DHS consists of a household questionnaire and a women's questionnaire (for women ages 15–49). The core questionnaire concentrates on basic indicators and is standardized across countries. The household questionnaire covers basic demographic data for all household members, household and dwelling characteristics, and nutritional status of young children and women ages 15–49. The women's questionnaire contains information on general background characteristics, reproductive behavior and intentions, contraception, maternity care, breast-feeding and nutrition,

Table A3.1 *Data Sources and Their Limitations*

Type of data	Examples	Advantages	Disadvantages
Survey data (household)	Living Standards Measurement Study (LSMS), Demographic and Health Surveys (DHS), Multiple Indicator Cluster Surveys (MICS), World Health Surveys (WHS)	Data are representative for a specific population (often nationally), as well as for subpopulations. Many surveys have rich data on health, living standards, and other complementary variables. Surveys are often conducted on a regular basis, sometimes following households over time.	Sampling and nonsampling errors can be important. Survey may not be representative of small subpopulations of interest.
Survey data (exit poll)	Ad hoc surveys, often linked to facility surveys	Relatively low cost of implementation. Provide detailed information about users of health services that can be related to provider characteristics. Data on payments and other characteristics of visit more likely to be accurate.	Exit polls provide no information about nonusers. Data often contain limited information about household and socioeconomic characteristics. Survey responses may be biased from "courtesy" to providers or fear of repercussions.
Administrative data	Health information system (HIS), vital registration, national surveillance system, sentinel site surveillance	Data are readily available.	Data may be of poor quality. Data may not be representative of the population as a whole. Data contain limited complementary information, for example, about living standards.
Census data	Implemented on a national scale in many countries	Data cover the entire target population (or nearly so).	Data contain only limited information on health. Data collection is irregular. Data contain limited complementary information, for example, about living standards.

children's health, status of women, AIDS and other sexually transmitted diseases, husband's background, and other topics. Some surveys also include special modules tailored to meet particular needs.

Aside from the standard DHS, interim surveys are sometimes implemented to collect information on a reduced set of performance monitoring indicators. These surveys have smaller sample sizes and are often conducted between rounds of the DHS. In addition, many of the DHS have included tools to collect community-level data (for example, Service Availability Modules). More recently, detailed facility surveys—Service Provision Assessments—have been implemented alongside household surveys with a view to providing information about the characteristics of health services, including their quality, infrastructure, use, and availability.

Further information, including a list of past and ongoing surveys, survey reports, questionnaires, and information on how to access the data, can be found at http://www.measuredhs.com.

The Living Standards Measurement Study (LSMS)   The LSMS was established by the World Bank in 1980 to explore ways of improving the type and quality of household data collected by government statistical offices in developing countries. LSMS surveys are multitopic surveys designed to permit four types of analysis: (i) simple descriptive statistics on living standards, (ii) monitoring of poverty and living standards over time, (iii) describing the incidence and coverage of government programs, and (iv) measuring the impact of policies and programs on household behavior and welfare (Grosh and Glewwe 2000). The first surveys were implemented in Côte d'Ivoire and Peru. Other early surveys followed a similar format, although considerable variation has been introduced over time.

The household questionnaire forms the heart of the LSMS survey. It typically includes a health module that provides information on (i) health-related behavior, (ii) the use of health services, (iii) health expenditures, (iv) insurance status, and (v) access to health services. The level of detail of the health section has, however, varied across surveys. Complementary data are typically collected through community and price questionnaires. In addition, detailed service provider (health facility or school) data have been collected in some LSMS surveys. The facility surveys have been included to provide complementary data primarily on prices of health care and medicines, and health care quality.

Further information, including a list of past and ongoing surveys, survey reports, questionnaires, and information on how to access the data, can be found at http://www.worldbank.org/lsms/.

UNICEF Multiple Indicator Cluster Surveys   The Multiple Indicator Cluster Surveys (MICS) were developed by UNICEF and others in 1998 to monitor the goals of the World Summit for Children. By 1996, 60 developing countries had carried out stand-alone MICS, and another 40 had incorporated some of the MICS modules into other surveys.

The early experience with MICS resulted in revisions of the methodology and questionnaires. These revisions drew on the expertise and experience of many organizations, including the WHO; the United Nations Educational, Scientific, and Cultural Organization; the International Labor Organization; the Joint United National Programme on HIV/AIDS; the United Nations Statistical Division; the Centers for Disease Control and Prevention; MEASURE DHS (USAID); and academic institutions. The MICS typically include three components: a household questionnaire, a women's questionnaire (for women ages 15–49), and a child (under age 5) questionnaire. The precise content of questionnaires has varied somewhat across countries. Household questionnaires often cover education, child labor, maternal mortality, child disability, water and sanitation, and salt iodization. The women's questionnaires have tended to include sections on child mortality, tetanus toxoid, maternal health, contraceptive use, and HIV/AIDS. Finally, the child questionnaire covers birth registration, vitamin A, breast-feeding, treatment of illness, malaria, immunizations, and anthropometry.

World Health Organization (WHO) World Health Surveys   The WHO developed a World Health Survey (WHS) to compile comprehensive baseline information on the health of populations and on the outcomes associated with investment in health systems. These surveys have been implemented in 70 countries across the full range of development in collaboration with the people involved in routine health information systems. The overall aims of the WHS are to examine the way populations report their health, understand how people value health states, and measure the performance of health systems in relation to responsiveness. In addition, it addresses various issues such as health care expenditures, adult mortality, birth history, various risk factors, and so forth.

In the first stage, the WHS targets adult individuals living in private households (age 18 or older). A nationally representative sample of households is drawn, and adult individuals are selected randomly from the household roster. Sample sizes vary from 1,000 to 10,000 individuals.

The content of the questionnaires varies across countries but, in general, covers general household information, geocoding, malaria prevention, home care, health insurance, income indicators, and household expenditure (including on health). In addition, a specific module is administered to household members who are trained or are working as health professionals. This module covers a limited set of issues, including occupation, location of work, hours of work, main activities in work, forms and amount of payment, second employment, reasons for not working (if applicable), and professional training. The individual questionnaire includes sections on sociodemographic characteristics, health state descriptions, health state valuations, risk factors, mortality, coverage, health system responsiveness, and health goals and social capital.

Further information, including country reports and questionnaires, can be found at http://www.who.int/healthinfo/survey/en/index.html.

WHO Multi-Country Evaluation of IMCI   Currently, the WHO is coordinating a multi-country evaluation (MCE) of the Integrated Management of Childhood Illness (IMCI). Integrated survey instruments for costs and quality have been developed and implemented (or are being implemented) in Bangladesh, Peru, Tanzania, and Uganda. The purpose of the MCEs is to (i) document the effects of IMCI interventions on health workers' performance, health systems, and family behaviors; (ii) determine whether and to what extent the IMCI strategy as a whole has a measurable impact on health outcomes (reducing under-five morbidity and mortality); (iii) describe the cost of IMCI implementation at national, district, and health-facility levels; (iv) increase the sustainability of IMCI and other child health strategies by providing a basis for the improvement of implementation; and (v) support planning and advocacy for childhood interventions by ministries of health in developing countries and national and international partners in development. Worldwide there are 30 countries at different stages of implementation of IMCI.

Further information, including country reports, questionnaires, and how to access data, can be found at http://www.who.int/imci-mce/.

RAND Surveys   RAND has supported the design and implementation of Family Life Surveys (FLS) in developing countries since the 1970s. Currently available country surveys include Indonesia (1993–94, 1997–98, and 2000), Malaysia (1976–77 and 1988), Guatemala (1995), and Bangladesh (1996). Further information about these surveys and information on how to access the data can be found at http://www.rand.org.

University of North Carolina Surveys   The Carolina Population Center at the University of North Carolina at Chapel Hill has been involved in a range of different data collection exercises. Much of the data is publicly available. Information can be found at http://www.cpc.unc.edu/projects/projects.php.

Cebu Longitudinal Health and Nutrition Surveys   The Cebu Longitudinal Health and Nutrition Survey is a study of a cohort of Filipino women who gave birth between May 1, 1983, and April 30, 1984, and were reinterviewed, with their children, at three subsequent points until 1998–99.

China Health and Nutrition Survey   The China Health and Nutrition Survey is a six-wave longitudinal survey conducted in eight provinces in China between 1989 and 2004. It provides a wealth of detailed information on health and nutrition of adults and children, including physical examinations.

Nang Rong (Thailand) Projects   The Nang Rong projects represent a major data collection effort that was started in 1984 with a census of households in 51 villages. The villages were resurveyed in 1988 and again in 1994–95. New entrants were interviewed and a subsample of out-migrants was followed.

Annex 3.2 Beneficiary Assessment

It is difficult to imagine a doctor recommending a course of treatment to a patient without first asking the patient a series of questions to understand the patient's ailments, medical history, allergies, and other key pieces of information. Treatment based on incomplete information may lead to poor health outcomes, a dissatisfied patient, and wasted time and resources for both the patient and the doctor. We then wonder why policy makers so often design and implement policies without first consulting the beneficiary group of the intended intervention. Policy makers who implement policies and programs intended to address the needs of a community without first gaining the views of the target population may do so inefficiently and at the expense of wasted funds, mediocre results, and a dissatisfied beneficiary population.

A beneficiary assessment (BA) is a qualitative analytic tool used to improve the impact of a planned or ongoing intervention by eliciting the views of the intended beneficiary population regarding the intervention that is intended to improve their lives. In addition to playing a critical role in the planning process, regular and routine assessment provides project managers a continual stream of feedback from the beneficiary group about the intervention, which enables them to routinely improve and modify the program to meet the ever-changing needs of the target population. Similarly, as in our doctor analogy, a physician who continually monitors the patient's course of treatment by regularly following up and asking the patient appropriate questions can modify medication and other treatment activity to best suit the patient's needs and tolerance. This approach, often described as "system listening" or "systematic consultation," ensures that the voice of the beneficiary population is heard and their concerns integrated into project development and implementation.

The long-term success and sustainability of a development project depend on the beneficiaries of an intervention eventually taking ownership of those projects that aim to improve their lives. Projects that originate from BAs are more likely to be accepted and used by beneficiary populations and therefore are more likely to achieve long-term success and sustainability. Often, the recipients of an intervention do not have a voice in its design and implementation. Communities that participate in the planning and implementation phases of a project feel more informed and involved. Because BA-based initiatives are anchored in the expressed needs of the beneficiary community, such projects have a higher likelihood of achieving full participation in program activities. Increased participation in project activities increases ownership among the beneficiary population.

This approach is useful in identifying and designing development activities, signaling constraints to participation faced by the target group, obtaining feedback on reactions of the target group to the interventions implemented, and uncovering new information that would otherwise not come to light. The scope of policy issues addressed by this approach is far-reaching. Several issues addressed by this approach and examples of each follow:

- *Better understand the popular perceptions of problems.* What do the poor see as the root cause of poverty? Understanding the root cause of poverty, as the poor perceive it, helps identify problems and improvement areas where development activities can be implemented.
- *Better understand the incentive and regulatory framework of the community.* What are the micro- and macro-level factors that affect the accumulation of human capital and access to land and credit as the poor see it in their country? What changes in the incentive system would be most welcomed by the poor? Understanding the incentive and

regulatory framework of a community helps policy makers design interventions in light of potential constraints to participation.

- *Gauge the effectiveness of public service delivery.* What factors affect the target group's use or non-use of public services? By understanding the factors that restrict access to certain services, improvements can be made so that these public services and institutions can become more valuable and relevant to the target group's situation.
- *Inform policies that intend to establish or improve safety nets for the poor.* What informal safety nets do the poor depend on? Which safety nets bring the poor the most benefit and which ones are the least relevant to them? Understanding informal safety nets brings to light new information that can be used to guide the design of effective safety nets.

The findings from the analysis are informative and lead to policy and operational changes that improve the impact of a project. The analysis reveals the population's concerns and problems; policy makers can use this information to immediately change and correct difficult situations faced by the target population. The beneficiary population in turn feels heard and is therefore inclined to trust and participate in program activities. The analysis also brings to light issues that were previously unknown by project managers and policy makers. New information can be used to investigate alternative designs and processes that were previously never considered and that better impact the lives of the target population.

When implementing a BA, it is important to consider the following factors:[16]

- Understand the context, including the sociocultural setting and institutional environment where the project is to take place.
- Set objectives that are feasible and realistic.
- Select institutions that are skilled neutrals to the project to ensure the credibility of the project. Select field researchers who are familiar with the culture, conversant in the language of the beneficiaries, sensitive to culture, respectful, unobtrusive, open and engaging, proficient at recalling interviews, skilled in writing, and good listeners.
- Prepare a Terms of Reference for the BA implementation.
- Develop interview guides that are open-ended and facilitate the elicitation of new information not previously considered by project

management. Three basic methods can be used to elicit the needs of the target population:

- Conversational interviews should use open-ended questions. Interviews should be one-to-one rather than conducted in groups if possible so individuals feel encouraged to speak freely.
- Focus group discussions should include 6 to 12 people with common characteristics unless the objective of the focus group is to elicit conflict between different stakeholders. Questions should be open-ended as well.
- Participant observation involves a field worker who spends three weeks to three months in the community of interest. The individual establishes enough involvement in the community to enable him or her to represent the conditions of the community.
- Determine a sample size large enough to provide an accurate understanding of the issues at hand. Do not limit interviews to the beneficiary group alone; key actors that have a stake in the issue should also be interviewed to provide a more comprehensive picture. For example, in a health project, health workers should be interviewed.
- Pretest the interview guide.
- Implement the assessment.
- Monitor and evaluate the assessment to determine if the BA is capturing the needs and priorities of the beneficiary population regarding the intervention.
- Write the report in a manner that allows project managers and policy makers to immediately integrate the information in the design, modification, or evaluation of the planned or ongoing intervention.

Annex 3.3 Recommendations for Further Reading

Selected from Goldman and others (forthcoming).

Boyle, M., Y. Racine, K. Georgiades, D. Snelling, S. Hong, W. Omariba, P. Hurley, and P. Rao-Melacini. 2006. "The Influence of Economic Development Level, Household Wealth and Maternal Education on Child Health in the Developing World." *Social Science and Medicine* **63 (8): 2242–54.**

A cross-sectional study estimating variations in child health (indicated by weight and height for age) relative to three variables—economic development (GDP in purchasing power parity terms), household wealth, and maternal education—found that national context had a strong modifying influence on the three estimates. Data from Demographic and Health Surveys conducted during 1984–2003 in 42 countries were used with information on mothers 15–49 years of age in 17,303 clusters (a cluster was defined as 20–25 rural, or 30–45 urban, households). A multilevel regression model was used to decompose unique versus shared variations in child health attributable to the three variables.

Filmer, D., and L. Pritchett. 2001. "Estimating Wealth Effects without Expenditure Data—Or Tears: An Application to Educational Enrollments in States of India." *Demography* **3 (8): 115–32.**
Information from India's National Family Health Survey (India's equivalent of the Demographic and Health Surveys) was used to generate an index (based on 21 asset indicators) that, in the absence of expenditure data, serves as a proxy for wealth. The index was in turn used to study the effect of wealth on children's school enrollment. The linear index was constructed with principal-components analysis (a simple technique for extracting from a set of variables orthogonal linear combinations of the variables that capture the common information most successfully). The survey data for 1992–93 covered 88,000 households (approximately 500,000 individuals) across India.

Fotso, J., and B. Kuate-Defo. 2005. "Measuring Socioeconomic Status in Health Research in Developing Countries: Should We Be Focusing on Households, Communities or Both?" *Social Indicators Research* **72 (2): 189–237.**
Examines and tests the various methodologies (household versus community level) used to calculate indexes of socioeconomic status in health-related research in developing countries. The authors rely on data from the Demographic and Health Surveys fielded in Burkina Faso, Cameroon, the Arab Republic of Egypt, Kenya, and Zimbabwe in the 1990s.

Gwatkin, D., A. Bhuiya, and C. Victora. 2004. "Making Health Systems More Equitable." *Lancet* **364 (9441): 1273–80.**
A cross-sectional analysis, using data from two studies, that demonstrates the continued relevance within and across countries of Tudor Hart's "inverse care law," in which the provision of medical care varies inversely with the needs of the poor. Successful cases are described in which the adaptation of targeted health programs, with poverty-relevant objectives, led to increases in coverage for the poor. Data from Filmer's 2003 study evaluating 21 developing or transitional countries are used to measure the role of government subsidies in bridging the gap in health care provision between the better-off and the poor.

Hadden, W., G. Pappas, and A. Khan. 2003. "Social Stratification, Development and Health in Pakistan: An Empirical Exploration of Relationships in Population-Based National Health Examination Survey Data." *Social Science and Medicine* 57 (10): 1863–74.
Regressions and Pearson correlations are used to investigate the relationship between individual socioeconomic status (gauged by education level and household ownership of consumer durables), an index of community social development (composed of data on education, the population structure, access to mass media, and economic diversity), and indicators of poor nutrition (low weight, anemia, dental caries, and monotonous diet). The study finds that low weight is related to economic status, anemia to education and social development, and both severe dental caries and a monotonous diet to both development and economic status, which interact with each other. The data for individuals are from the National Health Survey of Pakistan conducted from 1991 to 1994 and covering more than 6,000 adults.

Hoa, D., B. Höjer, and L. Persson. 1997. "Are There Social Inequities in Child Morbidity and Mortality in Rural Vietnam?" *Journal of Tropical Pediatrics* 43 (4): 226–31.
Investigates the relationship between various socioeconomic factors (poverty, education, occupation, maternal characteristics) and morbidity and mortality for children less than five years of age during a period of rapid social change in Vietnam. The study was a Vietnamese-Swedish collaborative effort and part of a household survey. Multistage cluster sampling was used on households with children in the subject age group, and five communes were randomly selected to represent different sources of income.

Lakshminarayanan, R. 2003. "Decentralisation and Its Implications for Reproductive Health: The Philippines Experience." *Reproductive Health Matters* 11 (21): 96–107.
In the 1990s, the Philippines transferred authority over the health system from the central government to local and intermediate governmental units. The paper examines the effects of the decentralization on the provision of reproductive health services and related health outcomes. The author's analysis of the Philippines' experience shows that decentralization does not always result in greater efficiency, equity, and effectiveness. Five years after the change, health outcomes in the Philippines were stagnant. Infant mortality hovered at 35 deaths per 1,000 live births, and immunization rates held at around 70 percent.

Laterveer, L., L. Niessen, and A. Yazbeck. 2003. "Pro-Poor Health Policies in Poverty Reduction Strategies." *Health Policy and Planning* 18 (2):138–45. Systematically assesses the extent to which the interim Poverty Reduction Strategy Papers (PRSPs) address the health issues of most pressing concern for the poor and vulnerable. Specifically, the authors review the interim PRSPs for (i) data on the distribution and composition of the burden of disease, (ii) evidence of policy proposals aimed at enhancing equity, (iii) information on health expenditures, (iv) evidence of pro-poor initiatives, and (v) other policies or data collection initiatives aimed at improving health outcomes for the poor.

Moser, K., D. Leon, and D. Gwatkin. 2005. "How Does Progress Towards the Child Mortality Millennium Development Goal Affect Inequalities between the Poorest and Least Poor? Analysis of Demographic and Health Survey Data." *BMJ* 331 (7526): 1180–82. Shows that progress toward the Millennium Development Goals (MDGs) for the mortality of children younger than five years of age (child mortality) can negatively affect equity. The MDG for child mortality is formulated as a national average, and the authors show that child mortality among the poorest populations deteriorates relative to that among the least poor as progress is made toward the child mortality MDG. The study compares 1991 and 2001 Demographic and Health Survey data from 22 low- and middle-income countries (in Africa, Latin America and the Caribbean, and Asia) that account for nearly 30 percent of the world's population.

Notes

1. These courses were "Achieving the MDGs: Reproductive Health, Poverty Reduction and Health Sector Reform" (a face-to-face course) and "Health Outcomes and the Poor" (a Web-based course).

2. The possible causes described here related only to the issue of inequality in the use of health services. The pathways framework can also be used to look at inequality in health outcomes, as was done in chapter 2 to understand why Safar Banu died.

3. A large segment of this section is adapted from a World Bank technical note (Technical Note 4C: Tools for Analyzing HNP Behaviors) written to support work on the Poverty Reduction Strategy Papers and a background document to Claeson and others (2003).

4. As noted in earlier chapters, most of the inequality data used in this book are recalculated from Demographic and Health Surveys that were not intended to measure inequality and did not include measures of household income or

consumption. These surveys did include asset questions that were used in Gwatkin and others (2007) and in other documents to construct quintiles of household wealth.

5. Two useful compendia of health service indicators exist, both of which present possible measures of availability. These are USAID (no date); and Knowles, Leighton, and Stinson (1997).

6. Annex 3.2 contains a brief discussion of beneficiary assessment as a tool for qualitative analysis of the needs of the poor.

7. This section is adapted from a World Bank technical note (Technical Note 4B: An Illustrative Example of Using Information about Clients to Better Manage Vaccine-Preventable Illness in Rural India), written to support work on the Poverty Reduction Strategy Papers and a background document to Claeson and others (2003).

8. This section is adapted from a World Bank technical note (Technical Note 4C: Tools for Analyzing HNP Behaviors) written to support work on the Poverty Reduction Strategy Papers and a background document to Claeson and others (2003).

9. O'Donnell and others (2007) provides detailed explanations of the use of regression analysis and other advanced statistical techniques (including computer programs) for analyzing inequality in the health sector.

10. This section is based on Soucat and others (2005) and on three other items from Agnes Soucat: (i) a World Bank technical note in support of the PRSP sourcebook [and a background paper to Claeson and others (2003)], (ii) a presentation by her on analyzing the health sector, and (iii) a module in the World Bank Institute's Web-based course "Health Outcomes and the Poor."

11. Chapter 1 includes a discussion of the use and interpretation of concentration curves.

12. This annex is based on O'Donnell and others (2007).

13. Other concerns of a technical nature can be found in chapter 2 of O'Donnell and others (2007).

14. For further information about the history of DHS, see http://www.measuredhs.com/aboutdhs/history.cfm. In 1997, the name was changed to *DHS+* to reflect the integration of DHS activities under the MEASURE program. Under this mandate, *DHS+* is charged with collecting and analyzing demographic and health data for regional and national family planning and health programs.

15. The World Fertility Surveys were a collection of internationally comparable surveys of human fertility conducted in 41 developing countries in the late 1970s and early 1980s. The project was conducted by the International Statistical Institute , with funding from USAID and the United Nations Population Fund.

16. For detailed guidance, refer to Salmen and Amelga (1998).

4

A Menu of Pro-Poor Policies

Over the years, many seemingly intuitive solutions to the problem of health care inequality have been implemented with only limited success. The lack of success may be attributed, in part, to the ideological and simplistic, rather than practical, nature of the solutions; but it is also a testament to the complex, situational nature of the problem and its many possible underlying causes.

In recent years, however, the literature has increasingly documented successful pilots and programs that provide a ray of hope and a growing arsenal of proven policy tools for attacking inequality. This chapter opens with a graphical summary of the successes experienced in many parts of the world in reducing inequality in the use of health services (some of which are summarized in the next 14 chapters). These cases reinforce the point that success can be achieved through programs developed with an empirical and exploratory spirit, crafted with input from the poor, responsive to specific local realities, and continually evaluated and adjusted to better achieve their goals. Yet if they are all locally determined, how can one glean from them lessons that might be applicable to a different place and time?

This chapter answers that question in three ways:

- First, it presents two conceptual schemes that provide more generally applicable strategies that seem to underlie the successes: (i) recurring themes and (ii) a framework of accountability. The accountability framework and how it relates to the findings from chapters 5–18 are in annex 4.1.

- Second, it organizes the most common successful policy actions into a matrix—a "menu" of pro-poor policies identified by their scope (macro, health system, or micro level) and by the five most common functions they address (finance, provider payment, organization, regulation, and persuasion).
- Third, from the menu, the chapter distills "rules of thumb" that suggest what may be the most productive avenues of attack in addressing inequality through the menu's five functions.

Again, however, there is no universal menu, only different lenses through which to view the various elements of the success stories.

Hope

In February 2004, the World Bank's Reaching the Poor Program (RPP) held a conference to present 36 examples of projects that evaluated the degrees of success or failure in redirecting health, nutrition, and population programs in lower-income countries to deliver more benefits to disadvantaged groups.[1] The context for the conference, and for RPP, was the increasing acceptance of the fact that, as summarized in chapter 1, health, nutrition, and population services in lower-income countries are much more likely to be directed to the better-off than to the poor.

At the end of the conference, panelist Cesar Victora presented a summary figure of the projects that captured the most important message of the meeting: despite the overwhelming evidence of inequality, health services can be made pro-poor (figure 4.1). For 28 of the 36 programs presented at the conference, figure 4.1 plots the share of benefits going to the poorest 20 percent in each country (horizontal axis) and the proportion of the poorest 20 percent receiving those benefits (vertical axis). And many, if not most, of the pro-poor programs were reaching at least half of the poorest 20 percent. Needless to say, those findings were extremely encouraging. The findings also demonstrated a need to better understand those islands of success.

Recurring Themes

The majority of the 14 examples of successful health sector programs summarized in chapters 5–18 are from the 2004 RPP conference. The examples were selected to highlight some of the main messages about what works and to serve as practical examples of a growing menu of pro-poor policy options. On the one hand, their diversity suggests that there is no one

Figure 4.1 Results from Studies Presented at RPP Conference

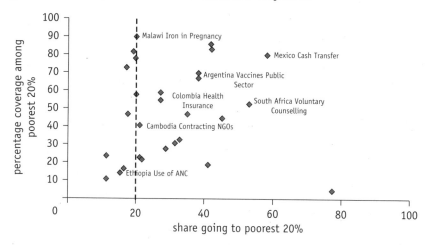

Source: Cesar Victora at the 2004 World Bank Reaching the Poor Program conference.

universal way to address inequality. Unique solutions were obtained variously from government intervention, public-private partnerships, improving the supply of services, community involvement, or changes in resource allocations.

On the other hand, the 14 cases also display some recurring themes regarding attitude and strategy. Here are five themes that one may discern from the examples of success (A.C.T.I.V.):

- *Analyzing the causes of inequality.* Analysis reveals the main factors that drive inequality in the use of services. Identifying the nature of the problem and prioritizing the main bottlenecks is the best way forward.

- *Customizing answers to address local constraints and capacities.* Just because a policy option works in one country does not automatically mean it will work in a different context. Successful programs take into account the specific local causes of inequality, the existing capacities of the health sector, and the cultural context influencing the poor and the health system.

- *Trying out new ways of doing business.* Systems fail for structural reasons that tend to be persistent and hard to change. Attacking inequality sometimes requires innovative thinking and the courage to attempt new ways of doing business.

- *Improving the results over time by learning from pilots and experimentation.* A by-product of the complex and persistent nature of poverty and inequality is the need for midcourse adjustments as new policies are implemented. Patience and a long-term view are required to modify the policy response as needed.
- *Verifying that the use of services by the poor is improving and that bottlenecks are being eliminated.* The road to hell is paved with good intentions. Merely starting a project to address inequality does not guarantee success—vigilance is critical.

A Menu of Pro-Poor Policies

The second answer to the question of how one can learn from the successes of seemingly idiosyncratic policy initiatives involves organizing them according to type. The policy instruments can be organized in a grid, or menu, according to two categories or typologies. The first typology ("vertical") categorizes policy actions according to their scope—the macro (overall policy and finance) level, the health system level, and the micro (community and facility) level (Claeson and others 2003). The second typology ("horizontal") categorizes actions according to a selection of five interrelated policy areas: finance, provider payment, organization, regulation, and persuasion (Roberts and others 2004). The policy instruments used in the success stories presented in the following chapters can then be mapped into the table formed by the vertical and horizontal typologies (table 4.1). Annex 4.1 provides an alternative way of presenting the menu of policy instruments. The accountability framework developed for the 2004 World Development Report (World Bank 2004) is used to show how each of the 14 cases covered in this book relates to one or more of the three basic accountability relationships between citizens, government, and health care providers.

Rules of Thumb

The third answer to the question of learning from "hand crafted" success stories involves judgment to extract intuitive basic principles. It is both difficult and dangerous to reduce a complex problem into such principles, or rules of thumb. However, some basic principles can be useful in helping decision makers wade through the many potential options for the reform of many health sector functions. The horizontal policy typology described above and used in table 4.1 can be used to organize six emerging rules of thumb for addressing inequality in the use of health services.

Table 4.1 A menu of Pro-Poor Policies

	Finance	Provider Payment	Organization	Regulation	Persuasion
Macro level (overall policy and finance)	Expand insurance coverage for the poor Geographic targeting (allocation) Needs-based targeting (allocation) Targeted conditional cash transfers (the cash part)		Integrated approaches (health, safety nets, education, roads, and so on)	Monitoring tools, PERs/BIA Poverty map creation and update	Charter of rights for the poor Targeted conditional cash transfers (the conditional part)
Health system level	Level of care targeting (allocation-input balance) Voucher systems for the poor	Contracting, incentives to serve the poor Equity-related performance-based allocation Hardship payments for locating providers	Pro-poor benefits package Balanced human resources allocation	Standards for facilities serving the poor Input market regulation (drugs, equipment, and the like)	Social marketing Health education focus Strengthening outreach Prioritizing demand generation
Micro level (community and facility)	Exemption policies for the poor Facility equity funds	Provider payment linked to use by poor Community-based mechanisms for identifying the poor	Local or community management of services Participatory planning Campaign mode delivery Mobile delivery approaches	Local or community oversight Supervision of facilities serving the poor Active identification of the poor	Community mobilization Health education campaigns

Source: Author.

Note: BIA = beneficiary incidence analysis; PER = Public Expenditure Review.

Finance Reforms—Both Resource Mobilization and Allocation

1. *Delink payment by the poor from use.* The main objective driving resource mobilization policy choices is the need to secure resources for the health sector. The choices made, however, can have unintended consequences for equity, efficiency, and quality of care. In a number of evaluated reforms, policy actions decreased inequality if they minimized or eliminated the financial disincentives for poor households to seek care. Examples include the expansion of health insurance coverage to the poor (Colombia, Mexico, Rwanda) and fee exemption mechanisms for cost recovery (Cambodia health equity funds, Indonesia health card program).

2. *Make the money follow the poor.* The number and size of fixed facilities, mainly hospitals, is the single most important driver of resource allocation in the health sector. Hospital services tend to be overwhelmingly pro-wealthy in most low- and middle-income countries. Some of the successful reforms reviewed included policy actions that reoriented resource allocation mechanisms to serve the poor. Examples include geographic targeting (Brazil), targeted conditional cash transfers (Chile, Mexico), vouchers, and targeting facility levels that serve the poor (the Kyrgyz Republic).

Provider Payment Reforms

3. *Link provider payment to use by the poor.* Facility managers and service providers respond to incentives, particularly financial incentives. There is overwhelming evidence that different provider payment mechanisms influence the types of services that are provided and the population served. The growing literature on the impact of reforms shows that creating explicit links between provider compensation and service use by the poor decreases inequality. Examples include incentives to municipalities increasing use by the poor (Brazil), incentives to contracted nongovernmental organizations (NGOs) that reach the poor (Cambodia contracting), and payment to hospitals serving the poor (Cambodia health equity fund).

Organizational Reforms

4. *Close the distance between the poor and services.* Organizational reforms cover a wide variety of actions, such as decentralization, service

delivery mechanisms, and service prioritization. The case studies confirmed that reforms that brought services geographically closer to the poor had a positive impact on inequality. One way to define the distance between services and the poor is the types of services offered. A number of programs defined a benefits package to serve the needs of the poor (Brazil, Cambodia contracting, Colombia, Mexico, Nepal, Rwanda). Social distance between providers and the poor is also an important factor. Effective methods to close the social distance in health services include use of familiar and trusted community members to provide health services (India Self-Employed Women's Association), engagement of the community in service management (Rwanda), and collaboration with the community in program design.

Regulatory Reforms

5. *Amplify the voice of the poor.* The poor and socially vulnerable suffer from a number of deficits when compared with the better-off. Two deficits that play critical roles in health service inequality are political voice and market power. Limited political voice weakens the *long route* of accountability while limited market power weakens the *short route*. A number of the evaluated policies successfully reduced inequality by engaging the poor in the design and implementation of health sector reforms. Examples include participatory planning (Nepal), community oversight (Rwanda), community identification of the poor (Cambodia health equity fund), research on the needs and preferences of the poor (Tanzania), household-level planning (Chile), and community mobilization (Kenya).

Persuasion Reforms—Behavior Change

6. *Close the gap between need and demand by the poor.* The pathways framework described in chapter 2 is based on the premise that households are the main producers of health. A critical element of this household production process is the consumption (use) of effective health services. The fact that health services are necessary does not automatically translate to demand. Rules of thumb 1 and 4 address a persistent gap between demand for services and the use of these services by the poor. That is, the poor may demand the services but there

are barriers to use (financial, geographic, and so on). Research findings increasingly point to a second "gap" between the needs of the poor and their demand for health services. Closing the need-to-demand gap may require information, persuasion, and incentives. Examples include conditional cash transfers (Chile and Mexico), social marketing (Tanzania), and outreach health education (Brazil, Cambodia, Chile, and Kenya).

Annex 4.1 Accountability Framework

At the same time that the RPP was financing and disseminating evaluations of policies that reduced inequality, the World Bank, in the 2004 edition of its *World Development Report*, was tapping available global knowledge to create a "basic accountability framework," a tool that would guide the development of policies to make services pro-poor (World Bank 2004).

The accountability framework is not a blueprint for specific policies. Rather, it portrays the basic relationships between the three essential groups in the service system—the public, the state (as the source of laws and policy), and service providers (figure A4.1). In doing so, it encourages thinking of services as embedded in those relationships and thus encourages thinking about which relationship holds the most promise for attacking any given service problem.

The framework portrays two layers of relationship: (i) the bilateral accountability relationships between the three entities and (ii) routes by which the public exercises influence over providers—the long route via the state and the short route via the public's bilateral relationship with providers.

Figure A4.1 *Service Delivery Accountability Framework*

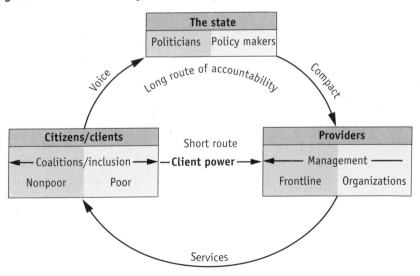

Source: World Bank 2004.

The three entities and their bilateral relationships are described in the following:

The Public (Citizens/Clients)   Members of the public have dual roles—as citizens and as clients of the service providers. As citizens, they participate individually in the political process or as part of a coalition (community, political parties, trade unions, business associations, and so on). As clients (in the case of the health sector), they hope to protect their health and the health of their families by demanding and receiving health services.

The State   The state uses its powers to regulate, legislate, and tax. Political circumstances vary greatly by country, from democratic governance to one-party control, from executive politicians in dominance to legislative rule. Policy makers also exercise the power of the state. In some countries, politicians and policy makers are one. In some, they are separate.

Providers   Service providers can be public organizations, such as ministries or departments of health, or private nonprofit or for-profit organizations. In a given area, the same service may be offered simultaneously by all these types of organizations and by several providers of one type. When the provider is in the public sector, one needs to be clear about the distinction between the policy maker and the head of the provider organization. The former sets and enforces rules of the game for all providers; the latter makes internal "policy" specific to the organization. Frontline providers are the service providers in direct contact with clients.

Ideally, the actors are linked through three relationships:

- As citizens, the public exercises *voice* over the state.
- The state has a *compact* with organizational providers.
- As clients, the public exercises *client power* over providers through interactions with frontline providers.

The two routes of accountability follow:

The Short Route   The short route is the basic market interaction; a consumer demands and the producer supplies the good or service. The markets for shoes, vegetables, or other competitive market transactions entail a clear system of accountability between the customer and the provider. Customers pay for the product or service. If customers are not satisfied, they can go elsewhere or seek legal recourse. For the most part, the short route has the customer—or client—exerting *client power* over the provider (holding the provider accountable) through payment.

In the health sector, the short route of accountability can fail the poor in two ways. First, the poor, by definition, have limited resources and hence less power over providers. Second, the health sector has considerable asymmetries of information and conflicts of interest. A variety of market failures—such as disease-related externalities and fragmented insurance markets—and concerns for equity often justify public intervention in financing health and nutrition services and a role for government.

The Long Route   The long route of public accountability, from poor clients to policy makers, then from policy makers to providers, is sometimes attempted when the short route fails to work. The client influences the policy maker (politician or bureaucrat) through *voice*, and the policy maker in turn exerts power, through the *compact* relationship, over the provider. The long route for services often breaks down in the health sector (and in other service sectors); in those cases, the two accountability relationships, voice and compact, need to be strengthened.

Successful policies for attacking inequality in the use of health services have to influence the accountability relationships between the three groups. The World Bank's 2004 *World Development Report* describes the client power, voice, and compact relationships in considerable detail and provides a number of examples of applicability to the health sector. The remainder of this annex links the main policy instruments described in chapters 5–18 to the accountability framework. The evidence from the 14 cases highlighted in this book and the published literature underscores the usefulness of thinking about the three main actors and the accountability relationships among them. The evidence also shows that successful programs did not try to address all the possible ways the accountability relationships can be influenced but used different combinations to address the barriers faced by the poor in the country of focus.

Choice: Increase Purchasing Power (Short Route)

Cambodia's health equity fund provides market power to the poorest by contracting with independent NGOs to manage a donor-financed fund that pays hospitals every time they provide a service to the poor. Poor households, especially those detected through active identification (before they seek care), have considerably more market power to seek care because they know it is in the provider's best interest to treat them.

Chile, Colombia, and Mexico (Seguro Popular) expanded health insurance for the poor, which increased the number of poor households with purchasing power in the health market. In all three countries, the health insurance umbrella is being expanded to cover an increasing percentage of the poor, giving them access to a benefits package and translating their use into payments to the providers.

Indonesia's health card program empowers the poor by giving access to health services for free (eliminating the cost-recovery component). While use is not directly linked to provider payments, there is a link between supplementary budgets received by providers and the percentage of the population that received health cards in their region.

Rwanda's community-based micro health insurance built a community purchaser function on behalf of the poor as well as expanded insurance coverage for the poor.

Tanzania's social marketing of treated bed nets lowered the cost of buying the bed nets by targeting subsidies to children and pregnant women.

Mexico (PROGRESA/Oportunidades) and Chile are going beyond simply lowering the financial barrier to seeking health care by using their conditional cash transfer programs to create incentives for poor families to use health care services.

Choice: Increase Coproduction (Short Route)

Brazil's family health program includes a strong outreach approach that highlights health education. Through health education, the program empowers poor households as the main producers of good health through both self-care and better choices.

Chile's Solidario program includes a component that works with individual households to create a development plan that, in part, strengthens the role of the household as a producer of good health.

India's SEWA health services program is mainly a community-driven service delivery program that closed the gap between the providers and the population served.

Kenya's immunization campaign included a considerable community mobilization effort, which strengthened the role of the poor community in the production of health and increased the likelihood of seeking services.

Rwanda's community-based micro health insurance program strengthened the role of the community as a coproducer of health services while lowering the financial barriers to care and strengthening financial protection.

Increase Leverage (Short Route)

Brazil's family health program uses outreach approaches to strengthen the leverage of poor clients through information.

Cambodia's health equity fund uses the outreach component of active identification of the poor to disseminate information about service availability and financial support.

Chile's Solidario program includes a demand component that highlights information and provides tools to translate information into demand for services. The development of household plans for each poor household has also been effective in strengthening participation.

Kenya's immunization campaign relies heavily on community structures and organization through sensitization to deliver information to the poor.

Nepal's participatory planning experiment focuses entirely on engaging the poor and vulnerable in the design of a health services package that includes clear delivery mechanisms.

Rwanda's community-based insurance program includes, in the governance structure, a role for the community in monitoring the implementation of the schemes.

Tanzania's social marketing of preventive services (bed nets) uses commercial marketing techniques, including information dissemination and demand creation, to ensure that critical information about the products reaches the poor to motivate their engagement and use.

The Long Route

Brazil's family health program made reaching the poor an explicit objective of the redesign of the service delivery approach. The program then developed outreach and health education components specifically for the poor. Moreover, the program targeted the poorest areas first in the phased implementation. To ensure that incentives drove the pro-poor objectives, the program included financial incentives for municipalities if they showed pro-poor use.

Cambodia's contracting with NGOs for delivery or management created incentives and an environment that increased the likelihood that the poor would be reached with services. The separation between policy/finance and delivery through contracting was part of the compact change but was also strengthened through incentives for NGOs to serve the poor. Information systems were created (before and during household surveys) to monitor pro-poor use. Another important component was the development of a pro-poor benefits package.

Cambodia's health equity funds mainly targeted strengthening the short route of accountability but also changed the incentives for hospitals to encourage use by the poor. Incentives were changed by creating a payment mechanism that linked the use of the hospital services by the poor to facility payment.

Chile's Solidario program also tackled many of the dimensions of the accountability framework through the short and long routes. A critical piece of the program was an aggressive outreach strategy that worked with households to improve access to existing but underutilized health services and to enroll them in health insurance.

Colombia's expansion of health insurance to the poor included several compact-strengthening actions, including using proxy-means testing for identifying the poor and improving targeting, subsidizing the premiums for the poor once identified (improved allocation), creation of a cross-subsidization function from the formal to the informal sector, and separating financing from provision through contracting.

Indonesia's health card program complemented the decrease of financial barriers by removing fees for card carriers and increasing resource allocation to facilities serving regions with large populations of health card holders.

The Kyrgyz Republic's health finance reform included several critical compact actions to improve efficiency and equality in the health sector. The reform strengthened pooling of resources, which, in turn, allowed for effective separation of financing and provision. Other actions included the use of new provider payment methods, redefinition of a benefits package, and the rationalization of facility-based care to strengthen lower-level facilities.

Annex 4.2 Recommendations for Further Reading

Selected from Goldman and others (forthcoming).

De Allegri, M., B. Kouyaté, H. Becher, A. Gbangou, S. Pokhrel, M. Sanon, and R. Sauerborn. 2006. "Understanding Enrolment in Community

Health Insurance in Sub-Saharan Africa: A Population-Based Case-Control Study in Rural Burkina Faso." *Bulletin of the World Health Organization* 84 (11): 852–58.

Seeks to identify the household and community factors that influence the decision to enroll in Burkina Faso's community health insurance (CHI) programs. CHI programs are an alternative to user fees and work by pooling risks and resources at the community level. The authors found a connection between existing inequalities and decisions to participate in CHI. To encourage participation in CHI, the authors recommend social marketing initiatives aimed at transforming attitudes about risk sharing.

Gakidou, E., S. Oza, C. Vidal Fuertes, A. Li, D. Lee, A. Sousa, M. Hogan, S. Vander Hoorn, and M. Ezzati. 2007. "Improving Child Survival through Environmental and Nutritional Interventions: The Importance of Targeting Interventions toward the Poor." *JAMA* 298 (16): 1876–87.

Investigates the extent to which interventions related to the UN Millennium Development Goals (MDGs) for nutrition and the environment (improving child nutrition and providing clean water, sanitation, and fuels) would advance the MDG of reducing the mortality of children younger than five years of age. The analysis covered Latin America and the Caribbean, South Asia, and Sub-Saharan Africa; the data came from the Demographic and Health Surveys of 42 countries in those regions, from the World Health Organization, and from epidemiology studies. The authors found that interventions that eliminate all risk of ill health from the nutrition and environmental factors for all children would bring the subject regions 30 percent to almost 50 percent closer to their MDG for child mortality. If half the risk reduction was achieved and applied to the poorest first, the mortality improvement would be more than 50 percent of the improvement under the full-risk-reduction scenario; and applying half the risk reduction to the poor first would produce a greater improvement in mortality than if applied to the wealthiest first.

Masanja, H., J. Schellenberg, D. de Savigny, H. Mshinda, and C. Victora. 2005. "Impact of Integrated Management of Childhood Illness on Inequalities in Child Health in Rural Tanzania." *Health and Policy Planning* 20 (S1): S77–S82.

The Multi-Country Evaluation of the Integrated Management of Childhood Illness (IMCI) strategy is an initiative designed to codify the prevention and treatment techniques of the most common childhood illnesses into simple guidelines for first-level health facilities and communities. Using concentration indexes and data on child health outcomes, the study focuses on IMCI's effect on the equity of health outcomes in rural areas of Tanzania between 1999 and 2002; to do so, it compares two districts with IMCI (Morogoro Rural and Rufiji) with two without (Kilombero and Ulanga).

Wagstaff, A., F. Bustreo, J. Bryce, and M. Claeson. 2004. "Child Health: Reaching the Poor." *American Journal of Public Health* **94 (5): 726–36.**
A review of the current literature that explores the inequalities in proximate determinants of child health outcomes, such as nutrition, and the underlying determinants, such as maternal nutrition status. The authors also aim to identify where programs to reduce inequality might be most effective.

Note

1. The RPP is a research project financed by the World Bank, the Bill and Melinda Gates Foundation, and the governments of the Netherlands and Sweden.

5

Brazil, Filling the Cracks in Universal Coverage

Brazil is among the 12 countries in the world with the greatest income inequality. Inequality in health outcomes has been recognized as a leading health problem in the Americas. Brazil has undertaken a number of health initiatives geared toward improving access to care among the poorest members of society, including universal primary health care programs. Universal health care programs are typically created with the objective of improving access to care for the poor and addressing persistent inequalities. In addition to the universal health care programs, Brazil has implemented specific health programs to target the poor; programs that provide cash incentives or rewards to municipalities that provide care to the poorest families; and cash incentives to the poorest families of municipalities for the proper use of available health and education public services.

Challenges

The following examples illustrate the challenges that Brazil is facing in its struggle to improve access to health care for the poorest members of its population.

The National Immunization Program

Brazil's National Immunization Program, established in 1973, is a universal program intended to eradicate vaccine-preventable diseases, for example, polio, measles, tuberculosis, diphtheria, pertussis, and tetanus. Services were delivered through the primary care preventive services at health facilities. To amplify program penetration, national immunization campaigns were carried out to increase awareness of the importance of vaccines in preventing diseases. In addition, availability of services was also enhanced through expanding delivery sites to include places where the poor usually visit or congregate, such as supermarkets, malls, and community centers.

Results of Brazil's immunization efforts showed that while there were significant increases in vaccine coverage during 1994–2000, the prevalence of incomplete immunization had its highest concentration in children living in households in the poorest 20 percent (or lowest quintile) of the population. In Sergipe, a city in Northeastern Brazil, a study conducted in 2000 found that children living in the poorest 20 percent of households received the least benefit from the services provided, as opposed to children in the wealthiest 20 percent of households, reflecting inequality in coverage. Table 5.1 illustrates the consistency in inequality for the poorest households with national data from 1996 and the Sergipe study.

The National Antenatal Care Program

The long-established National Antenatal Care Program also comes up short with respect to reaching the poorest women in Brazil. National use of antenatal care services is high, with more than 90 percent of women having at least one checkup and, on average, the number of consultations per person is

Table 5.1 *Prevalence of Incomplete Immunization among Children 12 Months and Older, by Wealth Quintiles, and Concentration Indexes (percent)*

Wealth quintiles	DHS (1996) $n = 3,827$	Sergipe (2000) $n = 1,436$
1 (poorest)	33.4	28.0
2	16.4	20.4
3	14.2	20.6
4	11.9	15.5
5	15.3	17.8
All	19.3	20.5
	$p < 0.001$	$p = 0.176$
	$CI = -21.8$	$CI = -10.8$

Sources: Data from BEMFAM (the Brazilian Family Well-Being Society) and DHS for Brazil 1996.
Note: DHS = Demographic and Health Survey; CI = concentration index.

Table 5.2 *Proportion of Mothers Receiving Inadequate Antenatal Care, by Wealth Quintiles, and Concentration Indexes*

Wealth quintiles	DHS (1996)	Sergipe (2000)
1 (poorest)	70.0	49.1
2	43.5	48.3
3	27.4	35.3
4	19.1	30.2
5	13.6	18.7
All	38.4	35.7
	$p < 0.001$	$p < 0.001$
	CI = −31.7	CI = −18.3

Sources: Data from BEMFAM (the Brazilian Family Well-Being Society) and DHS for Brazil 1996.
Note: DHS = Demographic and Health Survey; CI = concentration index.

more than six. While the overall coverage of the antenatal care program is good, mothers living in households of the least poor seemed to have benefited more from the services provided, reflecting inequality in coverage. The greatest concentration of women receiving inadequate antenatal care was from families in the poorest quintile, reflecting an inadequate pro-poor focus (table 5.2). Both the pro-poor focus and the level of coverage of the antenatal care program were found to be less than that of the immunization program.

Despite achieving major improvements in the nation's ability to address the issues associated with incomplete immunization and inadequate antenatal care, inequality persisted. The families in the poorest 20 percent of the population were consistently among those who did not receive services at all or the services received were incomplete or inadequate in comparison with families in higher income groups.

The Pastorate of the Child

The Pastorate of the Child is an example of a nongovernmental initiative targeted specifically to the poorest children. Launched in 1983 by the Catholic Church, this program is built on volunteer leaders, mainly women, recruited from the local community who give one day a month, delivering information and advice on maternal and child health care, including immunization. The Pastorate of the Child targets undernourished children and children from the poorest families. Despite its mission, research has demonstrated that this program had poor coverage overall and the greatest concentration of children benefiting were not from the poorest households, nor were they children who were the most undernourished. This program operated outside the existing public primary care system, was built on a foundation of volunteerism, and selected volunteer leaders from within the communities being served. This approach puts communities with the least developed organizational capacity and infrastructure, usually poorer communities, at a disadvantage with respect to benefiting from the service offered.

The experience of Brazil described here suggests that achieving equality in health outcomes requires complementing universal coverage with other strategies geared toward improving use of available services by the poor.

Policy Change: Supplementing Universal Health Coverage

Against this background, in 1994 the government of Brazil created the Family Health Program (PSF, or Programa de Saúde da Família) in an effort to reorganize primary care services and improve service to the poor. The principal objectives of PSF were to reach out to the universal population, particularly the poor. Two pro-poor features of the program follow:

- *Location of phased expansion.* As the program was implemented, it focused first on the poorest areas, as well as on those that had never before received primary care service.
- *Outreach.* PSF services were provided by health teams, each tasked with overseeing the health of selected households and families. Unlike traditional caregiving, in which the patient or family visits health facilities seeking services for specific problems, the teams reached out to their clients through home visits and community activities.

The teams were constructed to facilitate identification of the factors that represent possible threats to health in the community. Interventions were designed to address these threats as well as to educate community members about how these health threats can be prevented. Team staff included a general practitioner, a registered nurse, a nurse assistant, and four community health workers. A monetary reward was offered to municipalities, through the Ministry of Health, based on their ability to maintain 70 percent coverage of the population.

The PSF was implemented in phases across Brazil and in 1996 national coverage was estimated to be between 49.8 percent in the Northeast region and 26 percent in the Southeast region. In Porto Alegre in 2003, where the PSF had been newly implemented, the proportion of its facilities located in areas with families living in households from the poorest quintile was highest, with minimal representation from households in the top income quintile (figure 5.1). In the Sergipe program, in existence since 1996, the highest

Figure 5.1 *Distribution of Wealth Status for Residents of Areas Covered by the Family Health Program (PSF)*

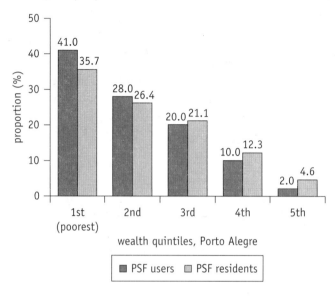

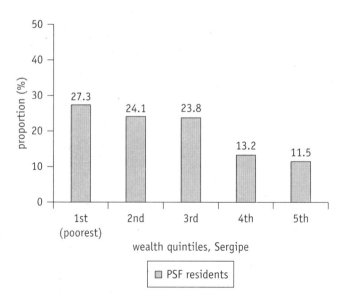

Source: Newmann and others 1999.

concentration of families was from the poorest quintile, although participation by families from the wealthiest income quintile was also considerably higher than in Porto Alegre.

While the program in both cities had a pro-poor focus, the pro-poor focus of the Porto Alegre program was stronger. The poorest households in Porto Alegre were nine times more likely to benefit from the program than the least poor. In Sergipe, the benefit ratio in favor of the poorest quintile was only 2.5. The differences are likely due to the different stages of implementation of the program at the two sites. At the beginning, coverage is low and the pro-poor focus is high, as observed in Porto Alegre. Later on, with increased overall coverage, the pro-poor focus decreases, but coverage is still higher among the poor.

Findings

Often, universal programs intend to make services available to all but do not necessarily achieve that goal. Brazil's universal programs for immunization and antenatal care highlight the fact that reaching the poor requires specific pro-poor actions to improve access by the poor and vulnerable. The PSF provides an excellent example of how to improve access by improving targeting of universal programs. Compared with the evaluated immunization and antenatal government programs and the targeted Pastorate of the Child program, PSF reaches the poor at a higher rate. The evaluation of the PSF suggests that maintaining focus on the poor, increasing awareness through individual and community educational efforts, and increasing service outreach through home visits and well-placed service sites, can produce greater participation by the poor in the health system. Future studies geared toward identifying factors that drive the various patterns of usage may provide some insight into these issues and help to foster the development of even better approaches to improving service use in the poorest sector of the population.

Note

This chapter was adapted from Barros and others (2005).

6

Cambodia: Contracting with Nongovernmental Organizations to Serve the Poor

Years of war and political turmoil exacted a heavy toll on Cambodia's health care infrastructure, particularly in the rural areas of the country. By the mid-1990s, it was clear that the primary health care system could not deliver adequate services. The number of paramedical and management personnel seemed sufficient, but their training was inconsistent and morale was low. At this time, only 4 out of 10 children between 12 and 24 months of age were fully immunized.

Policy Change: Contracting with NGOs

To address the inadequacies in its health care system, the Cambodian government obtained a loan from the Asian Development Bank. The primary health care system was reorganized and broadened. Small administrative districts were merged into larger, more viable units. Health care centers were built and old ones renovated, and each served 10,000 people. The centers delivered a newly defined package of preventive and curative services, including immunization, birth spacing, antenatal care, micronutrition, and simple treatments for diarrhea, acute respiratory tract infections, and tuberculosis. Contracting with international nongovernmental organizations (NGOs) to deliver these primary services was part of the implementation plan. This pilot was the largest of its kind with baseline, midstream, and end-of-project studies.

To make the pilot districts as comparable as possible, districts that were already receiving extra help with health care were excluded as candidate districts. The Ministry of Health (MOH) awarded contracts to NGOs in five districts. For comparison, four districts where the government provided health services were included in the trial, which started at the beginning of 1999.

The districts were then assigned to one of three health care delivery models:

- *Contracting out.* The contractors were given full line responsibility for service delivery, as well as for hiring, firing, and setting wages; procuring and distributing essential drugs and supplies; and organizing and staffing health facilities.
- *Contracting in.* The contractors worked within the MOH system to strengthen the existing administrative structure. They could not hire or fire health workers, although they could request that they be transferred. Drugs and supplies came through normal MOH channels. The contractors also received a nominal budget supplement for staff incentives and operating expenses.
- *Government provision.* The government district health management team (DHMT) continued to manage the services. Drugs and supplies came through normal MOH channels, and the DHMT also received a budget supplement for staff incentives and operating expenses.

The contractors, selected through international bidding, were awarded four-year contracts at a fixed annual price per capita for delivering specific primary health care services. All the winning bidders were international NGOs with previous experience in Cambodia.

Contracted-out districts had to purchase their own supplies and pay labor costs. These items were included in the MOH budget for contracted-in and government districts. In all nine test districts, construction, renovation, furniture, and equipment were provided by the MOH and not counted against the contract budgets.

Table 6.1 shows the average annual recurrent expenditure per capita over the two-and-a-half-year period for the three different arrangements. The higher expenditure for contracted-out districts is largely attributable to higher staff salaries.

Table 6.1 *Average Annual Recurrent Expenditure per Capita (US$)*

Expenditure category	Contracted out	Contracted in	Government provision
NGO technical assistance	1.28	0.77	0
Staff salaries[a]	1.32	0.55	0.53
Drugs, supplies, and operating expenses[b]	1.28	1.08	1.12
Total	3.88	2.40	1.65

Source: Schwartz and Bhushan 2005, table 8.2.
a. Salaries, bonuses, and other allowances.
b. Drugs, medical supplies, travel, fuel, per diem, office supplies, communications, building and vehicle maintenance and repairs.

District managers had different budget constraints, different baseline values for coverage and distribution of services, and possible differences in population demographics, all of which may have influenced resource allocation decisions. The study methodology controlled for these and other related factors to isolate the effect of contracting on distribution of services to the poor.

Findings

The research questions addressed were the following:

- Were primary health care services equally distributed before and after the contracting test? Which type of district made the largest gains in reaching the poor?
- What factors other than wealth are related to equitable distribution of primary health care services? Did the poor receive more health care services than the better-off in contracted or in government districts?

Answers were obtained through household surveys, comparison of test and control groups, and measurement of results through objectively verifiable indicators.

Household Surveys

Before the centers were built and equipment purchased, the government conducted a precontract baseline household survey in candidate rural districts in May–June, 1997. A follow-up household survey was conducted in June–August, 2001, two-and-a-half years after the contractors had started work.

In addition to information on child immunization, antenatal care, and birth providers, data were collected from all sampled households on socio-economic and demographic characteristics, as well as on the use of curative health care services by all household residents. The average household size in both surveys was between five and six individuals. In all, more than 20,000 individuals were included in each household survey. The information gathered constitutes a unique data set for comparing the distributional equity of primary health care services provided by contractors and by the government.

Using data from the baseline survey, health service indicators were measured for each district, and goals were set for improving service coverage. The equity goal of targeting services to the poorest half of the population was mandated for all districts.

Health Care Indicators

The indicators used to gauge service coverage are consistent with the priorities set in the United Nations Millennium Development Goals (MDGs) and in World Bank Poverty Reduction Strategy Papers. They target preventive child and maternal health care (table 6.2).

Contracted districts outperformed the government districts in changing the distribution of health care services from favoring the nonpoor at the outset to achieving a more equitable or pro-poor distribution.

At the 1997 baseline, distribution of services in all nine districts was found to be inequitable, largely to the disadvantage of the poor. Only one indicator, the use of public facilities for illness, in one district, distinctly favored the poor. Immunization, use of a trained birth practitioner, and use and knowledge of modern birth spacing were the other indicators that favored the poor before contracting. In the two districts selected for contracting out, five of the eight indicators showed the greatest inequality of the nine districts.

By 2001, the distribution of health care services seemed to have shifted toward a more equitable distribution, less favorable to the better-off across the nine districts, but with few exceptions, the distribution was not pro-poor. In all of the contracted-out and contracted-in districts, distributional equity improved. Three of the four government districts, however, still

Table 6.2 Health Service Indicators: Definitions and Coverage Goals

Indicator	Definition	Coverage goal (percent)
Fully immunized child (FIC)	Children ages 12–23 months fully immunized.	70
Vitamin A (VITA)	High-dose vitamin A received twice in the past 12 months by children ages 6–59 months.	70
Antenatal care (ANC)	At least two antenatal care visits, with blood pressure measurement at least once, for women who gave birth in the previous year.	50
Delivery by trained professional (TDEL)	Birth attendant was a qualified nurse, midwife, doctor, or medical assistant for women with a delivery in the past year.	50
Delivery in a health facility (FDEL)	Birth was in a private or public health facility for women with a delivery in the past year.	10
Use of modern birth-spacing method (MBS)	Women with a live child ages 6–23 months currently using a modern method of birth spacing.	30
Knowledge of modern birth spacing (KBS)	Women who gave birth in the previous 24 months and know four or more modern birth-spacing methods and where to obtain them.	70
Use of public health care facilities (USE)	Use of district public health care facilities (district hospital or primary health care center) for illness in the previous four weeks.	Increase[a]

Source: Schwartz and Bhushan 2005, table 8.4.
a. Percentage goal not specified.

favored the better-off in all health care services, and the trend had accelerated from baseline to 2001.

By 2003, contracted districts generally outperformed government districts, with concentration indexes showing a more equitable or pro-poor distribution of health care services (figure 6.1). There was a change toward a more pro-poor distribution in contracted districts for health services with only two exceptions (vitamin A for contract-out and delivery in a health facility for contract-in). Government districts, however, changed toward a more pro-poor distribution only for vertical programs (immunization, vitamin A, and modern birth spacing), and these changes were smaller than

Figure 6.1 *Changes in Concentration Indexes, 1997–2003*

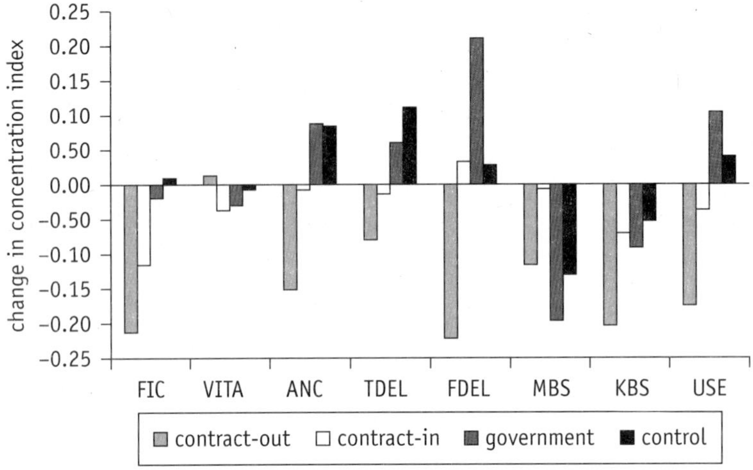

Source: Schwartz and Bhushan 2005.
Note: Negative values indicate a change toward a pro-poor distribution of services. FIC = fully immunized children; VITA = vitamin A; ANC = antenatal care; TDEL = trained birth attendant; FDEL = delivery in a health facility; MBS = modern birth spacing; KBS = knowledge of modern birth spacing; USE = use of health facility for illness.

the improvements made by the contracted districts. Government districts moved toward an even less pro-poor distribution for facility-based services, including antenatal care, trained birth delivery, birth in a facility, and use of public facilities for illness.

The contracting study is limited by its inability to detect differences in motivations, resource allocation decisions, incentives, and district managers' service delivery and monitoring methods. These shortcomings may have contributed to the observed differences in distribution of services in the contracted districts compared with the government districts.

Without further research, only speculation is possible about the reasons for the varied outcomes. The NGO managers may have been better trained than their local counterparts in management, implementation, supervision, and monitoring methods for targeting the poor. NGO district managers may have expected future personal rewards if they achieved all the goals set for them. This was the first large-scale contracting experience for the NGOs, and proven managers may have been assigned to Cambodia to increase the chances of success and follow-on contracts. Questions such as these need further investigation, particularly in other large-scale contracting projects.

In conclusion, Cambodia's experience with reaching the poor through contracting services is hard to generalize to other countries. The dearth of physical infrastructure and the large number of entrenched government health care workers in rural areas at the start of the contracting test were conducive to innovative approaches such as rational redelineation of operational districts and testing of new service delivery methods to rebuild the primary health care system. Circumstances are similar in densely populated urban areas in the four largest cities in Bangladesh and the rural areas of Afghanistan and Pakistan. The results of large-scale contracting projects in those countries might shed light on whether Cambodia's experience offers an effective model for other developing countries.

Note

This chapter was adapted Schwartz and Bhushan (2005).

7

Cambodia: Health Equity Fund for the Poor

In the late 1980s, on the advice of leading international agencies, developing country health ministries increasingly began to introduce user fees in their facilities as a way of helping deal with their dire financial situations. On paper, the ministry plans usually included a provision for exempting the poor, and sometimes these provisions were effective. But often, they were not. Implementation frequently consisted of little more than the distribution of circulars to facilities. Front-line providers tended to ignore or interpret these circulars very narrowly, especially when a significant portion of user fee revenue was retained at facilities and represented a badly needed source of health worker income. In such settings, few exemptions were granted, leaving poor people to bear the brunt of user fees along with everybody else.

The most obvious solution to this problem—to reimburse service providers for the income they lost in attending to poor clients—suffered from equally obvious difficulties. One was cost. As noted, governments had been attracted to user fees in large part because of their potential for revenue generation, but to the extent that fee income remained at the facility level, the resources of central health ministries remained the same. Few ministries felt they could afford the additional expense of reimbursing facilities for the income they had forgone in granting exemptions. Logistical challenges were an equally important factor. Even if ministries had been willing to bear the cost, most would have faced formidable challenges in developing systems to verify the accuracy and honesty of facility reimbursement claims, and to transfer funds promptly to the facilities concerned.

Cambodia was one of many countries confronted with this problem. Its health system had been virtually destroyed during the Khmer Rouge regime of the 1970s and the civil war that followed. Reconstruction had proven difficult, with the ministry unable to provide adequate and reliably steady financial support to its outlying facilities. Thus, user fees were introduced in 1997. To supplement salaries and help cover operational expenses, facility staff retained most of the revenue. The Cambodian government had issued a decree exempting the poor, but few exemptions had been issued. The resulting cost to the poor had become a major concern.

Policy Change: The Health Equity Fund

In response, some of the many external nongovernmental organizations (NGOs) active in Cambodia began experimenting with alternative approaches to health financing in the areas in which they were working. Among the approaches emerging from this experimentation was a "health equity fund" (HEF), a fund operating independently of the health system, whose staff identified people in particular need of financial assistance for health services, especially hospital care, and paid health service providers for the services provided to the needy.

By late 2006, there were 26 HEFs in operation. Each of the 26 projects is autonomous. All share the basic defining characteristic noted above, that is, all feature an independent organization identifying poor people and reimbursing service providers on their behalf. However, there is also considerable variation among them.

Administration

Although a few HEFs are administered directly by international agencies, most are managed by Cambodian NGOs. Many different types of NGOs are involved. For example, some are preexisting national organizations; others are local, created specifically to operate the HEF. In at least one case (Kirivong), Buddhist monks from local pagodas play a prominent role in the administering agency.

Definition of Eligible Population

All HEFs define the people eligible for support according to specified household characteristics. However, the procedures used in determining which characteristics apply are usually considerably less formal than the proxy means testing procedures (like those described for Colombia and Mexico PROGRESA, chapters 9 and 14, respectively) that use statistical analyses of household survey data to determine the characteristics most closely associated with poverty. More often, the Cambodia HEF procedures draw on the views of knowledgeable local observers concerning the characteristics that most clearly denote poverty. The characteristics most commonly identified include the occupation and marital status of the household head, the number of dependents, land ownership, housing construction materials, and possession of productive assets.

After a list of characteristics is drawn up, people lacking a certain portion of them are deemed eligible for HEF subsidies. In some cases, more than one poverty level is established, with those deemed "very poor" being eligible for greater benefits than those categorized as "poor."

Identification of Eligible Population

Once the criteria for HEF support have been defined, people meeting those criteria have to be identified. This is done either passively or actively.

Passive identification features determination of an individual's poverty status once the individual arrives at the health facility. HEF staff members stationed in the participating health facilities typically make the determination. If a patient reporting to the facility reception lacks the money to pay the facility's admission fee, the receptionist refers them to a HEF staff member, who asks a series of questions about the household. Should the responses indicate that the patient is poor according to the definition used, the HEF representative arranges for the provision of program benefits for that person. HEF staff members also often visit the facility wards to determine if there are other patients who qualify for benefits—for example, patients who were able to pay the admission fee only by borrowing heavily or by selling important productive assets. Where possible, HEF staff visit recipients of support in their homes after discharge. This allows the staff to verify the recipient's financial status and also provides them with some social support.

Active identification, also known as pre-identification, involves surveying a district's population to determine in advance who is poor enough to qualify for HEF assistance. Those who qualify are issued an identity document that they produce upon arrival at a participating health facility. In some cases, the survey is conducted by outside investigators using a formal questionnaire. In others, the procedure is considerably simpler, drawing on the local knowledge of respected community leaders.

The two approaches are not mutually exclusive, and some HEFs use a combination of the two. Each approach is recognized as having both advantages and limitations. Advocates of the passive approach cite its simplicity and low cost, its acceptability to people in the areas covered, and the possibility of implementation without the extended period often needed to establish a pre-identification system and the considerable effort to keep it up to date. At the same time, they acknowledge that the passive strategy risks missing the many poor people not aware of the financial support available who are reluctant to come for service. Practitioners of active identification argue that the greater complexity and cost of this approach are more than justified by the greater accuracy and coverage among the poor that it permits. See table 7.1 for information about the identification procedures and criteria used to identify beneficiaries for four hospital-based HEFs in Cambodia.

Proportion of Population Found Eligible

Application of the qualification procedures has led to varying percentages of the population found to be eligible for HEF support. In part, this reflects differences in economic conditions among the districts, and differences in the procedures used. In general, the percentage of the population found eligible ranged between 12 percent and 25 percent of the total. These percentages are usually well below the 35 percent to 75 percent of the population in the areas living below the $1/day poverty line.

Services Covered

The services supported by the HEFs are delivered through government facilities. Most HEFs deal primarily or exclusively with fees charged for services in district hospitals, which are considerably higher than those charged for primary care at lower-level facilities and thus further beyond the means of poor patients. Some of the HEFs have begun to extend the scope of their activities to include costs to patients of primary care provided at lower-level facilities.

Benefits Provided

The most common benefit offered by HEFs is payment of user fees on behalf of those found eligible for support. Often, the payment is for the full

Table 7.1 *Procedures and Criteria Used in Four HEFs to Identify the Poorest*

	Svay Rieng	Pearang	Kirivong	Sotnikum
Identification process				
Identification method	Household assessment	Household assessment	Household assessment	Household assessment
Selection place	Household	Household	Village	Hospital NGO office
Selection time	Ex ante	Ex ante	Ex ante	At the illness episode
Selection process	Pre-identification (proxy means testing) verification (database)	Pre-identification (proxy means testing) verification (database)	Pre-identification approval by Chief Monk Edition of entitled list	Passive identification (proxy means testing) at episode of illness, at hospital, by local NGO staff
Selection tool	Formal scored questionnaire	Formal scored questionnaire	Informal list of criteria for community-based targeting	Informal; nonformalized interview
Entitlement document	Equity certificate database	Equity certificate database	Voucher (nonpermanent) entitled list	None (except records in the books of the NGO)
Alternative process	Passive identification at episode of illness, at hospital, by hospital staff	Passive identification at episode of illness, at hospital, by NGO staff	Certification letter signed by the pagoda chief monk	None

(continued)

Table 7.1 (continued)

Criteria	Svay Rieng	Pearang	Kirivong	Sotnikum
Household characteristics	Occupation of household head Marital status Number of children < 18 years Number of elderly dependents	Occupation of household head Marital status Number of dependents	Number of dependents (alt. criteria)	Marital status Number of disabled members Number of dependents Number of children at work
Health status	n.a.	Length of severe illness during the previous year	n.a.	Chronic disease in household
Productive assets and belongings	Type of housing Transport means Size of land Number of cows, buffalos, and pigs	Roof and wall and m²/person Size of productive land Electronic items Transport means Farm assets and livestock Power supply Quantity of rice harvested	Type of housing Size of farmland Transport items (alt. criteria) Farm animals (alt. criteria) Electronic items (alt. criteria)	Size of land/rice fields Productive assets
Income/expenditures	n.a.	Cash income/expenditures Health expenditures during the previous year	Household income	Lack of food security
Others	n.a.	n.a.	n.a.	Appearance and social capital
Scoring	Score/criteria and threshold	Score/criteria and threshold	None	None

Source: Noirhomme and others 2007.
Note: n.a. = not applicable.

192

amount of the fees in question, but other patterns exist. In some cases, for example, the proportion of the fees covered varies according to just how poor the patient is. Some of the HEFs go beyond this by also providing transportation, food allowances, and other benefits when needed.

Cost

On average, the annual cost of operating the HEFs appears to be on the order of US$0.50 per person found eligible for support. However, this figure varies widely depending upon the benefits provided, the approach employed to identify beneficiaries, and other considerations.

Source of Funds

The funds required to cover these costs come primarily from external agencies. These agencies and international NGOs receiving their support have also played a leading role in introducing HEFs and the broader reforms of which they have been a part. A notable exception to this funding pattern is the Kirivong HEF, referred to above, where the Buddhist pagodas helping administer the project also raised a part of the required resources by soliciting donations from better-off families in the project area.

Findings

During their initial two or three years, most of the HEFs with available data recorded significant increases in the number of people receiving hospital services with HEF support. By the end of 2004, the latest period for which data are available, HEF support recipients varied between fewer than 10 percent to more than 50 percent of all patients in the hospitals concerned.

Data on hospitalizations for HEF beneficiaries and nonbeneficiaries in four hospital-based HEFs (Sotnikum, Svay Rieng, Pearang, and Kirivong) between the third quarter of 2000 and the last quarter of 2004 can be seen in figure 7.1. Increases in patients at three of the HEFs took place after these were launched (Sotnikum and Svay Rieng) or after household equity certificates were distributed (Pearang). According to data collected for the latter three hospitals, it seems that the HEF-supported patients are new clients who previously could not access the services for financial reasons. While it can be assumed that the creation of the HEF affected the patient numbers for these three hospitals, the proportion of patients using the hospital at

Figure 7.1 *Hospitalizations for HEF Beneficiaries and Nonbeneficiaries in the Four HEFs*

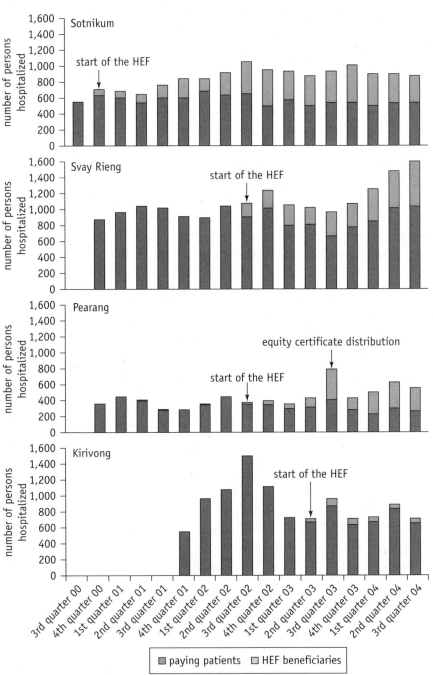

Source: Noirhomme and others 2007.

Kirivong was too small to draw any conclusions about HEF impact on hospital access in that area.

Although the HEFs have yet to be as rigorously evaluated as some other health equity projects, they appear to be achieving their objective of reaching Cambodia's lowest economic groups. In one rural HEF (Sotnikum), over 90 percent of the patients it supported were either poor or very poor, compared with 60 percent in Cambodia as a whole and 75 percent in the district where it operated. In another (Kirivong), HEF beneficiaries were significantly poorer than other district residents with respect to all of the dimensions measured: occupation, literacy, income, land ownership, and others. A further suggestion, or at least hint, that this is the case comes from data indicating that the number of paying hospital users has remained steady as the number of HEF beneficiary users has risen, implying that better-off people have continued to use their own funds rather than draw upon HEF resources.

The 26 HEFs established by late 2006 cover about a third of Cambodia's 76 health operational districts. The HEF concept has received strong governmental support, and has become part of the government's poverty reduction strategy. As a result of this and continuing donor interest, the number of districts covered by HEFs is expected to rise significantly over the coming years.

Note

This chapter is based primarily on a series of articles published in the journal *Health Policy and Planning*: Noirhomme and others (2007); Jacobs and Price (2006); and Hardeman and others (2004).

8

Chile: Integrated Services Program for the Poor

During the 1990s, Chile's gross domestic product grew at close to 5 percent annually. This growth, combined with a stable pattern of income distribution, led to a decline of over one-half (from 33 percent to 15 percent) in the proportion of the population living in poverty. However, not all the poor benefited equally. In particular, the poorest of the poor had largely been left out. The proportion of extreme poverty remained stubbornly fixed, at around 5 percent to 6 percent of the population.

Such extremely poor individuals and families lacked much more than adequate income. They also had little education, lived in inadequate housing, and suffered from poor health. For example, children born to the 5 percent of women with no education experienced an infant mortality rate of around 35 per 1,000 live births, as compared with a national average of fewer than 10.

These factors were reinforced by societal prejudices that tended to exclude the poor from participation in society at large. The disenfranchised segment of the population also lacked the support and protection against risk typically provided by families, neighborhood community associations, and other informal networks. Beyond such material and social factors were psychological issues: a lack of confidence or self-esteem, a distrust of social institutions, and limited interest in forward planning.

To deal with the problems of poverty, the Chilean government had earlier put into place a set of means-tested social programs like state-funded water, health insurance, and pension subsidies for the poor. But the programs, while relatively effective compared with those in neighboring countries, were not adequately reaching Chile's poorest households. To a considerable degree, this resulted from the failure of the poorest people to come forward and participate in the programs. Lack of participation was determined to be a result of a lack of knowledge about program existence or rules, a distrust of government services, and fear of discrimination. Another factor was the lack of significant incentives for the service-providing agencies, for which reaching the poor was but one of many mandates, to seek out difficult-to-reach indigent families.

Policy Change: Chile Solidario

Soon after taking office in early 2000, the Ricardo Lagos government decided to give high priority to overcoming these problems to improve conditions among Chile's 225,000 poorest households. To this end, after considerable discussion and experimentation, the government adopted a commonly espoused but rarely implemented approach: an integrated strategy that took seriously the multidimensional nature of poverty by simultaneously addressing the many different deprivations that afflict the poor. The resulting initiative was given the name Chile Solidario (Chile in Solidarity).

Identifying the Extreme Poor

As with other antipoverty initiatives in Latin America and elsewhere, the households eligible to participate in the Solidario program were identified through a proxy means test—a quantitative approach based on information from a census or large-scale survey to determine the household characteristics most closely associated with poverty. In the Chilean case, such a test was already in place, with the necessary information collected through the government's biannual national socioeconomic household survey (known by its Spanish acronym CASEN). In the version used at the time of Solidario's establishment, responses to 13 questions grouped in four areas—housing, employment, education, and income and assets—were combined to provide a score for each household surveyed. This established a threshold or cutoff score dividing the poorest households that qualified for Solidario participation from the better-off ones that did not. The result was a checklist (named CAS, after its Spanish initials) incorporating these same 13 questions. Field workers used the checklist to survey and score households, and invite households with scores below the threshold to participate.

Creating and Implementing a Household Development Plan

The first step in participation was agreement by the heads of eligible households to work with a Solidario family support counselor in developing and implementing a household development plan covering all family members. The plan's objective was to achieve 53 minimum conditions in seven areas of household life. In addition to health, they are personal identification (that is, possession of basic identity documents), education, family dynamics, housing conditions, employment, and income. (Box 8.1 provides illustrations of the minimum conditions to be met with regard to health and the other six areas.)

The content of the household plans varied according to each family's situation. A plan for a well-educated family whose members are without jobs, for example, might give highest priority to the area of employment; one for a family suffering from severe internal discord might focus on family dynamics.

Once a plan had been developed and agreed upon, the Solidario family support counselor worked to help the family implement it. At the core of the support was help with respect to the program's two principal components described further below: first, assisting the family members with gaining access to the broad range of government programs, many of them previously in existence, designed to help meet the members' needs; and second, enrolling families in the system of regular cash payments that they were eligible to receive for the duration of participation in the program.

The support was of limited duration, and took place in two phases. The first, intensive phase lasted for two years. The second, follow-up phase lasted for three years. During the first phase, the counselor visited the family regularly, once a week during the first two months, less frequently thereafter. During these visits, the counselor helped the family develop its plan, identify and access the services it needed, and enroll for the cash payments, and provided other psycho-social support. During the second phase, support from the counselor ceased, but the families continued to have priority access to the needed services and to cash payments. After the second phase, by which time the family had participated in the program for a total of five years, all support came to an end; and, if the program was successful, the

---

Box 8.1 *Illustrative Minimum Conditions to be Achieved by Chile Solidario Participants*

Health

- The family must be registered in the primary health care system.
- Pregnant women and children under age six should have medical check-ups and other services according to health ministry guidelines.
- Elderly family members and family members suffering from chronic diseases should be under the supervision of a doctor.
- Family members with physical disabilities who could benefit from rehabilitation should be participating in a suitable rehabilitation program.
- All family members should be provided with personal health care information.

Other Areas

- *Personal identification.* All family members should have an identity card issued by the Civil Registry (which is a prerequisite to the receipt of many social services).
- *Education.* Children of working mothers in households with no other adult caregiver available should attend a day-care program.
- *Education.* Adults and children over age 12 should be able to read and write, or be participating in educational programs designed to impart these skills.
- *Family dynamics.* The family should have a daily custom of discussing topics like habits and schedules.
- *Family dynamics.* There should be a fair distribution of household chores.
- *Family dynamics.* The family should be aware of the community resources and development programs available through local networks like sports clubs, senior citizens' centers, and community organizations.
- *Housing.* The legal status of the family's ownership or tenancy of their home should be clearly defined.
- *Housing.* The family should have access to clean water, adequate energy, adequate sewage, and a satisfactory waste disposal system.

---

family would be equipped to embark on an upward course leading out of poverty without further assistance.

Linking Participants to Programs and Services

As noted, Chile already had in place many social programs intended to benefit poor people. But their approach had been largely passive, marked by a readiness to serve people who applied, but with little effort to reach out and encourage use of the programs. Combined with the previously reported lack of knowledge and distrust on the part of indigent families, such passivity led to low uptake.

A central responsibility of Solidario counselors was to change this approach by ensuring that the families with whom they worked knew about and participated in the programs relevant to their needs. To this end, they acted as intermediaries between the families and the programs. For example, they worked actively to see that eligible families received the payments to which they were entitled from the several government agencies offering subsidies to the disadvantaged. These included regular payments available to children and youth in especially poor families, and pension assistance for the elderly poor and for the disabled.

In the case of health, this active assistance meant enrolling indigent families in the Chilean government's national health insurance program (Fondo Nacional de Salud, FONASA). Such enrollment entitled participants to free primary medical services provided principally through municipality health departments, with funds provided by the central government. Because these funds were provided largely on a per capita basis, increased enrollment of the indigent brought an increase in income for the service providers.

Providing Participants with Special Cash Allowances

In addition to the subsidies available through regular government programs, Solidario participants were provided a special financial allowance if they made satisfactory progress toward implementation of the family plan adopted at the outset. The allowances were modest, about a quarter of the size of those provided through the Mexico PROGRESA/Opportunidades program described in chapter 14. They began at the equivalent of about $15 monthly, then tapered down to about $5 monthly toward the end of the initial two-year phase. Families that successfully completed this intensive phase continued to receive payments during the three-year follow-up period.

Administrative responsibilities for the program were spread across a wide range of government agencies. At the core were two entities in the central government, and a unit in each of the more than 300 participating municipalities.

The first of the two central entities was Chile's planning ministry, which has overall responsibility for the program. The second was a national agency focused on poverty reduction: the Solidarity and Social Investment Fund (Fondo Solidario de Inversion Social, or FOSIS), which had been offering a wide range of community economic development and skill enhancement programs. As a first step, in early 2002 FOSIS organized a pilot project, the Programa Puente (Bridge Program) in 4 of Chile's 13 regions. Encouraged by the results of the program's initial experience, the government decided shortly afterward to expand it throughout the country as Chile Solidario, with FOSIS and Puente leading the drive to involve municipalities.

To administer Solidario on the ground, each participating municipality established a Family Intervention Unit. First, each unit undertook a survey to determine the number of indigent families within the municipality; they then recruited the number of family support counselors needed to serve them. Some of these were staff from other municipality departments, deputed for Solidario work on a part-time basis. Others were full-time, employed by FOSIS. By mid-2004, some 2,500 family support counselors were at work, each with an average caseload of 50–55 families.

In addition, the Family Intervention Units took responsibility for arranging participation of the several municipal departments responsible for the different services provided. Additional funding through Solidario to cover the municipalities' extra costs proved quite useful in persuading reluctant municipalities to participate, and gave Solidario extra leverage to ensure adequate treatment of its indigent participants.

Findings

Within 18 to 24 months of its establishment, Solidario had contacted some 125,000 to 130,000 indigent families, and over 95 percent of the contacted families had agreed to participate. As can be seen from figure 8.1, the participants were heavily concentrated among the poor: the enrollment rate was 11 percent among the poorest 5 percent of the population, and declined steadily with economic level, so that almost no families in the country's upper-income groups were included.

Since then, the program has expanded greatly, and has begun to evolve on the basis of experience during its initial years. For example, it has broadened its beneficiary identification approach to include vulnerability to impoverishment as well as poverty itself. Additionally, the government has developed a broader child development program into which Solidario is being integrated. In both urban and rural areas, preventive visits among

Figure 8.1 *Chile Solidario Participants by Economic Group, 2003*

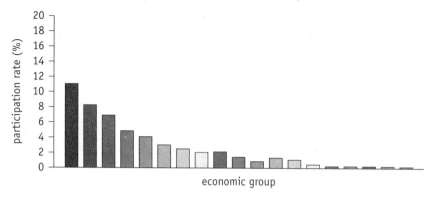

Source: World Bank 2008a.
Note: Each bar represents 5 percent of the population, from poorest (left) to richest (right).

Figure 8.2 *Estimated Chile Solidario Participants by Economic Group, 2006*

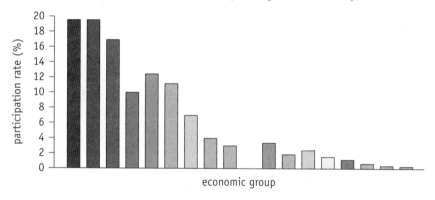

Source: World Bank 2008a.
Note: Each bar represents 5 percent of the population, from poorest (left) to richest (right).

children in Solidario households were significantly higher than among those in nonparticipating households. In rural areas, checkups for pregnant women were significantly higher as well.

The distributional results of these developments appear in figure 8.2, which provides estimated enrollment rates as of 2006. These rates stood at about 20 percent among the poorest 5 percent and the next-poorest 5 percent of the population, with notably lower coverage at higher levels. In all, about 15 percent to 20 percent of the total program benefits accrued to the population's poorest 5 percent, about 55 percent of the benefits went to the poorest 20 percent. While falling short of Solidario's ambitious goal to primarily reach the poorest 5 percent, this degree of focus appears to equal that of Mexico's PROGRESA/Opportunidades program, the most accurately targeted large-scale program on record.

Note

This chapter draws on many resources, most unpublished. Three of the most important were Government of Chile (2004); Galasso (2006); and Palma and Urzúa (2005).

9

Colombia: Expanding Health Insurance for the Poor

Before 1993, Colombia's Ministry of Health (MOH) was responsible by constitutional mandate for providing all Colombians with health care. Unfortunately, inefficiency, badly targeted public subsidies, and fragmented markets were endemic in Colombia's health care sector. In reality, only one Colombian in five had any protection against the financial risk of health shocks from serious illness, and only those with more financial resources could afford to join social security schemes or pay out of pocket for health care.

Colombia's shaky health care system was built on myths. Policy makers believed that Colombia's public health was well targeted to the poor; that public health services were free to all comers, but especially the poor; and that the poor did not have to go to private providers for health care. Public funds from the Treasury, raised through general taxation, supported a large network of public hospitals and clinics. In fact, a significant part of health care financing came from households spending out of pocket, while insufficient and inefficient social security schemes provided the rest. Faced with illness, the poor had three choices: (i) to try to get treatment from public health services, (ii) to pay private providers, or (iii) to go without any medical care. Left with self care as a last resort, the poor and less educated were at greater risk than the better-off because quality control in the pharmaceutical market was lax and medicine could be bought without a prescription in Colombia.

Cost was determined to be the most significant barrier to health care before 1993. In the poorest group, the first quintile, only one individual in six who fell ill in 1992 sought medical care. The poor had less access to health care than the rich, paid out of pocket for public as well as private health care services, and paid proportionately more of their income for any services they received.

The governmental health care delivery network did not adequately serve the poor, leaving already impoverished sick people with huge medical bills and the likelihood of abject poverty from which they could not recover.

Before 1993, the Colombian health care system allocated public subsidies directly to hospitals, rather than to users. Of patients treated in the public hospitals, only 20 percent came from the poorest income group and almost 60 percent from the upper- and middle-income groups. In 1992, 12 percent of hospitalizations and 20 percent of all surgeries done in the public sector were received by patients in the richest 20 percent of the population. Thus, middle- and higher-income individuals who could afford to use other private hospitals and medical services were crowding out the poor from public facilities.

More important, the poor who could get into public hospitals incurred out-of-pocket expenses more often than did middle- and upper-income patients, who were often covered by private insurance. Rarely did the poor receive free care in public facilities. In fact, 91 percent of the poorest inpatients incurred out-of-pocket expenses, while only 69 percent in the richest quintile did so (figure 9.1).

The private sector was important in both financing and delivering health services before the reform. According to the government's National Household Survey in 1992, 40 percent of all health interventions and 45 percent of all hospitalizations were done in the private sector. At that time, only 20 percent of the Colombian population had health insurance.

Policy Change: The 1993 Health Sector Reform

Law 100 of 1993 mandated the creation of a new national health care system with universal health insurance coverage and reorganized financing and delivery. Public subsidies would henceforth go directly to individuals, not institutions.

The reform introduced four main elements to reach the poor:

- A proxy means testing index to target public health subsidies to the neediest (SISBEN, Selection System of Beneficiaries for Social Programs; Nuñez and Espinosa 2004)

Figure 9.1 *Population Who Paid for Inpatient Care in Public Hospitals by Income Level*

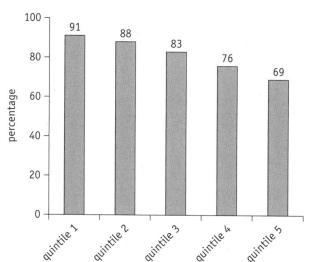

Source: Escobar 2005.

- Transformation of the traditional supply-side subsidies, which financed the public health care network, into demand-side subsidies, which subsidize individual insurance premiums for the poor
- An equity fund in which revenue from payroll contributions and Treasury resources cross-subsidize insurance premiums for the poor
- Contracting for health service delivery from both the public and private sectors

The new system is a universal health insurance coverage plan with two regimes:

- The contributory regime (RC) covers formally employed and independent workers who contribute to the scheme. Contributions are collected by the insurer of choice.
- The subsidized regime (RS) covers the poor and indigent individuals who cannot afford to make any insurance contribution.

SISBEN is a general purpose system for selecting beneficiaries for social programs in Colombia. It has a statistically derived proxy means test index that serves as an indicator of household economic well-being. The variables that determine welfare include availability and quality of housing and basic public services, possession of durable goods, human capital endowments, and current income (this last variable was excluded in the new revised SISBEN index because of its unreliability and lack of predictive power). The system includes a set of norms and procedures defined at the central level and operated at the municipal level to gather information necessary to calculate the welfare index and select beneficiaries for the numerous social programs. The Subsidized Health Insurance Regime is one of the programs where benefit incidence has been the highest for those targeted with SISBEN, and was benefiting over 11.4 million poor and vulnerable people by the end of 2002.

Payroll contributions go into a national health fund (Fondo de Solidaridad y Garantía, FOSYGA) with four separate accounts. The fund finances insurance premiums for all enrolled in the RC. In the RC-RS cross-subsidization process, a share of the contributions is allocated to finance the RS, together with Treasury transfers to the territories. Individuals who are eligible for enrollment in the RS but are still uninsured are to rely on public hospitals for care.

Every insured individual is free to choose an insurer and consult any provider in the insurer's network. Both regimes have a basic benefits package, but the POS (Plan Obligatorio de Salud) for the contributory regime includes every level of care while the POSS (Plan Obligatorio de Salud Subsidiado) has to be complemented with services provided by public hospitals and financed through traditional supply-side subsidies. According to Law 100, those supply-side subsidies were to be turned into demand-side subsidies over time to achieve universal insurance coverage with the same POS in both regimes.

Although Colombia still faces important challenges in expanding health insurance coverage to all the poor, such as improving service quality and providing a more complete benefit plan for the poor, some important accomplishments deserve attention.

Findings

SISBEN established a technical, objective, equitable, and uniform mechanism for selecting beneficiaries of social spending to be used by all government levels. It classified applicants for social programs in a rapid, uniform, and equitable way. It strengthened institutional development of municipalities with the establishment of a modern social information system and supported interinstitutional coordination within municipalities to improve the impact of social spending. It avoided duplication and concentrated efforts on the poorest. It developed socioeconomic diagnostics of the poor population to better prepare social insurance programs for the poor, and facilitated attainment of target goals for the various levels of government.

The reform of 1993 brought more opportunities for access to health care for the poor. Still, differences persisted between the insured and the uninsured. The insured still were more frequently treated than the uninsured in both urban and rural areas and also used more preventive care services.

The reform of 1993 increased financial protection for all, but especially for the poor and rural population. Before 1993, 23 percent of Colombians were financially protected against the risk of health shocks. A decade later, 62 percent of the population had access to health insurance, an impressive change when compared with all Latin American countries that had health care systems similar to Colombia's before 1993.

The reform improved equity in the system by introducing financial protection instruments to the poor, previously available only to the formally employed and the better-off (figure 9.2). Insurance coverage among the wealthiest group increased relatively modestly with the reform, from 60 percent in 1992 to 82 percent in 2003, while insurance coverage among the

Figure 9.2 *Insured Population, by Income Status*

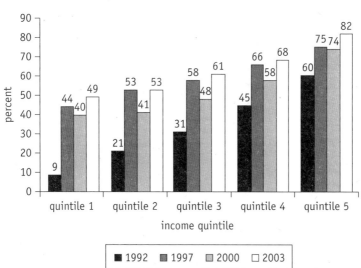

poorest group increased from 9 percent in 1992 to 49 percent in 2003. With the introduction of the subsidized insurance regime, access to health insurance was delinked from formal employment and income.

The reform reduced economic barriers to health care use for all income groups, but particularly for the insured poor. Lack of money was still the reason most often given by the poor, both insured and uninsured, for not seeking medical care (figures 9.3a and 9.3b). The economic barrier to health care access was more than twice as high for the uninsured poorest group as for the insured poorest.

Health care expenditure as a percentage of income is much larger for the uninsured than for people in either the contributory or the subsidized regimes. Formal insurance in Colombia reduced out-of-pocket expenditures on ambulatory care between 50 percent and 60 percent. The poor in the RS spent around 4 percent of their income on ambulatory care, but the uninsured poor more than 8 percent. Out-of-pocket expenditures on hospitalization among the uninsured poor absorbed more than 35 percent of their income in 2003. The poor in the RC spent a smaller proportion of their income on inpatient care than the poor enrolled in the RS. However, a health shock requiring hospitalization pushed 14 percent of those hospitalized and uninsured below the poverty line while that fate befell only 4 percent of inpatients covered by the subsidized regime (table 9.1).

The introduction of health insurance improved access to preventive care. While 65 percent of the insured saw a physician or a dentist at least once for preventive reasons and without being sick in 2003, only 35 percent of the uninsured did so.

Regulation gave preference to children, single mothers, the elderly, the handicapped, and the chronically ill for priority access to insurance enrollment in the RS. Empirically, those poor and insured were less healthy than their uninsured counterparts, which could be confused with adverse

Table 9.1 *Individuals Pushed below Poverty and Subsistence Lines by a Health Shock (percent)*

	Uninsured		Insured subsidized regime	
Health shock	*Poverty*	*Subsistence*	*Poverty*	*Subsistence*
Ambulatory care	5	6	4	3
Hospitalization	14	18	4	11

Source: Escobar 2005.

Figure 9.3 *Reasons for Not Seeking Health Care, 2003*

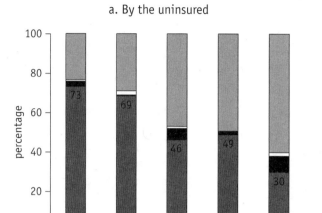

a. By the uninsured

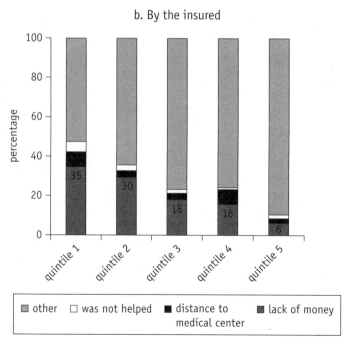

b. By the insured

■ other   □ was not helped   ■ distance to   ■ lack of money
                                 medical center

Source: Escobar 2005.

selection. In reality, however, individuals did not decide when to enroll in the RS, because annual extension of coverage depended on the availability of financial resources.

No longitudinal data existed to see whether access to health insurance among the poor affected their overall health status. However, some inferences could be made from data on infant mortality, institutional delivery, and prenatal care.

Consistent with findings in other countries, insured Colombians sought health care more often and faster than the uninsured. This activity was especially important in the cases of childbirth and child and maternal health. Lower infant mortality rates were observed among children of women who had access to medical care during pregnancy, used prenatal care, and had a medically assisted delivery. Colombia's Demographic and Health Surveys (DHSs) indicated a significant improvement in access to those services, particularly in the rural areas. According to the DHS (1986, 1990, 1995, and 2000), the following services saw increases: physician-assisted child delivery, 66 percent; institutional delivery, 18 percent; and prenatal care use among rural women, 49 percent. Changes after 1993 were influenced by improved access to health care services by the insured.

The DHS 2000 indicated that access to prenatal care and to institutional delivery reduced child mortality. Figure 9.4 shows a truly astonishing

Figure 9.4 *Impact of Institutional Delivery and Prenatal Care on Infant Mortality Rate*

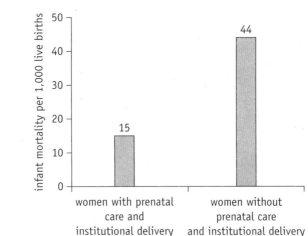

Source: Escobar 2005.

difference between infant mortality rates among children whose mothers had access to prenatal care and to institutional delivery compared with those whose mothers did not have access to such services.

Despite positive results, the Colombian social insurance scheme has been criticized for not having achieved universal coverage and for financing a less comprehensive benefits package for the poor (RS) than for the wealthy (RC). The slower-than-planned transformation in supply-side subsidies, which finance public hospitals, into demand-side subsidies to finance health insurance for the poor, has also come under fire for slowing down the expansion of the RS benefits package.

Several attempts to introduce legislation have failed to change the present system back into a government-owned and government-delivered health care system like the one in 1992. However, Colombia still has many challenges to surmount to complete the consolidation of the social insurance scheme, not only to cover the entire population, but also to improve the efficiency and quality of health care. The changeover to the new, insurance-based system has been difficult politically, administratively, and technically. The governmental decentralization process begun in the early 1990s has brought with it disadvantages as well as advantages for the implementation of the 1993 health reform.

Note

This chapter was adapted from Escobar (2005).

10

India: Community-Based Health Care Services

In India, as elsewhere, the poor die earlier, are more prone to illness, and have less access to health care than the better-off. Reaching this poor, largely illiterate, and geographically dispersed population, especially residents of remote rural areas, poses many challenges. Foremost among them are identifying and overcoming difficulties the poor face in obtaining health care.

India's public sector is vast but underfunded and not nearly large enough to meet current health needs. The private sector is growing quickly, but is unregulated. Lacking standards of care, it has many unqualified practitioners who likely provide too many inappropriate treatments. Patients pay out of pocket for much of their care, both public and private.

In Gujarat, relative to all-India, the private for-profit health care sector is thriving. The problems with publicly and privately provided care are the same in Gujarat as elsewhere in India. Most people, in both urban and rural Gujarat, use the private sector for outpatient and inpatient services. According to the 1995–96 National Sample Survey Organization (NSSO) survey, nearly 82 percent of outpatient treatments among rural residents` were obtained from private providers, as were 76 percent in urban areas. The private sector accounted for 71.0 percent of hospitalizations in urban Gujarat and 67.4 percent in rural Gujarat. Among the areas included in this study, the public health care system is strong only in Ahmedabad City, where four large government hospitals provide outpatient and inpatient care.

Distance and lack of financial resources are major barriers to health care seeking among the poor in Gujarat. Health care (particularly curative, expensive, inpatient care) is widely available in urban centers. But for village dwellers far from an urban center, the closest source of health care may be hours away. Some 12 percent of rural women have to travel at least 5 kilometers to reach the nearest health facility. Based on the 1995–96 NSSO survey, the wealthiest quintile of rural Gujaratis (measured by yearly household expenditure) was 4.6 times as likely to have been hospitalized over a one-year period as the poorest quintile. In urban areas, the ratio was 2.9.

Policy Change: The Self-Employed Women's Association (SEWA)

The Self-Employed Women's Association (SEWA), a trade union, was founded in 1972 in Ahmedabad, Gujarat State, India, to empower poor women who earn a living outside the formal sector through their own labor or small business. These women do not earn a regular salary and have no welfare benefits like those employed in the organized sector.

SEWA had two main goals: (i) to help these women achieve full employment that would offer security for work, income, food, and social protection; and (ii) to make them individually and collectively self-reliant, economically independent, and capable of making their own decisions. In addition to banking and credit services (SEWA Bank), and insurance (Vimo SEWA), SEWA became actively involved in public health services in the early 1970s, to provide its members and nonmembers with some form of preventive and primary health care. It aimed to serve the very poor, particularly those living in areas not otherwise served by government or nongovernmental organizations (NGOs). SEWA had to overcome many challenges to provide the needed health services to the very poor.

SEWA first became actively involved in the public health field in the early 1970s through health education and provision of maternity benefits. In the early 1980s, SEWA negotiated with the Indian government to help distribute maternity care to poor women. A focus of SEWA Health has always been to build capacity among local women, especially traditional midwives (*dais*), so that they become barefoot doctors in their communities. Today, SEWA's health-related activities are many and diverse. They include primary health care delivered through 60 stationary health centers and mobile health camps; health education and training; capacity building among local SEWA leaders and *dais*; provision of high-quality, low-cost drugs through drug shops; occupational and mental health activities; and production and marketing of traditional medicines. The evaluation financed by the Reaching the Poor program deals with the three activities summarized in table 10.1.

Table 10.1 The Three SEWA Health Services Covered by Reaching the Poor

Variable	Reproductive health mobile camps	Tuberculosis detection and treatment	Women's education sessions
Start-up date	1999	1999	1999
Target population	Women, reproductive age	Men and women, all ages	Women, reproductive age
Geographic coverage	Mainly Ahmedabad, Kheda, and Patan Districts	North and East Zones of Ahmedabad City (population 375,000)	Mainly Ahmedabad, Kheda, and Patan Districts (but also the other districts where SEWA Union has members)
Services	Education and training, examination and diagnostic tests (cervical examinations and Pap smears), treatment, referral, follow up	Diagnosis, treatment, medicines	Education: SEWA orientation, first aid, general disease and HIV/AIDS, immunization and child care, airborne and waterborne diseases and tuberculosis, sexual and reproductive health
Annual utilization rate	12,500 women	575 patients under treatment at the DOTS center; 23 served by barefoot DOTS workers	6,000 women
Cost to user	Rs 5 consultation fee; medicines sold at wholesale price (about one-third market price)	Services free, indirect costs only	Rs 5 SEWA Union membership fee
External donor	UNFPA and Indian government	WHO, Indian government, and Ahmedabad Municipal Corporation	Indian government, UNFPA, and Ford Foundation
Human resources	6 part-time physicians 50 barefoot doctors and managers	5 stationary centers (each with 2 to 3 staff) and 11 grassroots DOTS providers	35 grassroots workers and full-time staff

Source: Gwatkin, Wagstaff, and Yazbeck 2005, table 9.1.
Note: DOTS = Directly observed treatment, short course; UNFPA = United Nations Population Fund; WHO = World Health Organization. Rs = Indian rupees; $1 = 43.5 Rs.

In response to demand from people in remote and underserviced areas, SEWA Health began organizing reproductive health (RH) mobile camps for women in 1999. RH mobile camps are operated mainly in the slum areas of Ahmedabad City and in the villages of three districts and are funded largely by the United Nations Population Fund (UNFPA) and the government of India. More than 35 camps are operational per month, and the mean attendance per camp is 30 women, for a total of more than 12,500 patients per year. Physicians and 50 barefoot doctors and managers provide health care at the camps. The camps are repeated in each area, on average, once per year.

Activities at the RH mobile camps include health education and training, examination and diagnostic tests (including cervical examination and Pap smears), treatment, referral, and follow-up. Camps are usually held during the afternoon, and their duration is three to four hours. Those attending the camps are asked to pay a 5 rupee (US$0.11) contribution, and one-third of the total cost of medicines provided (although even these fees may be waived for those who are very poor).

Increasingly in rural areas, SEWA Health is conducting these camps in collaboration with the government of Gujarat. The camps are held right at government primary health centers, which are usually located in or near small villages. These camps differ from the standard "area" camps (described above) insofar as medicines are given for free, the range of medicines available is restricted to those on the government's formulary, and health care is provided by public doctors and nurses. Free transportation is provided by SEWA to women living in neighboring villages.

Findings

A sample of 376 urban and 158 rural women was surveyed to assess the socioeconomic status (SES) of the women using the RH mobile camps, as they attended randomly selected camps. They were compared with the general urban and rural populations of Gujarat, using recent, representative surveys. It was found that the RH mobile camps are very effective at reaching poor women in Ahmedabad City. A comparison based on a composite SES index showed urban camp users to be significantly poorer than the population of Ahmedabad. Camp users (and their families) were, for example, significantly less likely to possess a motorcycle or scooter (12 percent versus 43 percent), were more likely to rely on public (instead of private or shared) toilets (22 percent versus 9 percent), and were less likely to use natural gas as a source of cooking fuel (35 percent versus 66 percent). Figure 10.1a

Figure 10.1 *Frequency Distribution of SEWA Reproductive Health Mobile Camp Users, Urban and Rural, by Deciles of the SES Index Score*

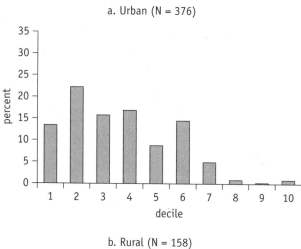

a. Urban (N = 376)

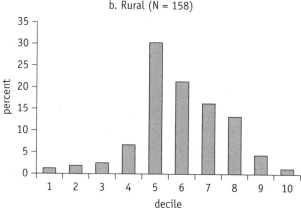

b. Rural (N = 158)

Source: Ranson and others 2005.

illustrates the distribution of urban camp users by deciles of the SES index score. The leftward skew of this figure indicates that camp users were more likely to be from poorer segments of the general population. The percentage of camp users falling below the 30th percentile of the SES score, which roughly approximates the poverty line in India, was 52 percent.

In rural areas, the camps were less effective in reaching poor women. Rural women did not differ significantly from the general rural population in their SES index score. Figure 10.1b indicates that the majority of rural camp users are from less poor deciles of the population. Only 5.7 percent of users fell below the 30th percentile—suggesting that SEWA Health's rural RH mobile camps do not effectively target the very poorest.

For the most part, the urban services seemed to be effectively targeting the poor. Reasons for this success are likely to include the following:

- SEWA personnel treat people with respect and warmth and give them detailed information.
- Services (especially RH mobile camps and women's education sessions) are offered "right at people's doorsteps"; that is, SEWA Health takes the services to the poor, rather than trying to bring the poor to the services.
- The services are delivered by women and by (or at least in part by) the poor themselves.
- The services are generally combined with efforts to educate and mobilize the community; for example, preceding the RH mobile camps, SEWA Health workers go door to door, educating people about the service, and educating people on how to use it.
- Services are free or low cost and medicines are much cheaper at SEWA facilities than in private shops.
- SEWA is an entity that people know and trust.

In-depth interviews with SEWA Health grassroots workers suggest that there are two main barriers that prevent poor rural women from using the RH mobile camps. First, the 5 rupee registration fee prevents some from attending the camps. Second, the camps may be difficult for women to attend because they often coincide with hours of work.

There are likely to be other, broader reasons underlying the difficulties in delivering services to the rural poor. Studies in other SEWA departments have documented similar discrepancies in the equity of use of rural versus urban services. For example, the poorest rural members of SEWA's insurance scheme (Vimo SEWA) have lower rates of claims than the less poor as a result of

- problems of geographic access, both to inpatient facilities and to Vimo SEWA's grassroots workers;
- weaker "links" between members and local Vimo SEWA representatives in rural areas (the contact between members and the organization is less frequent, and less intensive, in rural areas); and
- weaker capacity among Vimo SEWA grassroots workers in rural areas.

SEWA Health has taken steps to improve accessibility of the rural RH mobile camps. SEWA Health waives the registration fee and the medicines fee for those who appear to be particularly poor—typically a few women attending each camp. Perhaps these exemptions could be granted more liberally, and more objectively, for example, by providing exemptions to all who possess a Below Poverty Line card.

It must also be remembered that failure of a service to reach the poorest of the rural poor does not necessarily mean that the service has failed in "reaching the poor." Even those households that fall in the higher deciles of the SES index in rural areas should be considered "less poor" rather than "wealthy." Compared with their urban counterparts, these rural households have less in the way of cash reserves, material wealth, and thus economic security.

In conclusion, the findings of this study suggest that delivery of services through a broadly based, development-oriented union can facilitate equitable delivery of health care services. Government and donors can help to ensure that established NGOs with an interest in providing health services have the capacity and the resources to do so.

Note

This chapter was adapted from Ranson and others (2005).

11

Indonesia: Health Cards for the Poor

In the fall of 1997, Indonesia began to experience a dramatic decline in the use of public health services as a result of an economic crisis. The economic crisis led to a rise in the price of basic items such as food and medicine, which in turn led to an increase in poverty. The poor had to struggle to meet the basic needs of livelihood rather than seek health care. Ultimately, these events caused deterioration of the quality of Indonesian public health care facilities.

Policy Change: The Health Card Program

The Indonesian government mounted the Indonesian health card program in conjunction with social safety net programs (Jarang Pengaman Sosial, or JPS) to address the impact of the economic crisis on health services. Even though similar schemes existed, both the coverage and scope were changed and expanded as part of the JPS program.

The health care subsidies program provided health cards to poor households in all provinces in Indonesia at the district level. The health card was used to receive free health services from designated public hospitals, local health centers, and village clinics for medical or family-planning purposes. Free public services offered to the health card holders consisted of (i) outpatient and inpatient care, (ii) contraception for women of childbearing age, (iii) prenatal care, and (iv) birth assistance. Service providers were compensated for the additional workload by a lump sum transfer based on the number of health cards allocated to the district; this resulted in a loose

223

relationship between the use of the health card, which entitled the holder to the subsidy, and compensation of the health care providers.

Eligibility in this program was based on village-level lists, which primarily encompassed the National Family Planning Coordinating Board's (BKKBN's) "prosperity" rankings, with some modifications by local administration via a "health committee." A household was deemed in need when it had too little money to worship by faith; eat basic food twice a day; have different clothing for school or work and home; have a floor not made out of earth; or have access to modern medical care for children or modern contraceptive methods. Any one of these conditions qualified a household for a card. The BKKBN collected this information through the census. Local leaders were also permitted to distribute health cards to people they thought needed them. The health card could then be used by all members of the household.

Findings

After the health card program began in September 1998, poor beneficiaries' use of health services increased, and the better-off switched from private to public providers (figure 11.1).

Figure 11.1 *Outpatient Consultations, by Type of Provider (percent)*

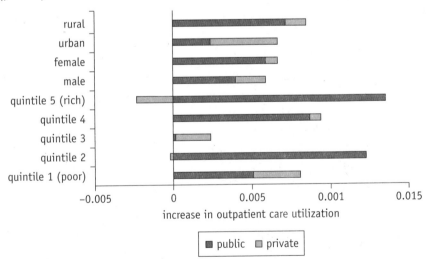

Source: Saadah, Pradhan, and Sparrow 2001.

Figure 11.2 Health Card Ownership versus Use for Outpatient Treatment

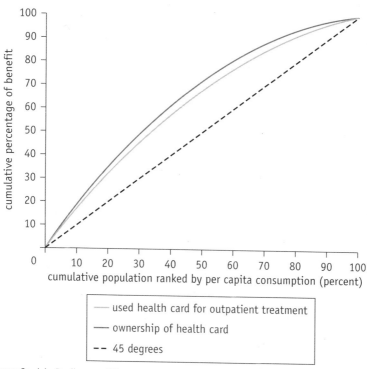

cumulative percentage of benefit

cumulative population ranked by per capita consumption (percent)

—— used health card for outpatient treatment
—— ownership of health card
-- 45 degrees

Source: Saadah, Pradhan, and Sparrow 2001.

Studies show that 10.6 percent of Indonesian households own health cards. Card holders appeared to be poorer, less educated, and more often employed in agriculture than people who did not have health cards. Their households were also more frequently headed by a woman.

Use of health cards was also pro-poor but slightly less so than card ownership, showing that the supply-side subsidy was less successful. Figure 11.2 compares ownership and use of health cards. The people receiving benefits were, on average, wealthier than the pool of card recipients. The poorest 20 percent of the population possessed 35 percent of the health cards, but there was a fair amount of leakage to the nonpoor. Considering that about 10 percent of Indonesian households received health cards, perfect targeting would mean that the poorest 10 percent of the population should have obtained all the cards. In fact, about 39 percent of the health cards were owned by households from the wealthiest three quintiles.

Table 11.1 Health Card Use
(percentage seeking care in previous three months)

Care-seeking action	Head of household reports owning health card	Head of household reports not owning health card
Received outpatient care	15.10	12.91
Went to public provider	10.61	6.75
Used health card	6.74	0.15
Did not use health card	3.88	6.60
Went to private provider	4.82	6.48
Did not seek health care	84.57	86.77

Source: Saadah, Pradhan, and Sparrow 2001.

In a three-month period of the distribution of the health cards, 15 percent of health card owners visited an outpatient provider, compared with 13 percent for those without health cards. However, health card holders did not always use their health cards—out of the about 11 percent of health card owners who sought care from a public provider, about one-third ($3.88 \div 10.61$) reported not using the card (table 11.1). Besides the technical reasons for why this could have happened, there were several possible explanations: Some public facilities reportedly limited the time spent with health card patients, and some patients thought care received with a card was of lower quality than services and medicines obtained without a card. In remote areas, lack of access to the nearest public facility may have deterred use.

Even though the design of the program had several limitations, the study found that the program (direct subsidies provided for basic health services for the poor) was effective in increasing use of these services. The scheme also tested mechanisms to channel funds directly to the facility level with increased budgetary support to the public sector to respond to the increased demand. However, there was a drawback in providing the subsidy only to public service providers and not to private providers.

Both ownership of the health card and services delivered under the health card program were shown to be pro-poor. The use of services was, however, less pro-poor than ownership. Conditional on ownership, the rich were more likely to use their health cards. The fact that the subsidy was provided to health care suppliers and not directly to households may have contributed to this result.

Ownership of a health card had a positive impact on the use of outpatient medical services for households from the poorest two quintiles. For all households, ownership resulted in a large substitution effect away from the private sector to the public sector. Because the health card was valid only with public service providers, health card holders used those services more frequently than those without cards.

The health card program resulted in a net increase in use for poor beneficiaries. For nonpoor beneficiaries, the program resulted mainly in substitution from private to public providers. The largest effect of the program seems to have come from a general increase in the supply of public services resulting from the budgetary support received through the JPS program. The budgetary increase may have also contributed in some measure to the quality of public services. Studies indicate that the health card program (card distribution and the supply-side subsidy) resulted in a 65 percent increase in the outpatient contact rate. The increased use by health card owners contributed only 25 percent to that increase in contact. If this is true, the revival of the public sector as a provider of outpatient care could be attributed to the health card program.

The program link between the delivery of services to health card owners and financial compensation to service providers was relatively weak. Service providers were reimbursed using a lump sum transfer based on the number of health cards distributed to their area. As a result, serving a health card owner did not result in a direct financial reward to the service provider.

Overall, the combined effects of the health card and the supply impulse have increased usage. However, more focus on demand-side financing and inclusion of both public and private providers could have enhanced the program's impact. Still, having a JPS helped. In the absence of the JPS program, the use of outpatient services would have been 5.4 percent lower relative to the observed contact rate. The results indicate that a closer link between health card use and funding would have resulted in a better-targeted program.

Note

This chapter was adapted from Saadah, Pradhan, and Sparrow (2001).

12

Kenya: Expanding Immunization Reach through Campaigns

In developing countries, immunizations are typically provided in the health clinics and hospital outpatient facilities that constitute the backbone of countries' regular health services. However, when health services are weak, as in much of Sub-Saharan Africa, many children are not reached. As of 2000, for instance, only about two-thirds of children were being immunized against measles in the 19 countries with reliable data.

This affected not only the one-third of children who were left unprotected, but also future generations of other children. The unvaccinated children were numerous enough to constitute a "safe haven," where the measles virus could reside undisturbed and subsequently reemerge to cause outbreaks at a later date in places where immunization coverage was allowed to slip.

This problem and the availability of simple, effective technologies led measles specialists to become increasingly frustrated by the slow development of routine health services and to begin seeking supplementary channels for delivering vaccines. Thus, in the late 1990s, the World Health Organization's African Regional Office developed an expanded strategy based on one previously implemented with considerable success in Latin America.

Kenya is one of the many countries in Africa that have sought to increase the immunization coverage achieved through its regular health services by undertaking mass campaigns—formally known as supplementary immunization activities (SIAs).

Policy Change: Immunization Campaigns

One central component of the strategy, both globally and as implemented in Kenya, was to offer children missed by regular health services a second chance to obtain a measles immunization, either through regular services or through a campaign that reached out to the missed children by organizing temporary, highly publicized stations providing immunizations closer to their homes. There were—and are—two types of campaigns:

- Catch-up campaigns, undertaken at the beginning of countries' intensified efforts. These are one-time efforts, seeking to handle the backlog of unprotected children by immunizing all children under age 15.
- Follow-up campaigns, undertaken every two to four years following the catch-up campaign. The objective is to reach unprotected children born since the time of the catch-up campaign.

Both types of campaigns follow the same basic approach, using intensive outreach activities to extend immunization services provided at regular government health facilities. Typically, the campaign managers organize intensive mass media and other publicity activities, and supplement them by creating social mobilization committees of influential groups and individuals in each local area to be covered. The committee members are provided the training and support they need to inform families about the value and availability of immunization at a specified time and place.

A team of two to four vaccinators and assistants then travel to the place indicated—usually a health center, school, church, mosque, or tent erected at a bus depot or marketplace—and immunize up to 200 children per day. Sometimes additional health services or products, such as other vaccinations, treated bed nets, or vitamins, are also provided. Depending upon the number of children to be seen, the team members remain at the site from a few hours to a few days, then move on to the next site and repeat the process until the entire region or country has been covered.

The approach is controversial. Its many advocates point to demonstrable accomplishments and to the platform that campaigns provide for delivering other health interventions. On the other side are the critics who note that these immediate accomplishments come at the cost of diverting scarce health personnel from their other important responsibilities, and equally scarce funds from routine activities. By doing so, the critics argue, campaigns detract from the key longer-term objective of strengthening health systems to provide immunizations and other services on an ongoing basis.

Findings

Despite criticisms, African governments have not been deterred from pushing ahead with immunization campaigns. Between 2001 and 2006, 42 African countries mounted catch-up measles campaigns and at least one follow-up measles campaign each, reaching over 300 million children. In 2007, 16 countries were implementing measles campaigns seeking to reach nearly 40 million more children. In 2005, 21 countries in the region mounted similar campaigns against polio.

On average, the measles campaigns reached nearly 95 percent of the children they targeted in the 19 countries with adequate data. By doing so, the campaigns can presumably claim credit for at least part, perhaps a majority, of the 90 percent decline in measles deaths reported in these countries between 2000 and 2006.

But such overall figures do not speak directly to the impact of campaigns on health equity. For that, one must look further, at the social and economic distribution of the children whom the campaigns reached. In this regard, the experience of measles campaigns in Kenya, where the distribution issue has been directly examined, is instructive.

In June 2002, Kenya's health ministry organized an initial nationwide catch-up campaign that sought to provide measles immunization and vitamin A supplementation to 13.5 million children. Shortly thereafter, the ministry undertook a large-scale household survey, also covering all parts of the country, to assess the campaign's results. The survey focused on determining whether children in the households covered had been covered through regular immunization activities or the campaign, drawing primarily on documentation provided to mothers at the time of immunization, supplemented by mothers' recall. The survey questionnaire also included enough information about household characteristics to permit an assessment of its assets or wealth, thereby permitting a comparison of the immunization experience among children living at different economic levels.

Overall, the campaign raised Kenya's measles immunization rate among children ages 9–23 months from 77 percent to 90 percent. As shown in table 12.1, the increases were largest in the lowest economic groups, regardless of whether the changes were measured in absolute or relative terms. Among children in the poorest 20 percent of households, for example, coverage increased by 32 percent or 21 percentage points, compared with a (statistically insignificant) decline of 2 percent or 2 percentage points among children in the best-off 20 percent of households.

Table 12.1 *Measles Immunization Coverage in Kenya before and after the 2002 Catch-Up Campaign*

Coverage	1st quintile (poorest)	2nd quintile	3rd quintile	4th quintile	5th quintile
Coverage rate before campaign (percent)	65	71	84	80	89
Coverage rate after campaign (percent)	86	92	91	92	87
Absolute change (percentage points)	+21	+21	+7	+12	−2
Relative change (percent)	+32	+30	+8	+15	−2
Change statistically significant?	Yes	Yes	No	Yes	No

Source: World Bank 2008b.

To be sure, many of the children immunized through the campaign already had a significant degree of protection through vaccinations they had previously received through regular health services. (Measles campaigns typically seek to immunize all children in the areas in which they operate, regardless of the children's previous immunization status. Although one dose of vaccine administered correctly at the optimal age provides 85 percent protection, the immunization fails to protect adequately in 15 percent of cases under even the best of circumstances—and circumstances in low-income country programs are rarely the best.) While these children received a potentially significant degree of extra protection, the greatest benefits accrued to children who had not previously received a measles immunization.

The distribution of coverage among these previously unprotected children also favored the poor. As can be seen from figure 12.1, almost 17 percent of immunized children in the poorest quintile of households had not been previously covered. This figure declines steadily across income classes, reaching a level of under 4 percent for children in the wealthiest quintile of households.

One reason for this pro-poor distribution of benefits appears to have been the lowered costs to families of obtaining immunizations for their children. While the estimated per-immunization cost to the government and participating donors was about the same (around US$0.90) for both the routine program and the catch-up campaign, bringing immunizations closer to

Figure 12.1 *Percentage of Children Covered by Kenya's 2002 Mass Campaign Who Had Not Previously Received Measles Immunization*

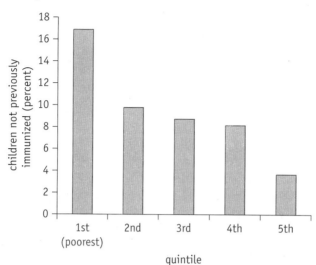

Source: World Bank 2008b.

families greatly reduced expenses for transportation and the time they had to take off from work. As a result, the average per-family cost of an immunization was only US$0.11 for vaccinations provided through the campaign, compared with US$0.86 for those made available through regular services.

How typical are these Kenyan results? There is no way to know for certain; but there is also no obvious reason to consider Kenya's regular immunization program and campaign, or the setting in which they occurred, notably different from those of the many other African countries that have also tried measles campaigns. Further suggestive evidence comes from careful studies in Ghana and Zambia showing that treated bed nets distributed through measles campaigns effectively reached even the poorest population groups, implying that the immunizations did so as well.

A further, general consideration is the likelihood that, in situations when the coverage before an SIA campaign is already high, unimmunized children will be disproportionately poor—as was the case in Kenya. This makes it difficult to significantly increase overall coverage without effective outreach to disadvantaged groups.

To the extent that such considerations and evidence are valid, the Kenya outcome would seem adequate to support a working hypothesis that the benefits of measles campaigns, and perhaps polio campaigns as well, undertaken elsewhere in Sub-Saharan Africa are likely to benefit primarily the poor. This appears especially likely in countries where a reasonably high level of overall coverage had been achieved before the campaigns' initiation.

Of course, this is not to deny the possible shortcomings of campaigns that critics have noted, as reported above. But it does point to a potentially significant advantage of the campaign approach that deserves consideration in any overall assessment of the approach's potential.

Note

This chapter draws on many resources. Four of the most important were Vijayaraghavan and others (2007), WHO (2006), Otten and others (2005), and the "Overview" section of the WHO African Regional Office Web site on measles (http://www.afro.who.int/measles/).

13

The Kyrgyz Republic: Health Financing Reform and the Poor

In 2001, over 50 percent of health expenditures in the Kyrgyz health system were paid for through out-of-pocket payments, mostly associated with inpatient care and outpatient drug purchases. To obtain hospital care, patients had to contribute toward medicines, syringes, intravenous tubes, bandages, linen, food, and even notebooks, light bulbs, and the like. These payments were in addition to informal payments to health care personnel (World Bank 2008c). In 2001, the mean out-of-pocket expense was 1,846 Kyrgyz soms (US$46) for those who reported any contact with the health system. This amount was equivalent to five times average monthly per capita consumption, raising questions of affordability for the large number of poor in the country.

The high share of out-of-pocket expenditures is a relatively new phenomenon in the Kyrgyz Republic that emerged in the postindependence transition period. Health services during Soviet times were free of charge except for occasional gifts to health care workers and cost sharing for heavily subsidized outpatient drugs. With the breakup of the Soviet Union and the general economic decline during transition, public spending on health dropped from 3.6 percent of GDP in 1991 to 1.9 percent by 2000 (World Bank 2008c). The extensive provider network built during Soviet times absorbed an increasing share of declining government expenditures. Staff and utilities consumed 75 percent of the health care budget, leaving few resources for direct medical expenditures such as medicines and supplies (World Bank 2008c).

Policy Change: The Kyrgyz Health Finance Reforms (2001–05)

The Kyrgyz Republic introduced far-reaching health finance reforms in 2001–05 as part of the 10-year Manas Health Sector Reform Program. One of the main objectives of the reforms was to reduce the negative financial impact of out-of-pocket payments on poor households. Given the limited fiscal space, it was clear that the health sector would not have additional public funds to reduce patient expenditures. The large hospital sector had to be downsized to achieve efficiency gains. Savings were reallocated to medicines, medical supplies, and better-paid personnel to reduce out-of-pocket payments.

The health finance reforms were based on a purchaser-provider split. The Mandatory Health Insurance Fund (MHIF) became the purchaser of most individual health services and the Ministry of Health (MOH) remained the purchaser of some individual health services (for example, for cancer and tuberculosis) and public health services. The MOH also continued to assume stewardship functions. The purchaser-provider split did not imply a change in the sources of funds, only in the flow of funds and purchasing arrangements. The MHIF became the purchaser of health services, predominantly using general tax revenues and a small payroll tax. The reforms were introduced in a phased manner starting with two oblasts (states) in 2001 and adding two oblasts per year until the roll-out was completed in 2005.

The reforms consisted of four key building blocks:

- *Centralization of health financing channels (pooling).* Before the reforms, providers—nearly all public—were funded from general tax revenues corresponding to hierarchical administrative structures: republican-level (federal) providers were funded from republican-level taxes, oblast facilities were funded from oblast taxes, and rayon (district) facilities were funded from rayon taxes. No funding or decision making occurred across these administrative boundaries, which led to duplication and lack of incentives for eliminating inefficiencies. The finance reforms centralized finance channels at the oblast level, and pooled tax revenues in the oblast departments of the MHIF. This decision eliminated rayon- and city-level resource pools and created the opportunity to reallocate resources across city-rayon boundaries within oblasts.
- *Prospective purchasing methods.* Before the reforms, providers were paid according to input-based norms formulated into strict line-item

budgets reflecting historical patterns. Managers could not reallocate across line-item categories if the need or the opportunity arose. In the context of the reforms, inputs based on line-item budgets were replaced with capitation payment for primary care providers and case-based payment for hospital care.

- *Explicit definition of benefits.* The third step involved clear regulation of entitlements through the State Guaranteed Benefit Package. The benefit package specifies free primary care for the entire population and referral care with formal copayment. Copayment consists of a flat fee payable upon admission. Exemptions are granted on the basis of certain disease categories that have high expected health care use, such as disability, cancer, recently experienced heart attack, tuberculosis, and so on, and for World War II veterans. Hospitals receive higher payments for treating exempt patients to prevent adverse selection. Hospitals also keep copayment revenues but are mandated to use 80 percent of collected copayments for the purchase of medicines, supplies, and food.

- *Downsizing the hospital sector.* These changes in health financing created an environment that enabled the downsizing of excess hospital facilities. Because most hospitals were built in a pavilion style, operating in 15–20 small buildings, within-facility downsizing had great potential to save fixed costs. The unnecessary buildings were demolished, rented out (to pharmacies, for example), or transferred to other public uses (such as health promotion units). During 2001–04, physical capacity in the hospital sector was reduced from 1,464 buildings to 784, with a concomitant change in total operational area, utility costs, and maintenance costs. At the same time, cross-facility downsizing involved merging facilities that served overlapping populations through administrative mechanisms.

Findings

The impact of the reforms on patient financial burden was evaluated using two household surveys. The first survey was conducted before the implementation of the reforms and the second one was conducted when the reforms had been rolled out to half of the oblasts.

The evaluation found that the reforms had a positive impact on patient financial burden for hospitalization, particularly for the poor. Out-of-pocket payments for hospital care increased significantly in control oblasts, by nearly 600 soms (US$15). In contrast, out-of-pocket payments increased by only 200 soms (US$5) in the reform oblasts during the same period. Assuming that the reform oblasts would have experienced the same trends as control oblasts, the reforms were successful in limiting the increase of out-of-pocket payments for hospitalization by 393 soms (US$10) for an average household.

Figure 13.1 shows that the reforms had a greater impact on lower-income groups. Conditional on hospitalization, the poorest 40 percent experienced a significant increase in out-of-pocket payments in control oblasts, and a slight decline in reform oblasts (quintiles 1 and 2). In contrast, out-of-pocket payments increased in both the reform and nonreform oblasts for the

Figure 13.1 *Effect of Reforms on Hospital Out-of-Pocket Payments, Conditional on Hospitalization*

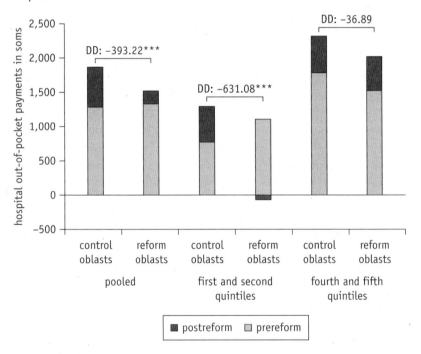

Source: World Bank 2008c.

Note: Results are predicted values from a two-part multiple regression model that estimates the reform effect on individual health expenditures, controlling for a number of individual, household, and regional characteristics. DD stands for difference-in-difference estimate and is the difference in the out-of-pocket expenditure trend between 2000 and 2003 in reform oblasts relative to control oblasts.

*** DD estimate is statistically significant at the 1 percent level.

richest 40 percent (quintiles 4 and 5), indicating that the reforms neither slowed nor increased the pace of growth in out-of-pocket expenditures for the rich.

Analysis of secondary data is consistent with the explanation that the positive impact on financial protection was facilitated by greater efficiency gains in the oblasts where the financing reforms were implemented:

- Restructuring was more intensive in reform oblasts, with a 44 percent reduction in beds during the period versus 18 percent in control oblasts.
- Personnel were reduced by 28 percent in reform oblasts versus 24 percent in control oblasts.
- There is also evidence that restructuring indeed allowed significant savings on utility expenditures, estimated at 60 percent where restructuring took place.
- In reform oblasts, nonmedical expenditures (utilities and staff) in hospitals were reduced from 83.6 percent of total expenditures in 2000 to 63.4 percent in 2003.
- Decomposed out-of-pocket payments show a differential decline for medicines in hospitals.

The study also highlighted that spillover effects for hospital visits and outpatient medicines took place at the same time. In reform oblasts, out-of-pocket payments for outpatient drug purchases and hospital visits increased relative to control oblasts and reversed the protective effect the reforms exerted for hospitalization. This trend was stronger for the nonpoor than for the poor. While this is a negative result from the perspective of financial protection, monthly out-of-pocket expenditures may have less catastrophic and impoverishing effects than large one-off expenditures incurred for hospitalization.

The Kyrgyz experience illustrates that limiting patient financial burden is possible in a poor country with limited fiscal space through more efficient use of public resources. This lesson is particularly encouraging for other transition economies of the Commonwealth of Independent States struggling with low levels of public financing and significant inefficiencies.

The Kyrgyz reforms involved the introduction of copayments for hospitalization. Typically, the introduction of cost-sharing is associated with a negative impact on financial protection. The Kyrgyz experience shows that when copayments are introduced in an environment of high informal payments (to personnel but also for medicines and supplies), there is not necessarily an associated increase in patient financial burden. Copayment can create clarity and transparency in entitlements and can explicitly protect the poor through exemption schemes.

Finally, the Kyrgyz results also reinforce the notion that there are no magic bullets for improving financial protection. The Kyrgyz experience was based on a complex systemic approach rather than on isolated reform instruments. Implementation of a complex systemic approach is quite challenging and requires a longer time frame and consistent political support.

Note

This chapter was written by Melitta Jakab with support from WHO/EURO and based on her paper "An Empirical Evaluation of the Kyrgyz Health Reform: Does It Work for the Poor?" Harvard University/WHO (2007). The sources of information include World Bank 2008c. WHO also funded data collection for the paper.

14

Mexico: Paying the Poor to Use Health Services

Despite food subsidies and other poverty relief programs, Mexico continued to experience a stubbornly high poverty rate into the 1990s. Ultimately, the existing poverty relief programs were found to be poorly targeted, expensive, and inefficient. Administrative expenses constituted a third of the poverty relief budget. Rather than teaching skills that could help poor people break out of poverty, the old programs simply gave them handouts, merely temporary relief.

Policy Change: Conditional Cash Transfers in Health and Education

To combat the country's stubbornly high poverty rate and replace the poverty relief programs that did not work, Mexico launched the Health, Nutrition and Education Program (known by its Spanish acronym PROGRESA) in 1997. PROGRESA replaced subsidies with conditional cash transfers to encourage and enable households to invest in education, nutrition, and health care.

Since its inception, PROGRESA has grown steadily. It managed to survive a landmark shift in power away from the political party that established it (the title of the program was changed to Oportunidades in 2001). It now serves over 20 million people or approximately one-fifth of Mexico's population. The accomplishments were achieved with relatively modest administrative costs. Overall, administrative expenses have been held to under 10 percent of the program's total expenditures.

Beneficiary Selection

To make sure program benefits actually go to poor people, PROGRESA first selected beneficiary villages, then families. Poor villages were identified through a community score, based on national census data, using factors such as educational attainment, occupation, housing, and health conditions. The lowest-scoring villages located within reachable distance of educational and health facilities were selected for participation. Within eligible villages, families were selected by a proxy means test. Information closely associated with income was collected from households through special community censuses and combined to provide a poverty rating. The lowest-rated households qualified for inclusion. Originally, about half the households in eligible villages were included. However, after local protests, PROGRESA revised the selection criteria, and about 80 percent of the households in selected communities qualified. Thus, the selection of communities became much more important in determining PROGRESA's targeting effectiveness than the identification of households. In 2001, when PROGRESA became Oportunidades, the program was extended to urban areas.

Benefits Determination and Delivery

Program benefits were designed to further long-term human development and poverty alleviation, as well as to give immediate poverty relief. Women in beneficiary families were eligible for regular cash payments only if they acted to improve their own and their families' educational, health, and nutritional status. Thus, the benefits paid under the program were "conditional" cash transfers, paid to participants if they kept their children in school and obtained health care for their families:

- *Health.* An eligible family received a monthly food-transfer payment of 125 pesos (US$12) *if* each child had two to four health checkups a year and each adult had one annual checkup. Pregnant women, however, had to have seven pre- and post-natal checkups. Nutritional supplements were available for young children.
- *Education.* Up to 305 pesos (US$28) a month were paid for each child in grades three through nine, *if* the child attended at least 85 percent of his or her classes. Payments were higher for higher grades and also higher for girls.

The Oportunidades program extended education grants to the high school level. The Fox administration also announced a new component of Oportunidades called Youth with Opportunities (Jovenes con Oportunidades), a savings plan for participating high school students that grows with each year, from ninth grade through graduation.

The program based each beneficiary's payment amount on attendance information submitted electronically by school teachers and health personnel at the facilities where the beneficiary registered upon enrollment in the program. The funds were telegraphed to local distribution points where beneficiaries collected their payments. When the funds arrived, beneficiaries were notified by their elected community volunteers, who also performed many other liaison functions between the program administrators and benefit recipients. Overall, these conditional cash transfers represent about 20 percent of participating family incomes.

Findings

We will first look at the implementation challenges, then focus on program accomplishments, especially in health and education.

Implementation Challenges

Executing a program so drastically different from its predecessors posed many challenges. The complex, technocratic proxy procedure used to identify beneficiaries had to be explained to community residents so that they could understand and accept its legitimacy. This was one reason the program administrators felt compelled to include more people than originally envisaged, thereby diluting (but by no means completely negating) the targeting effectiveness.

Timely payment of benefits was another challenge. At first, delays cropped up at several points: within the community in submitting completed forms to program authorities, and at the central office in issuing payments once the forms had arrived. A related limitation was in the number of fund distribution points, which were often far from the beneficiaries' homes. More distribution points than planned were eventually opened to satisfy disgruntled beneficiaries.

Other issues involved keeping lists of eligible households up to date and monitoring the effectiveness and integrity of the procedures used to identify and pay beneficiaries. Early evaluations did not identify any major problems in procedural effectiveness or integrity, but the issues remained as major concerns to program administrators.

Program Accomplishments

Despite these constraints, the program grew steadily and remained strong after the Fox administration came to power. The program was evaluated by household surveys just before its initiation and two years after, in 320 villages that had received services and 186 villages that had not. These and other evaluation studies suggested that most program benefits have gone to poor families and that the program produced (i) noteworthy increases in school enrollment, especially in middle school enrollment; (ii) declines in levels of child malnutrition and illness; and (iii) reductions in poverty.

Record on Reaching the Poor

The program serves more than 20 million people, currently a fifth of Mexico's population. Payments through the program make up 20 percent of the income of the households receiving them.

PROGRESA's record in reaching the poor is summarized in figure 14.1. As can be seen, almost 60 percent of people reached by the program

Figure 14.1 *PROGRESA/Oportunidades's Success in Reaching the Poor*

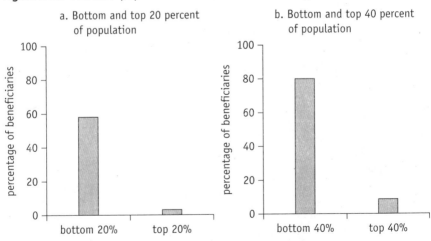

Source: Coady, Filmer, and Gwatkin 2005.

belonged to the poorest 20 percent of Mexico's population, and 80 percent of the beneficiaries were in the poorest 40 percent of the country's population. The program also produced some enviable improvements in outcome indicators, a 45 percent reduction in the severity of poverty being one of them.

The main factors behind these highly progressive results were the selection of poor villages, and conditions tying payment of benefits to children's participation in education and health programs (because poor people have more children than do the better-off). The focus on choosing poor families within villages was less important (because most of the families in the selected villages were poor, and the program was not introduced in higher-income areas).

Record on Adult and Child Health

Illness profoundly affects child development and adult productivity. As a result of improved nutrition and preventive care, PROGRESA/Oportunidades children have fewer illnesses than non-PROGRESA/Oportunidades children from infancy to age five. It was reported that there was a 16 percent increase in the annual growth rate of children in their first 12 to 36 months, and a 20 to 25 percent reduction in the incidence of illness among children from infancy to age 5. Adults in program households have 17 percent fewer incapacitating days of illness than non-PROGRESA/Oportunidades adults.

Record on Education

The program expanded enrollment of boys and girls at both primary and secondary levels. At the primary level, where enrollment was high at the outset, the program boosted the rates 1.07 percent for boys and 1.45 percent for girls. At the secondary level, enrollment grew 8 percent for boys and 14 percent for girls. The increase in educational attainment for both boys and girls was an estimated 10 percent, from a starting point of about 6.2 years for the average 18-year-old.

The students within the program begin school younger, repeat fewer grades, and drop out less frequently, especially between primary and secondary school, than children from other groups in Mexico. Despite the higher financial incentives given to girls to continue their education at the secondary level, the program seemed to encourage more boys than girls to stay in school.

Although the program has increased the number of children staying in school, any impact it may have had on performance at school is hard to quantify. Test scores did not improve noticeably, but teachers and other school personnel interviewed thought students had nonetheless benefited from the program. Employment of both boys and girls in salaried and nonsalaried jobs fell because more were staying in school in PROGRESA/Oportunidades villages.

In conclusion, the positive impacts of PROGRESA/Oportunidades show that a conditional cash transfer program can be an effective, feasible instrument in both reducing current poverty and improving the future of children through increased investment in their health and education. The experience of PROGRESA/Oportunidades also shows that it is feasible to carry out a targeted conditional cash transfer program on a very large scale even within poor, isolated areas with few services, and in particular, in a developing country with a limited welfare state.

Among the important factors behind the success of the program was that an initial evaluation was planned from its beginning. This ensured the feasibility of having a control group and also ensured that results were available at an early juncture in the program, when program changes are easier to carry out and when programs may be more susceptible to budget cuts. Involving prestigious academics in the evaluation was also important, making the credibility of the results difficult to question.

Note

This chapter was adapted from Coady, Filmer, and Gwatkin (2005), and Coady (2003).

15

Mexico: Providing Subsidized Health Insurance to the Poor

In the 1940s, Mexico solved the problem of providing insurance coverage to formal sector workers through the typical Latin American arrangement of social security institutions for employees of private and public establishments. These institutions collect premiums from employees and their employers, obtain additional funding through subsidies from general government revenue, and use these resources to provide services to the covered employees. This system has worked relatively well for the half of the Mexican population who have access to it.

The better-off are usually employed in factories, governmental organizations, and other institutional settings, which are more likely to offer health insurance. Consequently, this segment of the population has greater knowledge of, easier access to, and more frequent health insurance coverage. The poorer half of the population is far less fortunate. The poor tend to work in smaller and poorly regulated establishments, to be self-employed menial laborers, or to be without work at all, as in the case of many female-headed households. Because they are outside the formal labor market, they generally do not have access to health insurance through the workplace or cannot afford to pay for it. This segment of the population was left to seek lower-quality services provided, at a fee, through health ministry facilities, or through the expensive and often unregulated private sector.

The Mexican health system was seriously unbalanced and underfunded. Government health programs were not able to address the challenges presented as the country's health profile shifted in a modernizing economy. Overall per capita spending on health care in Mexico was less than the average in Latin America. More than half of the money spent on health was out of pocket and higher than in many other Latin American countries. Funding was not distributed efficiently or equitably—close to half of the population was uninsured, yet only a third of the federal funds for health went to them. More richer people had health insurance coverage, while coverage among the poor was very low—maybe 10 percent. There was great risk of impoverishment as a result of health spending; two million to four million households spent 30 percent of annual disposable income on health.

Policy Change: Subsidized Health Insurance for the Poor through Segura Popular

The government that took office in 2000 assigned a high priority to correcting this imbalance. It introduced a set of reforms that featured a new health insurance program, Seguro Popular (SP), for all those not covered by existing social security plans. The purpose of the voluntary program was, and is, to provide these people with subsidized insurance coverage comparable to that available to social security beneficiaries.

The health ministries of Mexico's 32 state governments have primary responsibility for identifying, enrolling, and serving eligible SP participants. The program was designed to focus on the poorest families first. Regular premium payments are subsidized on a sliding scale by the state, and the families from the poorest 20 percent of the population do not pay. Participants are entitled to treatment *at no additional cost* through some 250 interventions at specified institutions (mostly the same state government facilities at which participants had previously paid for such services as had been available to them). SP participants are also eligible for 17 interventions at a network of higher-level tertiary care institutions operated by the federal and state governments.

The gap between income from premium payments and the program's total cost is covered by government subsidies. The majority of the funding comes from the federal government, through payments to the state governments allocated through a formula that factors in the level of development of the state, with poor states receiving more than better-off ones. The formula also accounts for the number of families enrolled, giving states an incentive to improve the quality of services and increase the number of participating families. The state governments bear the remaining costs from their own resources.

The financial requirements of the SP program constitute a primary reason for the recent increase of the previously limited volume of federal government resources allocated to health. For example, the budget of the federal health ministry increased by about 53 percent between 2000 and 2005, largely attributable to the program's implementation. Universal health insurance is projected to add 1 percentage point of the public investment budget to public investment in health. Public investment in health rose to 66.5 percent in 2006.

Ensuring Participation by the Poor

The SP program aspires to universal coverage by 2010, reaching better-off and poor uninsured people alike. However, it is designed to ensure that the disadvantaged are served first, rather than last (or never) as occurs in many universal coverage programs.

The legislation underlying the program calls for increased coverage among deprived groups to receive highest priority during the seven-year (2004 through 2010) roll-out period. To move this statement of intent beyond rhetoric, the program design includes three related measures. One is a scale of premium rates that is graduated by economic status and exempts the poor from payment. The second is a mechanism permitting acceptably accurate identification of poor families that qualify for premium subsidies or exemptions. The third is a system for paying implementing agencies that gives them an incentive to focus on enrolling the poor families thus far identified.

Subsidized Premiums for the Poor

The system is based on prepayment for a package of services that will expand as demand and funding permit. The premium payments for participation in the program, which is voluntary, vary according to the participants' economic status. Families pay up to 5 percent of disposable income (defined as total spending after basic needs are covered). The premium falls and the government subsidy rises further down the economic ladder, with people in the poorest 20 percent of the population paying nothing at all.

Identification of the Poor

The states have several options available for identifying the people qualifying for different levels of subsidy. One option is to follow the lead of the already-existing, highly progressive PROGRESA/Oportunidades program, described more fully in chapter 14, whose enrolled participants (in principle, also from the poorest 40 percent of the population) are automatically eligible for SP coverage at no cost. Another is to apply a method for identifying prospective beneficiaries, similar to that of PROGRESA/Oportunidades, prepared by the SP program itself. Alternatively, the states are free to use approaches taken by several other federal subsidy programs, or to enroll all members of specified groups without evaluation of the groups' individual members.

The PROGRESA/Oportunidades and SP approaches both use a proxy means test, (described in chapter 14 for eligibility for Mexican cash transfers and in chapter 9 for eligibility for Colombia's universal health insurance plan). Such a test involves identifying the poor based on information about the assets of households and the people living in them, not on the basis of income or expenditures, which until recently were the standard measures of economic status. Field workers score each item on the basis of guidelines developed through statistical studies of household economic status, sum the results, and compare the overall outcome with that of other members of the population. A family's SP premium is based on where the family fits on the economic spectrum thus identified: the lower the family is, the less it pays.

The proxy means test is applied only to members of poor villages who may not be enrolled in other social service programs, identified on the basis of census information about factors such as employment conditions, civic amenities, and educational levels. The result is thus a two-stage process, involving first the determination of poor communities, then the identification of the poorest people within those communities.

Incentive for Enrolling the Poor

Federal SP support to state governments largely and gradually replaces federal assistance provided on the basis of prior-year levels and the number of state health workers. This shift makes the volume of federal assistance dependent on the number of people the states serve rather than on the number of people they employ and the facilities they operate. The result is an incentive for the states to enroll as many people as possible in SP to maximize and stabilize their federal subsidies. The fact that the poor do not have to pay premiums, unlike higher-income groups, makes them likely candidates for enrollment earlier than the better-off, who will have to be persuaded to pay for participation. The poor thus potentially become the most lucrative enrollees from the perspective of the administering agency, rather than the least attractive group as they are to administrators of other programs because of the greater difficulty and expense often involved in reaching them.

Findings

By the end of 2005, the second of the seven years in the roll-out period, SP had enrolled about 11.5 million people, just under 20 percent of the 65 million to 75 million Mexicans not covered by the social security system. About 40 percent of these enrollees were in the poorest 20 percent of the population, compared with under 3 percent in the population's best-off 20 percent (figure 15.1). By 2004, insurance coverage among the poorest 20 percent of Mexican families had risen to 37 percent, up from 7 percent in 2000. SP participants in need of health services were significantly more likely to obtain them than were those who did not participate.

These results have made SP far more progressive than the social security programs it is designed to complement—the social security program

Figure 15.1 *Enrollment in Mexico's Seguro Popular Program by Economic Level*

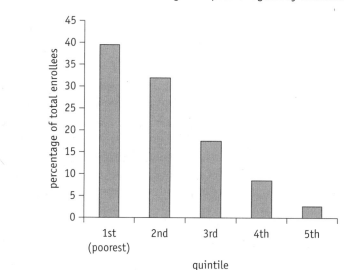

Source: Gakidou and others 2006.

beneficiaries remain heavily concentrated among the higher-income groups. Conversely, SP's initial record has been notably less progressive than that of PROGRESA/Oportunidades's conditional cash transfers. As shown in chapter 14, PROGRESA/Oportunidades had reached some 80 percent of the poorest 20 percent of the Mexican population seven years after its 1998 initiation; and nearly 60 percent of its beneficiaries at that time were in this poorest group.

To some extent, this difference can be attributed to the differing objectives of the two programs: PROGRESA/Oportunidades was intended for only the poorest 20 percent of the population, while SP is designed to reach all uninsured, many of whom lie outside this group. Two other possible considerations relate to the differences in the amount of time the two projects have been in operation, and the income levels of the states and the fact that they joined the program at different times. By some accounts, another significant factor has been the decision of some states to follow less precise beneficiary identification measures than those used by the centrally administered PROGRESA/Oportunidades. (The government of Mexico's Federal District, for example, opted to use the notoriously inaccurate system used by a long-standing program for the distribution of subsidized milk.) To the extent that this is the case, it illustrates a disadvantage of decentralizing program design in a setting where local authorities appear less progressive than central ones.

In the time since collection of the above-cited data, the SP program has moved to the approximate half-way point in its seven-year roll-out period. What about the future? Informed observers point to two of the principal challenges that SP is likely to face:

- First is continuation of the federal government's provision of the funds the project will require over the years ahead. National elections led to a change of government in late 2006. One can rarely take for granted the willingness of any new government to continue a project created by and closely associated with its predecessor. Nonetheless, one of the first decisions of the new government was to insure all children born as of the start of the administration, thereby indicating its commitment to the program.

- Second is the interest of people outside the poorest 20 percent to pay the premiums required of them to participate in SP. These people will constitute an ever-increasing proportion of the additional people who will have to be enrolled in the coming years if SP is to meet its objective of universal care. Failure to attract these people would leave

SP in the highly unusual situation of being a universal coverage program whose failure to completely achieve its objective leaves it as an initiative that disproportionately benefits the poor and ultimately misses the mark on providing *universal* care.

Note

This chapter is based primarily on a 2006 series of six articles on health reform in Mexico published in *The Lancet*, particularly the first and fifth in that series: Frenk and others (2006) and Gakidou and others (2006). Other source material includes Knaul and Frenk (2005) and Secretaría de Salud de México (2006). Additional information came from Scott (2006).

16

Nepal: Participatory Planning

The developing country of Nepal is an excellent example of the worldwide health dilemma affecting the largest generation of youth the world has ever seen. The world now has more than a billion young people between the ages of 10 and 19, most living in developing countries. Many of these adolescents marry and start families, but because of social and moral assumptions and judgments concerning youth sexuality and service needs, they do not have access to reproductive health information and services. The most disadvantaged segment of the population is female—and poor, rural, and uneducated. The gaps in services and information affect not only the lives of these individuals but also the future well-being of their societies.

Policy Change: The Nepal Adolescent Project

In Nepal, a country where young people's reproductive health needs are especially acute, a grassroots participatory approach was instituted to bridge the gap in reproductive health outcomes for young people with disadvantaged backgrounds. The Nepal Adolescent Project (NAP) was a five-year project conducted from 1998 to 2003, in collaboration with an international service delivery organization (EngenderHealth), an international research organization (International Center for Research on Women), and local Nepali nongovernmental organizations (New ERA Ltd. and BP Memorial Health Foundation). The development communities see participatory approaches as effective in increasing empowerment and accountability—two of the key factors in improving health services for the disadvantaged.

To test the effectiveness of participatory versus nonparticipatory approaches to youth reproductive health, the project implemented programs in urban and rural study and control sites, with a total of four sites.

In the study sites, there was a focus on involving the community and actively engaging disempowered groups, such as the poor, young women, and ethnic minorities, at every stage of the program. NAP took into account broader development priorities voiced by diverse members of the community. Thus, interventions aimed at improving youth-friendly services, peer education, and counseling were linked with broader interventions that had been prioritized by the community aimed at improving the socioeconomic environment and opportunities for youth. These interventions included adult education programs, activities to address social norms, and access to economic livelihood opportunities. Consequently, the entire intervention package addressed structural, normative, and systemic barriers to youth reproductive health. Furthermore, youth, parents, and other community members were actively engaged in implementing study site program activities through a wide variety of community-based groups set up during the project. In contrast, in the control sites, project staff designed and implemented standard reproductive health interventions that addressed only the most immediate risk factors, such as sexually transmitted diseases or unwanted pregnancies. Socioeconomic disadvantages—based on gender, rural or urban residence, wealth, ethnicity, schooling status, and marital status—were a specific focus of the intervention design and approach in the study sites, whereas this was not the case in the control sites.

Poverty by household asset ownership was measured. Although poverty is critical, it is not the only disadvantage that keeps young people from accessing appropriate information and services for reproductive health. The study looked at multiple types of disadvantage among young people in addition to poverty—gender, rural or urban residence, and education status. Prenatal care, delivery at a health facility, and knowledge of HIV transmission were chosen as important reproductive health outcomes for examining the impact of various types of disadvantage among young people. Data for this study came from baseline (965 households) and endline (1,003 households) cross-sectional quantitative surveys, as well as from qualitative and participatory methods. The target age group at baseline was 14- to 21-year-old males and females, married and unmarried. At the end of the intervention program, data were collected on 18- to 25-year-olds, so as to capture all youth who could have participated in or benefited from the project.

Findings

The participatory approach was generally more successful in reducing advantage-based differences in youth reproductive health outcomes. Results were measured for three indicators: institutional delivery, prenatal care, and knowledge of HIV/AIDS transmission. In both groups, the overlap between household wealth status and urban or rural status was almost synonymous with rural or urban residence, and the gap between the two groups was wide. Two other measures of disadvantage—education and ethnicity—also overlap substantially with both wealth and rural or urban residence.

Delivery in a Health Facility

At baseline, both the study and control sites showed substantial differences between rich and poor young women's access to a health facility for pregnancy delivery (figure 16.1). By the endline, poor young women in the study sites were closer in their access to a health facility for delivery when

Figure 16.1 *Delivery in a Medical Facility: First Pregnancy, Poor and Nonpoor Young Married Women, Nepal*

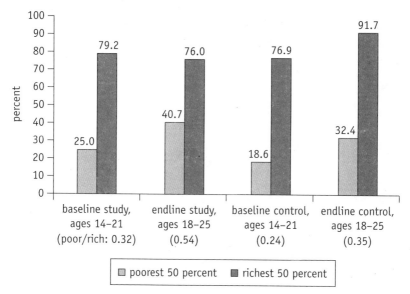

Source: Nepal Adolescent Project, 1999 baseline adolescent and household surveys and 2003 endline adolescent and household surveys.

compared with better-off women, but a similar change was not evident in the control sites. As figure 16.1 shows, this is because the improvement in access to delivery at a health facility was entirely among the poorer 50 percent of the population in the study site, whereas in the control sites, both the rich and the poor gained.

Prenatal Care

Regression results show that before the intervention, an urban young woman in a study site was 16 times more likely to get prenatal care than her rural counterpart. By the end of the project she was only 1.2 times more likely to receive prenatal care. The control sites do not show a similar improvement of access to prenatal care among rural young women (Malhotra and others 2005).

Accurate Knowledge of HIV Transmission

In all the sites at baseline, girls were less likely than boys to be able to correctly identify at least two modes of HIV transmission. In the urban study site, the intervention led to such a substantial improvement in knowledge among girls that the proportion of girls who were knowledgeable about HIV actually surpassed the proportion of boys. A similar change was not observed in the control sites. At the same time, however, neither type of intervention was able to substantially reduce the difference in knowledge regarding HIV between the educated and the uneducated (Malhotra and others 2005).

Success of the Participatory Approach

The participatory approach succeeded mainly because of three of its aspects: (i) facilitating coproduction of services, (ii) empowering young people and increasing the accountability of service providers and policy makers to the community, and (iii) increasing community demand for information and services.

Coproduction   The nature of adolescent reproductive health makes it especially amenable to coproduction and self-service by clients, and the participatory intervention design facilitated such coproduction. Well-informed and trained peers, and reliable social networks, emerged as sources of service provision. The study site interventions tapped and strengthened social networks for information exchange and counseling, while the control site interventions did not. Young people's understanding of what the services mean and how best to use them also showed greater improvement in the study sites than in the control sites.

Empowerment and Accountability   An active effort was made to impart information and build decision-making structures and coalitions. The participatory approach was more successful in empowering youths and adult community members and increasing the accountability of providers and policy makers to the communities. Committees, task forces, and youth clubs set up in the study sites fostered community skills in consensus building, decision making, planning, organizing, consulting, and demanding resources and accountability from the various participants. For example, adults and young people learned to negotiate with the village development committee and came to feel that *jointly* they could demand government funds to continue project activities. Providers were trained by the program to be youth friendly, courteous, and responsive, and young people were made aware that they could insist upon these expectations.

Community Demand   In the study sites, the focus was not just on altering reproductive health outcomes but also on changing basic social norms and institutions, as a major factor in increasing demand for information and services among the disadvantaged. The participatory approach generated a new mind-set in the communities, marked by a deeper, more sophisticated understanding of youth reproductive health and its implications for a range of life outcomes. The communities are also clearer about how family, gender, social structures, and norms constrain healthier sexual and reproductive behavior. This enriched understanding is an assurance for sustainable demand in youth reproductive health services.

In conclusion, small-scale community efforts can achieve empowerment and accountability. Specifically, participatory approaches can successfully provide youth, especially disadvantaged youth, the means to negotiate for appropriate, accessible, and accurate information and services from parents, providers, and policy makers. The critical need for broader definitions of disadvantage should be recognized. There is no dispute that poverty is a key and powerful measure of disadvantage. Nonetheless, in many rural communities in the developing world, those who are most disadvantaged owe this disadvantage to complex and interwoven interactions between various contextual factors that need to be considered. Analyses of poverty as a measure of disadvantage need to be accompanied by analyses of rural or urban residence, gender, and educational access as other important markers of social, cultural, and economic differentials.

Note

This chapter is adapted from Malhotra and others (2005a, 2005b) and Malhotra, Mathur, and Pande (2005).

17

Rwanda: Community-Based Health Insurance

In 1994, Rwanda experienced a genocide during which nearly a million people died. Gradually, the social fabric of the country is being stitched together with support from the international community. The economy is recovering and between 1995 and 2001 GDP grew at a yearly rate above 6 percent. In more recent years, GDP continued to grow at a yearly rate of between 4 and 6 percent. Despite these encouraging indications of recovery and growth, Rwanda remains one of the world's poorest countries, with GDP per capita of less than US$300 a year. Six out of ten Rwandans live in poverty. In rural areas, where 90 percent of the population lives, 66 percent are impoverished.

This level of impoverishment has forced Rwandans to develop coping strategies regarding health care. These strategies have been devised in neighborhoods, villages, and larger communities. Mutual aid and community solidarity value systems, born of great need, have long been traits of Rwanda's society. For example, associations of *hamac* (systems of mutual self-help) carry the sick to health facilities; resources are collected in neighborhoods to meet emergencies; and structured tontines are organized at cell level to meet priority needs, particularly for medical care.

As user fees were reintroduced in public and mission health facilities to help defray operational costs, additional mutual aid initiatives emerged in communities. This resilient cultural trait of Rwandan society did not receive much attention before 1994, but more recently health authorities and nongovernmental organizations (NGOs) have built on these community initiatives and transformed these spontaneous coping schemes into a deliberate strategy for community-based health insurance (CBHI).

Policy Change: Emergence of Community-Based Health Insurance Schemes

In 1998, the Ministry of Health (MOH) initiated pilot experiments in the health districts of Byumba, Kabgayi, and Kabutare. These pilots played a key role in the design and organization of CBHI schemes around the country, provided a platform for compiling information to evaluate CBHI results against health system objectives, and familiarized health sector participants and partners with strategies that would support their extension.

CBHI schemes in Rwanda are health insurance organizations based on a partnership between the community and health care providers. To regulate contractual relations between members and the mutual organization, CBHI schemes develop their own bylaws and organizational structures (general assemblies, boards of directors, surveillance committees, executive bureaus). Participation in a CBHI scheme is voluntary and based on a membership contract between the CBHI scheme and the member. CBHI schemes also develop contractual relations with health care providers for purchasing the health care services included in their members' benefits packages. Both the bylaws and the contracts with health care providers include measures for minimizing risks associated with health insurance (adverse selection, moral hazard, cost escalation, and fraud).

The target population of each CBHI scheme includes everyone living in the partner health center's catchment area. Low-risk events (included in the "health center package") in the CBHI benefits package are shared at the partner health center catchment area population. In each health district, CBHI schemes form a federation and perform a risk-pooling function for high-risk events (the "hospital package"). The district federation also plays social intermediation and representation roles for individual CBHI schemes in their interactions and contractual relations with health care providers and external partners. The federation also provides individual schemes with training, advice, support, and information services.

Members make annual contributions to the CBHI scheme. Members can sign up as a family for US$7.60 a year with a maximum of seven members. Membership entitles family members to a benefits package that includes all preventive and curative services, prenatal care, delivery care, laboratory exams, drugs on the MOH essential drug list, and ambulance transport to the district hospital. With a health center referral, members also receive a limited package of services at the district hospital. Sick members make a copayment of US$0.30 for each health center visit. At the hospital, referred members have direct access to the hospital package without any copayment. Health centers serve as gatekeepers to discourage inappropriate use of hospital services.

Since its inception in 1998, an ongoing learning process about CBHI has been taking place in Rwanda, involving CBHI schemes in the pilot districts and in other districts, with members and promoters identifying and designing the legal tools needed to support mutual health organizations, exchanging experiences, sharing information on strategies and tools, and learning from best practices. This learning environment has fostered innovative strategies for strengthening CBHI schemes in pilot districts and establishing new CBHI schemes in other parts of the country. These local initiatives, while maintaining the technical design of the pilot phase, have capitalized on the decentralization movement under way in Rwanda, incorporating partnerships between local administrative structures, grassroots associations, and microfinance schemes to strengthen local CBHI support systems and expand enrollment.

Findings

CBHI schemes have taken off in Rwanda. From a single CBHI scheme in 1998, the number increased to 60 in 2001 as a direct result of the pilot phase supported by the MOH. Starting in 2001, an adaptation phase, drawing on lessons learned and recommendations from the pilot phase, extended the number of CBHI schemes and increased enrollment rates in individual schemes. By July 2003, 97 CBHI schemes covered a half million Rwandans. In 2004, 214 CBHI schemes had arisen across the country as a result of the combined promotional efforts of central authorities (MOH and Ministry of Local Affairs), provinces, districts, local health personnel, local opinion leaders, and NGOs. In mid-2004, national coverage of CBHI schemes was estimated at 1.7 million Rwandans, about 21 percent of the population.

With the removal of financial barriers to health care by CBHI schemes, plan members are four times more likely than nonmembers to seek modern health care when sick. The household survey results of the pilot phase, summarized in figure 17.1, have been replicated based on routine data from health centers gathered during the pilot phase, and more recently from health centers in the same pilot districts, as well as from results in health

Figure 17.1 *Proportion of Sick Seeking Care from Modern Provider, by Income Quartile, 2000*

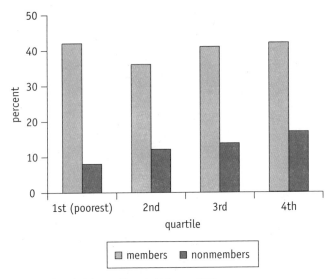

Source: Byumba, Kabgayi, Kabutare Household Survey 2000.

centers in the districts that set up CBHI schemes between 2001 and 2003. CBHI has also increased the use of reproductive health services, including prenatal care and delivery care. It had no effect, however, on the use of family planning services.

As a result of their insurance function, CBHI schemes prevent members from falling into poverty as a result of illness through two mechanisms. First, sick members seek care earlier in their illnesses than the uninsured, resulting in efficiency gains in the consumption of health care services. Second, sick members pay small out-of-pocket copayments at the health centers. Consequently, out-of-pocket payments are reduced significantly for CBHI members (figure 17.2).

Promoting CBHI

Greater access of the poor to CBHI benefits is being promoted through two main strategies: microfinance and subsidies.

Microfinance   Building on partnerships between CBHI schemes, grassroots associations, and microfinance schemes (*banques populaires*), members of

Figure 17.2 *Out-of-Pocket Illness-Related Expenditures*

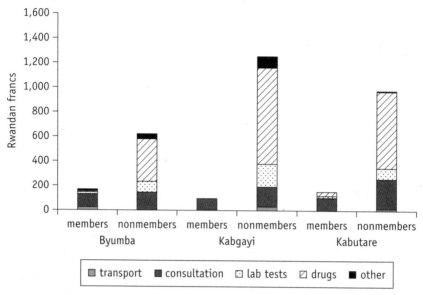

Source: Patient Exit Survey 2000.

grassroots associations, new and old, are motivated to enroll as a group in the CBHI schemes. Microfinance schemes then make small loans to the associations' members to pay for their annual dues to the CBHI schemes. Microfinancing has boosted enrollment of the poor in the CBHI schemes. It has also opened opportunities for poor CBHI members to access larger microloans and finance income-generating activities. Such financial arrangements developed as a consequence of the institutional arrangements between CBHI schemes, microfinancing schemes, and health centers, and innovations introduced by local actors.

Subsidies NGOs and administrative districts are using the institutional bridges between the community, the CBHI schemes, and health care providers to finance the enrollment of the poorest, the indigent, and vulnerable groups (orphans, widows, and people living with HIV/AIDS). Under these demand-based subsidy schemes, community leaders exercise administrative functions in identifying the poorest, the indigent, and vulnerable groups; the CBHI schemes manage health care use for these groups; and the subsidies are financed by NGOs and administrative districts that serve as intermediaries for primary sources of finance, such as state funding and external aid.

Learning from the Rwanda CBHI

CBHI in Rwanda is still a work in progress, but experience there since 1999 affords some valuable lessons for the extension of micro health insurance schemes throughout the country as well as for adaptation by other developing countries.

Lesson 1   CBHI in Rwanda is being built using an incremental approach, drawing lessons from internal experience as well as external experience of prepayment schemes in southern Africa and mutual health organizations in western Africa. The MOH provided the leadership to initiate the pilot phase and secured technical assistance from the U.S. Agency for International Development (USAID)/Rwanda and Abt Associates Inc. to improve the technical design and organization of already-functioning CBHI schemes. The MOH kept a respectful distance from scheme design and management, giving communities and local health providers autonomy and operating room. The pilot generated information on scheme performance and convened multiple forums for stakeholders to exchange experiences and to debate the consequences and implications of CBHI for the Rwanda health system. The incremental approach provided a learning platform and opportunities to derive policy direction for the development of CBHI.

Lesson 2   As consensus on the benefits of CBHI increased, multitiered leadership developed in the country to support its adaptation and extension. National political leaders, starting with the president, called upon all stakeholders to mobilize the implementation of CBHI schemes throughout the country. Local communities were motivated by MOH support, and this support in turn boosted promotional activities by the Ministry of Local Affairs. At the province and district levels, préfets and mayors actively coordinate promotional activities originated by the Ministry of Local Affairs. At the grassroots level, cell and sector representatives, together with health personnel and local opinion leaders, are active in sensitization activities. This multilevel leadership and activism have strengthened the legitimacy of CBHI and won intersectoral support for it.

Lesson 3   Intersectoral action was mobilized with the involvement of decentralized entities and NGOs in CBHI promotional activities under a policy environment in which community development was a central theme. The resulting local initiatives improved access of the poor to CBHI benefits. Partnerships between local microfinance schemes, CBHI schemes, and grassroots associations have widened access for the poor to microfinance credit and to CBHI. NGOs and administrative districts are using CBHI schemes as intermediate local solidarity funds to target demand-based subsidies for the most underprivileged in the health sector, thereby broadening their access to CBHI.

Note

This chapter was adapted from Diop and Butera (2005).

18

Tanzania: Social Marketing for Malaria Prevention

Malaria infects over 500 million people worldwide each year. The most vulnerable segments of the population are infants, young children, and pregnant women. Infants and young children are vulnerable because they have not developed immunities to malaria. Pregnant women experience a decrease in immunity, particularly during their first and second pregnancies, which results in an increased vulnerability to malaria. The World Health Organization (WHO) and the United Nations Children's Fund (UNICEF) estimated that in 2003, malaria caused more than 3,000 child deaths a day, mostly in Africa.

In 2000, African leaders came together at the African Summit on Roll Back Malaria and signed the Abuja Declaration, which called for protecting 60 percent of children with insecticide-treated bed nets by 2005. Insecticide-treated nets have been shown to effectively reduce malaria mortality on average by 18 percent among children in Sub-Saharan Africa and increase the proportion of improved birth outcomes. The principal challenge to achieving the Abuja Declaration goal was to develop an efficient, equitable, and sustainable mechanism to deliver insecticide-treated nets to the poor and most vulnerable segments of the population.

Policy Change: The KINET Project

The Kilombero Treated Net Project (KINET) sought to increase coverage of insecticide-treated nets for a defined population in Tanzania, targeting pregnant women and the mothers of children under age five through combined social marketing and community participation techniques. Initiated in 1997, KINET was implemented by the Ifakara Health Research and Development Centre (IHRDC) in the Kilombero and Ulanga districts in southwestern Tanzania. Located on the low terrain of the flood plain of the Kilombero River, both districts experience high levels of rainfall annually from November to May and are high transmission areas for malaria, particularly during the rainy season.

Social marketing employs the principles and practices of commercial marketing techniques to deliver socially beneficial goods at affordable, and often subsidized, prices to particular groups. Social marketing of insecticide-treated nets through a public-private partnership and meaningful community participation successfully and quickly increased the distribution of mosquito nets among the poorest populations in Tanzania, particularly children and pregnant women. This program resulted in improved health outcomes with respect to the morbidity and mortality impacts of malaria on children.

To determine the project's effectiveness in benefiting the poor, it had a built-in evaluation component, collecting baseline information on demographics, risk factors for child mortality, and knowledge about childhood diseases. Marketing research determined access, knowledge, and preferences relating to mosquito nets and their usage. These data provided a reference point for evaluating the achievements of the initiative.

The information collected showed that although villagers perceived a link between mosquitoes and malaria, the link between malaria and children's deaths was not as evident to them. Many people did not believe enlarged spleen, convulsions, or high fever were caused by malaria.

Marketing research established the availability of nets and that mosquito nuisance was the main reason for their use in the 37 percent of homes found to have at least one net in 1996. Insecticide treatment of nets was rare, though people were familiar with the idea. Thus, though knowledge about the availability of nets existed, their use was viewed mainly as a convenience rather than as a disease prevention tool. These findings highlighted another challenge to net ownership—the need to change the mind-set of individuals regarding the purpose of the nets; these findings served as the basis for the subsequent planning of the project.

Community participation in the early stages of the program and the continued involvement of communities in development of the product contributed greatly to the emergence of an effective social marketing strategy as well as to the success of the project. Sensitization meetings allowed community leaders to express their concerns about the project while allowing researchers the chance to identify opportunities for using strengths within the communities, as well as weaknesses and potential threats to the success of social marketing efforts requiring their attention. The selection of products; the development of a marketing strategy, including the message to be disseminated; and the product delivery method represented a true collaborative effort between the marketing research team and the targeted population. This process differs from traditional marketing methods in which decision making is generally controlled by the seller.

The KINET project worked closely with local health and education authorities to develop an information, education, and awareness strategy guided by fundamental social marketing principles. These principles included promoting certain messages along with a product carrying an appealing brand name and logo; having a consumer orientation; and targeting specific populations (Andreasen 1995). The knowledge and understanding gained by the KINET team regarding the preferences and the socioeconomic status of community members, along with the community's awareness of the importance of having a successful program, created a foundation for collaboration and dialogue between the team and community members in exploring the concepts of sustainability and cost recovery.

Product Choice and Pricing

The brand name chosen for the treated nets and insecticide was Zuia Mbu (which means "prevent mosquitoes" in Kiswahili). The actual products selected were dark green, high-quality polyester nets in two sizes; and a water-based formulation of lambda-cyhalothrin (ICON TM) insecticide for treating the mosquito nets. The insecticide was packaged in a 6 ml sachet, enough to re-treat one net, thus eliminating the potential danger of exposing children or other individuals in the household to excessive insecticide.

Product pricing was determined through a combination of village sensitization meetings and past experience of affordability in other areas. Marketing research revealed that local people were willing to pay near cost recovery for the nets and a little less than cost recovery for the insecticide sachets. The nets were sold for T Sh 3,000 (US$5.00 in 1997) and the insecticide sachets for T Sh 250 (US$0.42 in 1997).

Product Promotion through Effective Communication

Seeking to improve general awareness and knowledge about the association between malaria and ill health and the protective nature of insecticide-treated nets, the IHRDC and the District Health Management Team developed a promotional campaign and materials designed based on the findings from the research conducted about community perceptions of severe childhood disease. The promotional schemes included setting up posters and billboards, distributing leaflets and exercise books used in schools, and so on. Mass communication campaigns were organized around sporting events; local drama presentations; other forms of entertainment, such as singing and dancing; and product-launch parties. This strategy was disseminated to the sales agents and resource people from the villages (including leaders, primary school teachers, and maternal and child health aides). Clinic health aides were trained to speak to pregnant women and mothers of young children. Interpersonal interaction during message delivery is an important component of social marketing.

Distribution

The products were distributed through a combination of public and private outlets. Sales agents were nominated from each village by community leaders and members in conjunction with program personnel in open meetings. These agents included health workers, parish priests, community leaders, and shopkeepers. They were remunerated on a commission basis, and a reward system was established for retailers who met or exceeded targets. The agents were trained to treat the nets and keep sales records. Subsequent biannual training and review sessions were conducted. Initially, project personnel distributed the product to sales agents. As the program's coverage area grew, wholesalers assumed this role.

Findings

One important feature of the project was the identification of a specific area to provide a sampling frame for evaluation of the program. A demographic surveillance system was established in 1996 using a complete census of the population covered in Phase I of the project, which included 55,000 people living in 11,000 households in 18 villages. The census collected baseline vital statistics data on the population, and mapped residences as well as temporary structures that farmers erect to be close to their fields. Each household interviewed at baseline was visited every four months to record changes in the composition of the population, such as migration into or out of the area, births, pregnancies, and deaths. In addition, data about ownership of nets and other assets, such as a tin roof, a radio, or a bicycle, were collected and a socioeconomic status score was calculated for each household. With the scores, the approximately 10,000 households surveyed were ranked by quintiles. Over the life of the program, a variety of surveys and assessments were conducted to provide baseline data and record changes. Post-implementation research evaluated the program's success in increasing the percentage of net use as well as the impact of increased usage on childhood malaria morbidity and mortality outcome indexes.

Distributional Outcomes

Between 1997 and 2000, this social marketing program was able to bring about an increase of over 100 percent in the use of insecticide-treated nets for individuals living in the first through fourth asset quintiles. Net use in the poorest quintile was at 20 percent in 1997 and rose to 73 percent in 2002. The ratio of the poorest to the least poor (an indicator of equity) went from 0.30 at baseline to 0.75 after five years. Net ownership in 1997, 2000, and 2002 is displayed by economic status in figure 18.1.

Further evidence of the social marketing program's success is the overall increase in net ownership (whether insecticide treated or not) from 58 percent to 83 percent. Use of treated nets rose from 10 percent to 61 percent.

Cost Effectiveness

The cost effectiveness of the KINET insecticide-treated net distribution project in Tanzania was also evaluated. The cost for insecticide-treated nets was US$1,560 per death averted and US$57 per disability-adjusted life year (DALY) averted. When untreated nets were factored in, the costs dropped to US$1,018 per death averted and US$37 per DALY averted. The cost per death averted falls in the range of the results of randomized controlled trials in Ghana and Kenya, of US$2,304 and US$3,228, respectively, per death averted.

Figure 18.1 *Household Net Ownership before and after Social Marketing Program, by Socioeconomic Status*

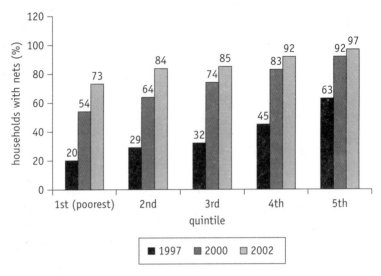

Source: Nathan and others 2004.

Health Outcomes

Insecticide-treated nets were successful in protecting children from malaria and associated conditions. Several studies assessed child survival and morbidity after program implementation. One study documented an increase of 27 percent in survival among children between the ages of 1 month and 4 years who were insecticide-treated net users. Another demonstrated that while both insecticide-treated and untreated nets showed protective efficacy with respect to malaria morbidity, and specifically anemia (classified as hemoglobin level of less than 80 g/l) and enlargement of the spleen, the protective efficacy of the treated nets was always greater (see table 18.1).

Social marketing was successful in accomplishing an important objective of the project—making the nets available to the poorest of the poor, as well as reaching the target populations of pregnant women and children. By 2000, the program covered a population of close to 350,000 people in 122 villages in Tanzania. This effort's results highlight social marketing as an efficient, cost-effective methodology for controlling malaria infection and its associated morbidity and mortality impact in children.

Table 18.1 *Protective Efficacy of Insecticide-Treated and Untreated Nets in Kilombero and Ulanga Districts of Southwestern Tanzania, 1999 (percent)*

Condition	Insecticide-treated nets	Untreated nets
Parasitemia (presence of malaria parasite)	62	51
Anemia (hemoglobin < 80 g/l)	63	37
Enlarged spleen (splenomegaly)	76	71

Source: Abdulla and others 2001.

This model of social marketing with public-private partnership implies that, unlike private sector commerce, the monetary return on the government's investment, if any, may not be great. Nonetheless, it transfers goods through the commercial system, thus seeking to develop a sustainable distribution method, accomplishing a social goal, while supporting commerce. Besides the immediate successful outcomes, there are also other longer-term and less tangible benefits that a social marketing scheme, such as the KINET project, can potentially provide. These include education, community organization, and perspective transformation at the individual level. The long-term impacts can also result through the achievement of in-country human and technical resource capacity building. The community infrastructure could potentially serve as a framework for other community health prevention initiatives.

Note

This chapter was adapted from Abdulla and others (2001), Andreasen (1995), Hanson and others (2003), Nathan and others (2004), and Schellenberg and others (1999, 2001).

19

Vigilance

The Reaching the Poor Program, which began in 2001, was launched in part because of inequality in the health sector—the overwhelming evidence that, relative to other groups, the poorest were much less healthy and made much less use of the health care system. Another motivation, and the problem underlying this chapter, was the scarcity of published evidence on whether health policies and reforms were working to reduce that inequality.

The lack of evidence on what works did not reflect a lack of concern. Indeed, virtually all countries and development agencies highlight the importance of reaching and helping the poor through the health and education sectors. The missing link has been a systematic attempt to measure whether reforms within the health sector were actually decreasing inequality and reaching larger segments of the poor.

The health sector is not unique in this regard. Global development efforts are notably weak in providing measurement frameworks that monitor progress against stated objectives. In far too many cases, even baseline information is not available for critical outcomes. A number of factors may play an important role in the overall weakness in the monitoring of development programs. Two important factors are rooted in the very conditions of low- and moderate-income countries—limited capacity and the challenges of measuring economic status:

Limited capacity. The lack of "monitoring and evaluation" (M&E) components in health projects can be traced in part to the limited capacity of the countries for collecting, analyzing, synthesizing, and disseminating data. The problem has led to the creation of an industry devoted to "teaching"

M&E, and several globally run vertical support programs have arisen to supply M&E capacity.[1]

Difficulty of measuring wealth or income. Measuring wealth or income in low-income or low-capacity countries is not straightforward. Over the years, substitutes for measures of "means" have been developed, including location of residence and gender of the head of household, but such proxies provide only weak support for analysis of health sector data stratified by economic status.

Two other difficulties are more political in nature:

Limited investment in measurement. Governments appear reluctant to invest in the measurement of performance. The M&E components of projects tend to be the last to be implemented; in many cases, they never take off and are eventually canceled. The lack of governmental "ownership" of M&E may be due, in part, to conflicting commitments by development agencies or donors. Conflicting commitments have led donors to bypass government budget arrangements and directly finance components, such as M&E, that are not strongly owned by the government.

Lack of incentives. A factor related to the issue of reluctance is that governments face a political risk in measuring the results of their own programs. In relatively poor countries, the top leadership may be especially reluctant to fund a review that might show failure in changing the pro-wealthy orientation of their health sector. Middle levels of management also face disincentives in that measured failure may have consequences for their budgets, and facilities may see a zero-sum game in which the cost of evaluations comes out of system expenditures.

Those are but a few of the likely explanations for the paucity of monitoring and evaluation in many reform projects in the health sector. Regardless of the reasons, a by-product of the resulting information vacuum is a heavy reliance on intentions and assumptions instead of outcomes. Another by-product is a general practice of measuring inputs and processes instead of inequality in service use. The overwhelming evidence on inequalities in the health sector of low- and middle-income countries demonstrates that good intentions are not enough, that untested assumptions can lead us astray, and that unfocused monitoring of overall inputs and processes may be a waste of resources.

In short, despite the obstacles, the advancement of effective health sector reforms depends in major part on progress in the area of monitoring. Fundamental to such progress is the development of monitoring mechanisms that are seen as credible by virtue of their impartiality and the high quality of the data they generate. Such credibility is especially important considering the political sensitivity of the topic of inequality.

The design of a credible monitoring framework responds to the following issues:

- *What to monitor.* The monitoring plan cannot measure everything; it must choose a subset of indicators that measure changes in inequality that are attributable to the policy change.
- *How to monitor.* How will the data be gathered, how often, and how will it be processed? What is the strategy for disseminating results?
- *Who to involve in monitoring.* The way this question is answered has an especially large effect on the perceived transparency and independence of the mechanism.

What to Monitor

We will focus on the response to the first issue—what to monitor. The process of developing a policy—which includes the definition and analysis of a problem and prioritizing a list of policy actions—naturally produces indicators to be monitored. In the case of reforms to reduce inequality in the use of health services, the policy development process yields three indicators. First, the definition of the problem (the inequality of use of health services) yields a list of possible outputs regarding service use. Second, the analysis of the underlying causes of the problem generates a list of bottlenecks at the household and health system levels. And third, prioritization specifies the changes in resource allocation that are desired. These three sets of indicators to be monitored can be restated as the following three questions in the monitoring framework—that is, the issue, "What to monitor" resolves itself into three questions of greater specificity:

1. Is the inequality of service use changing?
2. Are the supply-side or demand-side bottlenecks being eased?
3. Are resource allocation patterns changing?

Below are selections from the 14 case studies covered in chapters 5–18 that identify potential elements of an effective monitoring framework across the three dimensions of service use, bottlenecks, and resource allocation.

Is the inequality of service use changing? All 14 programs summarized in this book included a measurement of service use by wealth group. Here are a few examples selected to highlight different approaches:

- Cambodia (chapter 6). Service use by socioeconomic group was monitored for seven critical preventive and curative services at the primary care level.

- India (chapter 10). Use of community-run health services by socio-economic status was monitored for three services in both urban and rural populations.
- Indonesia (chapter 11). Use of the health card program by socioeconomic groups and by card holders was monitored for use of primary care services.
- Kenya (chapter 12). Coverage by socioeconomic group of campaigns for immunization was tracked to measure effectiveness in serving the populations that are difficult to reach.
- Mexico (chapter 14). Use of basic health services for children and pregnant women under the conditional cash transfer program was tracked to monitor the extent to which the program increased the demand for and use of these services.
- Nepal (chapter 16). Monitoring of participatory planning for reproductive health services included not only the use of critical reproductive health services by different socioeconomic groups, but also knowledge about HIV/AIDS by the same groups.

Are the supply-side or demand-side bottlenecks being eased? Monitoring the extent to which these bottlenecks were addressed should be an integral part of the monitoring framework. All 14 programs identified specific bottlenecks faced by the poor—here are some examples:

- Brazil (chapter 5). Two important bottlenecks in family health programs were identified. The first was a mismatch between needs and the services provided. The second was a lack of health knowledge among poor households. In such a case, a monitoring framework should track the extent to which facilities adjust their packages of services to address the needs of the poor as well as monitor the effect of health education on behavior change in poor households.
- Cambodia (chapter 7). The critical bottleneck addressed by the health equity fund was the financial barrier faced by the poor seeking care at hospitals. A monitoring framework could assess the extent to which active or passive identification of the poor, by local nongovernmental organizations administering the funds, eliminated the bottleneck. The same framework could also be useful in identifying other household-level bottlenecks.
- Chile (chapter 8). The integrated program addressed a number of household and system constraints. A monitoring framework could look at the effectiveness of the following program features: (i) identifying

the poor through proxy means testing (a supply-side constraint), (ii) motivating behavior change through the outreach program and the household development programs (a demand-side constraint), and (iii) motivating behavior change through conditional cash transfers.

- Colombia (chapter 9). Under the expansion of health insurance for the poor, the system bottleneck of concern was identifying the poor, and the demand-side bottleneck of concern was the financial barrier to care.
- Mexico (chapter 15). In this case, a monitoring framework should capture the extent to which proxy means testing correctly identified the poor and monitor the changes in insurance coverage for the poor.
- Tanzania (chapter 18). A critical factor in the plan for social marketing of bed nets for malaria prevention was the limited awareness and knowledge of the poor about the association between malaria and ill health and the protective nature of insecticide-treated nets. An effective monitoring program could track how the social marketing campaign changed awareness and knowledge among the poor.

Are resource allocation patterns changing? A critical element of reforming health systems is changing resource allocations. As was noted in chapters 1 and 3, tools for public expenditure review (PER), such as benefit incidence analysis, can be used to measure the extent to which the needs of, and the programs for, the poor are given the highest priority in public spending. Likewise, PERs can monitor the extent to which reforms influence spending choices. Examples of PER findings from the 14 cases are as follows:

- Colombia (chapter 9). In extending health insurance coverage for the poor, the extent of the subsidy from the formal to the informal employment sector grew over time.
- The Kyrgyz Republic (chapter 13). Under the program to reform the health sector, a PER measured the extent to which out-of-pocket spending by the poor decreased as a result of the reforms. The PER was also used to track changes in the allocation of inputs, including human resources and hospital beds.
- Rwanda (chapter 17). Under the expansion of community-based micro health insurance, household expenditure reviews measured the changes in out-of-pocket spending by poor households after they enrolled in the insurance scheme.

Other Elements of Monitoring Frameworks

The literature on monitoring addresses three additional topics that are directly related to the development of monitoring frameworks—the use of tracer services, the importance of listening, and tracking expenditures.

Monitoring Tracer Services

The World Bank's 2004 *World Development Report*, which focused on making services work for the poor, identified three clusters of health services that are based on service-specific characteristics (figure 19.1). The monitoring

Figure 19.1 *Three Classes of Health Services*

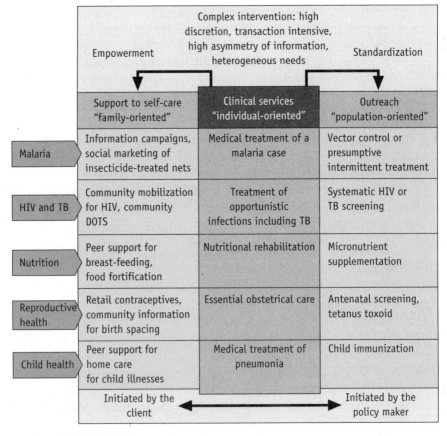

Source: World Bank 2004.

framework must include "tracer" services—services to be monitored—from each of the three clusters. That is, each class of services presents a different challenge in reaching the poor, so the monitoring framework must be able to capture successes and failures in each of the clusters. Monitoring mechanisms must also recognize differences between the three classes of services in the role of clients in the monitoring process.

Making Listening a Habit

The crucial act of listening to the poor to understand why the health system fails them was highlighted in chapter 3. The same active and passive listening techniques, described as part of an analytical approach for understanding and prioritizing policy actions, can also be effective for building a robust monitoring system that tracks constraints and bottlenecks. Here are some elements of participatory monitoring:

- Consultations with representatives of the poor (from civil society and grassroots movements) can influence the selection of the monitoring indicators and methods of tracking.
- Representatives of the poor from civil society can lead the implementation of the monitoring process with funding by the government, by donors, or by both.
- Representatives of the poor from civil society can play a critical role in the dissemination of the results and the review process to increase transparency.

Following the Money: Expenditure Tracking

One of the earliest attempts at expenditure tracking was the monitoring of spending on drugs in several African countries in the 1980s (World Bank 1994). The analysis found that only an estimated US$12 out every US$100 budgeted for drugs reached the intended clients (figure 19.2).

The Africa example is fairly old and is not focused on inequality. But it demonstrates that following the money through the system—from the budget development stage all the way through final use of the funds—is critical to determining whether all resources reach their intended targets and thus to assessing the efficiency of the project.

A specific tool for "following the money," the public expenditure tracking survey (PETS), has considerable potential to monitor and analyze inequality in the movement of resources from budgeting to final use;

Figure 19.2 *Tracking Drug Expenses in Africa in the 1980s*

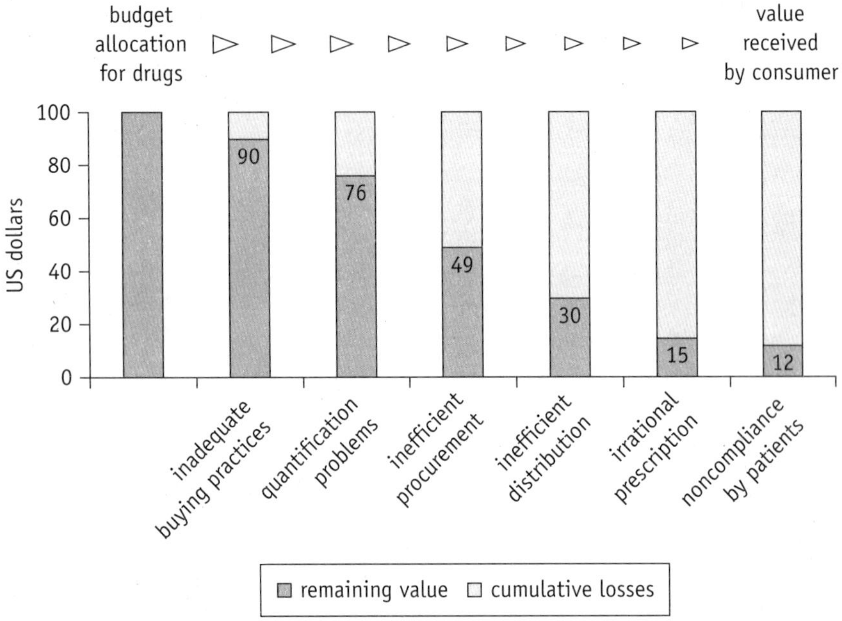

Sources: WHO and World Bank data.

however, successful implementation is dependent on two key conditions. First, the surveys require access to data at all operational stages of the expenditure process. A recent publication reviewing evidence from PETS in the health sector found that a lack of complete data was a critical limitation in the applicability of this tool (Lindelow 2008). Second, the analysis must be focused on facilities that typically serve the poor. That focus was present in the groundbreaking work that helped identify the extent to which schools in Uganda received the resources promised in the budget (Reinikka and Svensson 2004).

Annex 19.1 Recommendations for Further Reading

Selected from Goldman and others (forthcoming).

Cissé, B., S. Luchini, and J. Moatti. 2007. "Progressivity and Horizontal Equity in Health Care Finance and Delivery: What about Africa?" *Health Policy* 80 (1): 51–68.
Concentration curves and indexes are estimated to assess horizontal inequity and progressivity in health care financing and delivery systems in this cross-sectional study using 1998–99 household survey data on health care expenditures and utilization in four West African capitals (Abidjan, Bamako, Conakry, Dakar). Results strongly suggest regressive health care payments in all four West African capitals. Other research in developed countries shows similar regressivity, but its extent is limited in magnitude in comparison with the findings in this study.

Haddad, S., A. Nougtara, and P. Fournier. 2006. "Learning from Health System Reforms: Lessons from Burkina Faso." *Tropical Medicine and International Health* 2 (12): 1889–97.
This study analyzes the consequences of Burkina Faso's macroeconomic adjustment program (MAP) on the provision of health resources and the consequences of health policies implemented within the context of MAP on health outcomes. The analysis relies on data spanning the years 1983–2003 and includes documents from national and international sources, a database of secondary socioeconomic data, as well as questionnaires and interviews with health staff, key health informants in upper management, and patients. Data from surveys of households and health facilities are also included.

McMichael, C., E. Waters, and J. Volmink. 2005. "Evidence-Based Public Health: What Does It Offer Developing Countries?" *Journal of Public Health* 27 (2): 215–21.
Focuses on issues surrounding the relevance of evidence-based public health and systematic reviews in the context of health in developing countries. Authors argue that systematic reviews relevant to the health priorities of developing countries are lacking; many reviewed interventions cannot be implemented in resource-poor settings; and primary research conducted in developing countries is limited. These issues limit the usefulness of currently available systematic reviews and primary research for decision makers in developing countries. Authors review systematic reviews of the Cochrane Library and systematic reviews published in peer-reviewed

journals and make suggestions for overcoming challenges related to limited evidence-based systematic reviews in the developing-country context.

O'Donnell, O., E. van Doorslaer, R. Rannan-Eliya, A. Somanathan, S. Adhikari, B. Akkazieva, D. Harbianto, and others. 2008. "Who Pays for Health Care in Asia?" *Journal of Health Economics* 27 (2): 460–75.
Estimates the distributional incidence of health care financing (through taxes, social insurance, or direct payment) in 13 Asian countries and territories of varying levels of development in relation to ability to pay. Data on health expenditures and use are derived from official health accounts estimates, household expenditures, and socioeconomic surveys.

Wagstaff, A. 2007. "Health Systems in East Asia: What Can Developing Countries Learn from Japan and the Asian Tigers?" *Health Economics* 16 (5): 441–56.
This cross-sectional study of 2005 Organisation for Economic Co-operation and Development and WHO health data provides an analytical overview of health system financing and delivery mechanisms relative to income groups in Japan and the Asian Tigers (Taiwan, the Republic of Korea, Hong Kong [China], and Singapore). Policies and institutional arrangements were linked to outcomes of interest (health spending, unit costs, use of services, and so on) for five health systems in Asia in an effort to glean lessons for other developing Asian countries. The author examines the following factors: health finance burden distributed across income groups; progressivity of health financing mechanisms; protection of the poor from catastrophic health spending; and service utilization rates according to income groups. Results are interpreted in light of schemes aimed at cushioning the poor from copayments.

Wirth, M., D. Balk, E. Delamonica, A. Storeygard, E. Sacks, and A. Minujin. 2006. "Setting the Stage for Equity-Sensitive Monitoring of the Maternal and Child Health Millennium Development Goals." *Bulletin of the World Health Organization* 84 (7): 519–27.
Bivariate analyses (simple stratification) are used to explore the relationships between 11 health indicators and 6 social stratifiers related to the U.N. Millennium Development Goals (MDGs) for children's health. The purpose of the analysis is to demonstrate the need for equity-sensitive monitoring of the health-related MDGs. The social stratifiers (sex, education status, urban or rural residence, ethnicity, wealth, and geographic region of residence) are deployed to ascertain whether differentiations in child health outcomes are

associated with differentiations in socioeconomic condition. Each stratifier is meant to substitute for an equity-based factor of interest.

Note

1. The largest of the support programs is the Health Metrics Network financed by the Bill and Melinda Gates Foundation, http://www.who.int/healthmetrics/en/.

References

Abdulla, S., J. A. Schellenberg, R. Nathan, O. Mukasa, T. Marchant, T. Smith, M. Tanner, and C. Lengeler. 2001. "Impact on Malaria Morbidity of a Programme Supplying Insecticide Treated Nets in Children Aged under 2 Years in Tanzania: Community Cross Sectional Study." *BMJ* 322: 270–73.

Andreasen, A. 1995. *Marketing Social Change: Changing Behavior to Promote Health, Social Development, and the Environment.* San Francisco: Jossey-Bass.

Ashford, L., D. Gwatkin, and A. Yazbeck. 2006. *Designing Health and Population Programs to Reach the Poor.* Washington, DC: Population Reference Bureau.

Barros, A. J. D., C. G. Victora, J. A. Cesar, N. A. Neumann, and A. D. Bertoldi. 2005. "Brazil: Are Health and Nutrition Programs Reaching the Neediest?" In *Reaching the Poor with Health, Nutrition, and Population Services: What Works, What Doesn't, and Why,* ed. D. R. Gwatkin, A. Wagstaff, and A. Yazbeck, 281–306. Washington, DC: World Bank.

Beegle, K., E. Frankenberg, and D. Thomas. 2001. "Bargaining Power within Couples and Use of Prenatal and Delivery Care in Indonesia." *Studies in Family Planning* 32 (2): 130–46.

Campbell White, A., T. Merrick, and A. Yazbeck. 2006. *Reproductive Health, The Missing Millennium Development Goal: Poverty, Health and Development in a Changing World.* Washington, DC: World Bank.

CIET (Community Information, Empowerment and Transparency)-Canada. 2001. "Health and Population Sector Programme, 1998–2003, Service Delivery Survey, Second Cycle." Ministry of Health and Family Welfare, Dhaka, Bangladesh.

Claeson, M., C. Griffin, T. Johnston, A. Soucat, A. Wagstaff, and A. Yazbeck. 2003. "Health, Nutrition, and Population." In *A Sourcebook for Poverty Reduction Strategies*

Vol. II: Macroeconomic and Sectoral Approaches, ed. Jeni Klugman. Washington, DC: World Bank.

Coady, D. 2003. "Alleviating Structural Poverty in Developing Countries: The Approach of PROGRESA in Mexico." Background Paper for the 2004 *World Development Report*, World Bank, Washington, DC.

Coady, D. P., D. P. Filmer, and D. R. Gwatkin. 2005. "PROGRESA for Progress: Mexico's Health, Nutrition, and Education Program." *Development Outreach* 7 (2): 10–12.

Diop, F. P., and J. D. Butera. 2005. "Community-Based Health Insurance in Rwanda." *Development Outreach* 7 (2): 19–22.

Ensor, T., and S. Cooper. 2004. "Overcoming Barriers to Health Service Access: Influencing the Demand Side." *Health Policy and Planning* 19 (2): 69–79.

Escobar, M.-L. 2005. "Health Sector Reform in Colombia." *Development Outreach* 7 (2): 6–9.

Evans, R. G. 2002. "Financing Health Care: Taxation and the Alternatives." In *Funding Health Care: Options for Europe*, ed. E. Mossialos, A. Dixon, J. Figueras, and J. Kutzin, 31–58. Philadelphia: Open University Press.

Filmer, D. 2004. "The Incidence of Public Expenditures on Health and Education." Background paper for *The World Development Report 2004*. Washington, DC: World Bank.

Filmer, D., and L. H. Pritchett. 2001. "Estimating Wealth Effects without Expenditure Data—or Tears: An Application to Educational Enrollments in States of India." *Demography* 38 (1): 115–32.

Frenk, J., E. González-Pier, O. Gómez-Dantés, M. Lezana, and F. Knaul. 2006. "Comprehensive Reform to Improve Health System Performance in Mexico." *Lancet* 368 (9546): 1524–34.

Gakidou, E., R. Lozano, E. González-Pier, J. Abbott-Klafter, J. Barofsky, C. Bryson-Cahn, D. Feehan, D. Lee, H. Hernández-Llamas, and C. Murray. 2006. "Assessing the Effect of the 2001–06 Mexican Health Reform: An Interim Report Card." *Lancet* 368 (9550): 1920–35.

Galasso, E. 2006. "'With Their Effort and One Opportunity': Eliminating Extreme Poverty in Chile." Development Research Group, World Bank, Washington, DC.

Gaudin, S., and A. Yazbeck. 2006. "Immunization in India 1993–1999: Wealth, Gender, and Regional Inequalities Revisited." *Social Science and Medicine* 62 (3): 694–706.

Goldman, A., G. Azcona, G. Pammie, R. Crawford, and A. Yazbeck. Forthcoming. *Health Inequalities in Developing Countries: An Annotated Bibliography*. Washington, DC: World Bank.

Government of Chile. 2004. "An Introduction to Chile Solidario and El Programa Puente." Prepared for the World Bank International Conference on Local Development, Washington, DC, June 16–19. http://www1.worldbank.org/sp/LDConference/Materials/Parallel/PS2/PS2_S13_bm1.pdf.

Grosh, M., and P. Glewwe. 2000. *Designing Household Survey Questionnaires for Developing Countries: Lessons from 15 Years of the Living Standards Measurement Studies.* Washington, DC: World Bank.

Gwatkin, D., S. Rutstein, K. Johnson, E. Suliman, A. Wagstaff, and A. Amouzou. 2007. *Socio-Economic Differences in Health, Nutrition, and Population.* Washington, DC: World Bank.

Gwatkin, D., A. Wagstaff, and A. Yazbeck. 2005. *Reaching the Poor with Health, Nutrition, and Population Services: What Works, What Doesn't, and Why.* Washington, DC: World Bank.

Hanson, K., N. Kikumbih, J. Armstrong Schellenberg, H. Mponda, R. Nathan, S. Lake, A. Mills, M. Tanner, and C. Lengeler. 2003. "Cost-Effectiveness of Social Marketing of Insecticide-Treated Nets for Malaria Control in the United Republic of Tanzania. *Bulletin of the World Health Organization* 81 (4): 269–76.

Hardeman, W., W. Van Damme, M. Van Pelt, P. Ir, H. Kimvan, and B. Meessen. 2004. "Access to Health Care for All: User Fees Plus a Health Equity Fund in Sotnikum, Cambodia." *Health Policy and Planning* 19 (1): 22–32.

IIPS (International Institute for Population Sciences). 1995. *National Family Health Survey: India 1992–93.* Bombay: IIPS.

———. 2000. *National Family Health Survey (NFHS-2): India 1998–99.* Bombay, India, and Calverton, MD: IIPS and ORC Macro.

Jacobs, B., and N. Price. 2006. "Improving Access for the Poorest to Public Sector Health Services: Insights from Kirivong Operational Health District in Cambodia." *Health Policy and Planning* 21 (1): 27–39.

Jakab, M. 2007. "An Empirical Evaluation of the Kyrgyz Health Reform: Does It Work for the Poor?" PhD Dissertation, Harvard University, Cambridge, MA.

Jalan, J., and M. Ravallion. 2001. "Does Piped Water Reduce Diarrhea for Children in Rural India?" Policy Research Paper No. 2664, World Bank, Washington, DC.

Jejeebhoy, S. 1995. *Women's Education, Autonomy, and Reproductive Behaviour: Experience from Developing Countries.* Oxford: Clarendon Press.

Knaul, F., and J. Frenk. 2005. "Health Insurance in Mexico: Achieving Universal Coverage through Structural Reform." *Health Affairs* 24 (6): 1467–76.

Knowles, J. C., C. Leighton, and W. Stinson. 1997. "Measuring Results of Health Sector Reform for System Performance: A Handbook of Indicators." Special Initiatives Report No. 1. Partnerships for Health Reform, Abt Associates, Bethesda, MD.

Lindelow, M. 2008. "Tracking Public Money in the Health Sector in Mozambique: Conceptual and Practical Challenges." In *Are You Being Served?* ed. S. Amin, J. Das, and M. Goldstein, 173–90. Washington, DC: World Bank.

Loevinsohn, B., and A. Harding. 2005. "Buying Results? Contracting for Health Service Delivery in Developing Countries." *Lancet* 366 (9486): 676–81.

Mahal, A., J. Singh, F. Afridi, V. Lamba, A. Gumber, and V. Selvaraju. 2002. "Who Benefits from Public Sector Health Spending in India? Results of a Benefit Incidence Analysis for India." Background Paper for *Better Health Systems for India's Poor*. National Council for Applied Economic Research, New Delhi.

Malhotra, A., S. Mathur, R. Pande, and E. Roca. 2005a. "Do Participatory Programs Work? Improving Reproductive Health for Disadvantaged Youth in Nepal." *Development Outreach* 7 (2): 32–5.

———. 2005b. "Nepal: The Distributional Impact of Participatory Approaches on Reproductive Health for Disadvantaged Youths." In *Reaching the Poor with Health, Nutrition, and Population Services: What Works, What Doesn't, and Why*, ed. D. Gwatkin, A. Wagstaff, and A. Yazbeck, 211–41. Washington, DC: World Bank.

Mustard, C. A., S. Derksen, J.-M. Berthelot, M. Wolfson, and L. L. Roos. 1997. "Age-Specific Education and Income Gradients in Morbidity and Mortality in a Canadian Province." *Social Science and Medicine* 45 (3): 383–97.

Nathan, R., H. Masanja, H. Mshinda, J. A. Schellenberg, D. Savigny, C. Lengeler, M. Tanner, and C. G. Victora. 2004. "Mosquito Nets and the Poor: Can Social Marketing Redress Inequities in Access?" *Tropical Medicine and International Health* 9 (10): 1121–26.

Neumann N. A., C. G. Victora, R. Halpern, P. R. Guimaraes, and J. A. Cesar. 1999. "A Pastoral da Criança em Criciúma, Santa Catarina, Brasil: cobertura e características sócio-demográficas das famílias participantes." *Cad Saude Publica* 15 (3): 543–52.

Noirhomme, M., B. Meessen, F. Griffiths, P. Ir, B. Jacobs, R. Thor, B. Criel, and W. Van Damme. 2007. "Improving Access to Hospital Care for the Poor: Comparative Analysis of Four Health Equity Funds in Cambodia." *Health Policy and Planning* 22 (4): 246–62.

Nuñez, J., and S. Espinosa. 2004. "Asistencia Social en Colombia: Diagnósticos y Propuestas." Unpublished, National Department of Statistics, Bogotá.

O'Donnell, O., E. van Doorslaer, A. Wagstaff, and M. Lindelow. 2007. *Analyzing Health Equity Using Household Survey Data: A Guide to Techniques and Their Implementation.* Washington, DC: World Bank.

Otten, M., R. Kezaala, A. Fall, B. Masresha, R. Martin, L. Cairns, R. Eggers, and others. 2005. "Public-Health Impact of Accelerated Measles Control in the WHO African Region 2000–03." *Lancet* 366 (9488): 832–39.

Palma, J., and R. Urzúa. 2005. "Anti-Poverty Policies and Citizenry: The Chile 'Solidario' Experience." Management of Social Transitions Policy Paper No. 12. UNESCO, Paris.

Pande, R., and A. Yazbeck. 2003. "What's in a Country Average? Wealth, Gender, and Regional Inequalities in Immunization in India." *Social Science and Medicine* 57 (11): 2075–88.

Peters, D., A. Yazbeck, R. Sharma, G. N. V. Ramana, L. Pritchett, and A. Wagstaff. 2002. *Better Health Systems for India's Poor: Findings, Analysis, and Options.* Washington, DC: World Bank.

Ranson, M. K., P. Joshi, M. Shah, and Y. Shaikh. 2005. "India: Assessing the Reach of Three SEWA Health Services among the Poor." In *Reaching the Poor with Health, Nutrition, and Population Services,* ed. D. Gwatkin, A. Wagstaff, and A. Yazbeck. Washington, DC: World Bank.

Reinikka, R., and J. Svensson. 2004. "Local Capture: Evidence from a Central Government Transfer Program in Uganda." *Quarterly Journal of Economics* 119 (2): 679–704.

Roberts, M., W. Hsiao, P. Berman, and M. Reich. 2004. *Getting Reform Right: A Guide to Improving Performance and Equity.* New York: Oxford University Press.

Saadah, F., M. Pradhan, and R. Sparrow. 2001. "The Effectiveness of the Health Card as an Instrument to Ensure Access to Medical Care for the Poor during the Crisis." Paper prepared for the Third Annual Conference of the Global Development Network, Rio de Janeiro, Brazil, December 9–12.

Salmen, L., and M. Amelga. 1998. "Implementing Beneficiary Assessment in Education: A Guide for Practitioners (with Examples from Brazil)." Working Paper No. 20945, World Bank, Washington, DC.

Schellenberg, J., S. Abdulla, H. Minja, N. Rose, O. Mukasa, T. Marchant, H. Mponda, N. Kikumbih, E. Lyimo, T. Manchester, M. Tanner, and C. Lengeler. 1999. "KINET: A Social Marketing Programme of Treated Nets and Net Treatment for Malaria Control in Tanzania, with Evaluation of Child Health and Long-Term Survival." *Transactions of the Royal Society of Tropical Medicine and Hygiene* 93 (3): 225–31.

Schellenberg, J., S. Abdulla, R. Nathan, O. Mukasa, T. Marchant, N. Kikumbih, A. Mushi, H. Mponda, H. Minja, and H. Mshinda. 2001. "Effect of Large-Scale Social Marketing of Insecticide-Treated Nets on Child Survival in Rural Tanzania." *Lancet* 357 (9264): 1241–47.

Schwartz, J., and I. Bhushan. 2005. "Cambodia: Using Contracting to Reduce Inequity in Primary Health Care Delivery." In *Reaching the Poor with Health, Nutrition, and Population Services: What Works, What Doesn't, and Why,* ed. D. R. Gwatkin, A. Wagstaff, and A. Yazbeck, 137–62. Washington, DC: World Bank.

Scott, J. 2006. "Seguro Popular Incidence Analysis." In "Decentralized Service Delivery for the Poor," vol. 2, 147–66. World Bank, Washington, DC.

Secretaría de Salud de México. 2006. *Salud: México 2001-2005: Información para la rendición de cuentas.* Federal District, Mexico. http://www.salud.gob.mx/unidades/evaluacion/saludmex2005/sm2005.htm.

Soucat, A., R. Levine, A. Wagstaff, A. Yazbeck, C. Griffin, T. Johnston, P. Hutchinson, and R. Knippenberg. 2005. "Assessing the Performance of Health Services in

Reaching the Poor." In *Public Services Delivery*, ed. A. Shah, 153–92. Public Sector Governance and Accountability Series. Washington, DC: World Bank.

USAID (United States Agency for International Development). No date. *Health and Family Planning Indicators: A Tool for Results Frameworks*. USAID, Washington, DC.

Victora G., J. Vaughan, F. Barros, A. Silva, and E. Tomasi. 2000. "Explaining Trends in Inequities: Evidence from Brazilian Child Health Studies." *The Lancet* 356 (9235): 1093–98.

Vijayaraghavan, M., R. Martin, N. Sangrujee, G. Kimani, S. Oyombe, A. Kalu, A. Runyago, G. Wanjau, L. Cairns, and S. Muchiri. 2002. "Measles Supplemental Immunization Activities Improve Measles Vaccine Coverage and Equity: Evidence from Kenya." *Health Policy* 83 (1): 27–36.

Wagstaff, A., and M. Claeson. 2004. *The Millennium Development Goals for Health: Rising to the Challenges*. Washington, DC: World Bank.

WHO (World Health Organization). 2006. "Measles SIAs Field Guide." WHO Regional Office for Africa. www.afro.who.int/measles/guidelines/measles_sias _field_guide_revised_jan2006.pdf.

———. 2008. "Indicators for IMCI at First-Level Facilities and Households. Revision 1, 2001." WHO, Geneva.

World Bank. 1993. *World Development Report 1993: Investing in Health*. Washington, DC: World Bank.

———. 1994. *Better Health in Africa: Experience and Lessons Learned*. Development in Practice series. Washington, DC: World Bank.

———. 2003. *A Sourcebook for Poverty Reduction Strategies Vols. I and II*. Washington, DC: World Bank.

———. 2004. *World Development Report 2004: Making Services Work for Poor People*. Washington, DC: World Bank.

———. 2008a. "Chile: Reaching the Poor with Health Services through Provision of Multidimensional Support." Reaching the Poor Policy Briefs, World Bank, Washington, DC.

———. 2008b. "Kenya: Immunization Reaching the Poor through Mass Campaigns." Reaching the Poor Policy Briefs, World Bank, Washington, DC.

———. 2008c. "Reducing Financial Burden of Health Care for the Poor—the Case of Kyrgyz Health Financing Reform." Reaching the Poor Policy Briefs, World Bank, Washington, DC.

Yazbeck, A. 2004. "Real and Perceived Threats to Reproductive Health: A Way Forward." *Reproductive Health Matters* 12 (24): 25–34.

———. 2007. "Shining the Spotlight on Inequality in Health." Guest blog, Public Libraries of Science. http://www.plos.org/cms/node/283.

Yazbeck, A., and D. Peters. 2003. *Health Policy Research in South Asia: Guiding Reforms and Building Capacity*. Washington, DC: World Bank.

Index

Boxes, figures, notes, and tables are indicated by *b, f, n,* and *t,* respectively.

A

Abdulla, S., 275*n*
Abuja Declaration, 269
accessibility/availability of health services to poor. *See also under* specific countries
eight steps to effective use of health services by the poor, 84, 85, 116–117, 118*f*
facility placement, 131
regression analysis revealing, 114–115
as supply-side cause of health inequality, 104
accountability framework for pro-poor health policies, 157, 160, 165–170, 165*f*
accountability of available health services, 87, 125–126, 126*f*
active listening, 108, 111
Adhikari, S., 286
administrative data, 142–143, 144*t*
adolescent fertility, 1, 76*n*1
levels of health inequality in, 4–8, 5*f,* 7*b*
summary table of data by country and region, 36–41*t*
Africa. *See* Middle East and North Africa; sub-Saharan Africa
African Summit on Roll Back Malaria, 269
agricultural policies as factors in health inequality, 98
AIDS. *See* HIV/AIDS
Akkazieva, B., 286
allocation and mobilization of resources, 88–89, 131
Amelga, M., 155*n*16
Andreason, A., 271, 275*n*
ANMs (auxiliary nurse-midwives) in India, 112–113
antenatal care, 1. *See also under* specific countries
pro-wealth bias in health services, 9–11, 9*t,* 10–11*f,* 12–13*b*
summary table of data by country and region, 54–59*t*

Anwar, I., 99–100
Armenia, 16*f*
Arokiasamy, P., 74
Asia. *See* East Asia and Pacific; Europe and Central Asia; South Asia
Asian Development Bank, 179
asset indexing, 3, 24–28, 25–28*t,* 28*f*
attended delivery, 1, 76*n*2. *See also under* specific countries
pro-wealth bias in health services, 9–11, 9*t,* 10–11*f,* 14*f*
summary table of data by country and region, 66–71*t*
auxiliary nurse-midwives (ANMs) in India, 112–113

B

Balk, D., 286–287
Bangladesh
BIA data, 16*f*
FLS for, 147
further reading recommendations, 75–76, 99–100
IMCI survey of, 147
poverty and health inequality in, 81, 82–83*b,* 84
transportation factors leading to health inequality, 96
Banu, Safar, 81, 82–83*b,* 84, 101*n*1, 154*n*2
Barros, F., 76, 178*n*
Becher, H., 170–171
bed nets, insecticide-treated, 164, 168, 269–275
Beegle, K., 97
behavioral and cultural factors leading to health inequality, 81–82, 105
beneficiary (patient) assessments, 148–151
benefit incidence analysis (BIA), 15–17, 16*f,* 18*b,* 72–74, 127–131, 128–130*f,* 133
Benin, 122–123, 122*f*
Bhuiya, A., 152
Bhushan, I., 185*n*
BIA (benefit incidence analysis), 15–17, 16*f,* 18*b,* 72–74, 127–131, 128–130*f,* 133
Bill and Melinda Gates Foundation, 172*n*1, 287*n*1